LiBretto, Ellen V.

High/low handbook.

$48.00

DATE			

High/Low Handbook

HIGH/LOW HANDBOOK

◆

Best Books and Web Sites for Reluctant Teen Readers

4th Edition

ELLEN V. LIBRETTO

CATHERINE BARR

2002
Libraries Unlimited
A Division of Greenwood Publishing Group, Inc.
Westport, Connecticut

ISBN: 0–313–32276–7

Libraries Unlimited
A Division of Greenwood Publishing Group, Inc.
88 Post Road West
Westport, CT 06881
1–800–225–5800
www.lu.com

Contents

Preface

ON JUNE 11, 2001, *USA Today* reported that President George W. Bush considers reading the key to all learning. Calling literacy "the new civil right," Bush and Education Secretary Ron Paige spoke out about the need for higher literacy standards. With an estimated 27 million functionally illiterate adults in the United States, literacy is indeed a national priority.

High/Low Handbook: Books and Web Sites for Reluctant Teen Readers is a practical guide to the selection of high-interest low-reading-level books and Web sites that will inspire a love of reading in teenagers (ages 12–18) who read below grade level and fall within the category of "reluctant readers."

Uses

This fourth edition of *High/Low Handbook* provides easy accessibility to the really wide range of materials available to students with poor reading skills and to librarians, teachers, tutors, and others who work with them. This volume will be especially useful for professionals in school and public libraries charged with building collections of suitable titles. It also serves as a quick ready reference for professionals seeking to guide teens to suitable materials on topics of high interest.

In addition to books, this new edition includes Web sites. The World Wide Web did not exist when the last edition of *High/Low Handbook* was written. Since its creation in 1993, the Web has come to be a powerful—if erratic—educational tool. Web sites can be very attractive to teens who are reluctant to tackle books. Information is often presented in small chunks and combined with images and even sound and interactivity.

The Web sites recommended in the Core Collection are included as an extension of the print materials. This can work in both directions. Students who enjoy a print product may want to explore further but may reject the idea of tackling another book; many of these Web sites will offer an alternative. On the other hand, the Web sites may generate enough interest to induce a reluctant reader to venture into a book. Teachers and librarians are using this collaborative approach with great success.

Arrangement

Part I: High/Low Books and Web Sites: A Core Collection is organized by broad subject area, for easy browsing. It recommends high-interest books that, for the most part, are written and published specifically for the reluctant reader aged between 12 and 18. These titles are written at a low reading level (grades 1 to 5) and are short in length (25 to 75 pages). Web sites extend the usefulness of the books selected for inclusion in the Core Collection. They allow readers who have become interested in a topic to explore further. The Core Collection includes 426 main entries. An additional 100 titles are cited within the main entry annotations.

Part II: Young Adult Materials for the Reluctant Reader recommends standard young adult materials (books and magazines) that are popular with all teens. These books (often 200 pages long), many of which are award winners, are not written to a high/low formula. They just happen to be easy to read and their content is compelling. These are the books that jump off the shelves into the hands of all teens, whatever their reading ability. Librarians and teachers who are unfamiliar with YA literature can use this list to recommend surefire good reads. There are 128 books listed here.

Periodicals have a special allure for reluctant readers. This section provides a handy subject breakdown of recommended periodicals as well as a more detailed annotated list.

Two appendices give practical information. The first lists Web resources for the professional working in the area of teen literacy, including Webquests and "keypal" programs. The Publisher List in Appendix II provides contact information for publishers of high/low titles, easing acquisition of these sometimes hard-to-find books.

Finally, the indexes offer access by author (books only), title, and subject. Those in search of suitable materials on narrower topics will find easy access via the Subject Index. Those who are looking for additional titles by favorite authors will want to use the Author Index.

Selection Criteria

Central to the selection of titles in the Core Collection are the concerns of the typical teenager: dating, parental conflict, friendship, health concerns, and gangs, as well as career choice and money management. Adventure stories, biographies and memoirs, historical fiction, and books illustrated in the graphic novel style also mirror teenagers' interests.

The titles chosen are inspiring. They show teens that there can be a bright future despite poverty, war, racial or sexual abuse, physical disability, or illness. Many titles in history, natural science, and the social studies are also useful as curriculum tie-ins. Fiction titles are frequently emotionally gripping, life-affirming, and sometimes just plain fun.

There are ample titles for both boys and girls, and every attempt has been made to select titles and Web sites that reflect the growing ethnic diversity of the American teenage population.

Acknowledgments

The editors would like to thank Deanna McDaniel (Middle School Media Specialist at Genoa Middle School, Westerville City Schools, Westerville, Ohio) for her excellent contributions on teens' favorite fiction and nonfiction and on magazines that entice reluctant readers. Thanks are also due to school librarian Gordon Riley for his help in writing annotations for the Core Collection; to the publishers who supplied review copies of books; and to the staff at Libraries Unlimited—in particular Barbara Ittner, for her support and guidance.

Part I

◆

High/Low Books
and Web Sites:
A Core Collection

Selecting the Core Collection

ELLEN V. LIBRETTO AND CATHERINE BARR

THE CORE COLLECTION consists of carefully selected high-interest, low-reading-level books and Web sites with appeal to reluctant teen readers.

The Web sites provide additional information on many topics covered in the recommended books and will encourage additional online and offline reading by adolescents. Professionals working to inspire poor readers can combine the books and Web sites in many innovative ways.

In its Teen Read Week Initiative, the American Library Association refers to *The Summary of Adolescent Literacy, A Position Statement for the Commission on Adolescent Literacy of The International Reading Association* (1999), which—in its opening recommendations for focusing on the literacy needs of adolescent learners—states that teens should be provided with "access to a wide variety of reading material that appeals to their interests." In an additional position paper titled *Supporting Young Adolescents' Literacy Learning: A Joint Position Paper of the International Reading Association and National Middle School Association*, the associations advocate "ample opportunities to read and discuss reading with others—to achieve this goal, schools for young adolescents must have ready access to a wide variety of print and non-print resources that will foster in students independence, confidence, and a lifelong desire to read."

The editors of *High/Low Handbook* believe that teens who are drawn to the computer can be introduced to subjects of interest on the Web and then guided to printed material on the same topic. Teens who may not have easy access to the Web, or who prefer books, will find a wide array of interesting print titles in these lists. When they have exhausted the print options, they can progress to the Web to explore further. The magazines listed in Part II offer an additional point of access.

The books and Web sites are arranged under the following broad subject categories, providing an at-a-glance look at the rich variety of teen interests represented in the Core Collection:

Fiction
Poetry and Drama
Folklore and Mythology
Biography and Memoir
Careers
Celebrities and Entertainment
Disasters
Health and Fitness
History
Inspirational
Love, Sex, and Relationships
Nature and the Environment
Reference
Science, Technology, Space Exploration
Sports and Recreation
Teen Culture and Issues
Transportation
The World Around Us

Under each subject heading, you will find the books listed first, organized alphabetically by author, followed by the Web sites, organized alphabetically by title.

Users seeking more detailed access by subject will find this in the Subject Index. Author and Title indexes are also provided.

High/Low Books

ELLEN V. LIBRETTO

TITLES INCLUDED IN the Core Collection, for the most part, are written at the fifth-grade reading level and below. The vast majority of the titles have been identified by their publishers as high-interest, low-reading-level materials. The titles listed here are a sampling of the best in their category. Although the titles selected reflect the commonality of the adolescent experience in a low-literacy-level context, many are appropriate for adults and will be useful for teachers and librarians working with adolescents and adults enrolled in ESL programs.

Interest in locating books for teens with reading problems peaked in the 1970s. At the June 1978 American Library Association annual conference, held in Chicago, the Young Adult Services Division (now the Young Adult Library Services Association) and the Association for Library Services to Children cosponsored a preconference, "Dispelling the High/Low Blues." Attended by 300 public and school librarians, this preconference was aimed at identifying suitable reading material for reading-disabled teenagers, defined as twelve- to seventeen-year-olds whose reading scores fell below the fourth-grade level.

This writer was the primary planner of this preconference. Prior to the event, 160 publishers were surveyed in order to identify and develop a list of those publishers who were actively producing high/low materials. Forty-seven publishers responded to the survey and contributed books and catalogs for display at the preconference. The exhibit of materials was informative for the participants and served to demonstrate the need for more books written at the lower levels on a variety of fiction and nonfiction subjects. In the 1970s—and in the new millennium—these titles are considered transitional books. Librarians, teachers, and tutors see them as bridges to more advanced reading.

At the close of the conference, the Young Adult Services Division established the High Interest/Low Reading Level Materials Evaluation Committee. The committee members represented the reading needs of teens from rural, suburban, and urban areas of the United States; this writer served as the first chair. The charge of the committee was to compile an annual list of high-interest, low-literacy-level (high/low) books aimed at teenagers. Most of the titles selected were designated by their publisher as high/low. Teachers, tutors, and librarians working with the teenage reluctant reader recommended these titles to their students. By 1990, the committee—renamed the Quick Picks Committee—had shifted gears and had started to recommend titles based on teen interest observed by committee members. The list, produced annually, is now called Quick Picks for Reluctant Young Adult Readers.

This edition of *High/Low Handbook* compiles transitional titles that offer reading choices on a wide range of subjects and interest levels to a population that shows reluctance to read and/or scores below grade level on reading tests. Many librarians object to high/low books because the books do not seem to meet the same standards as children's and YA literature, but high/low books have evolved in both content and style and most now do meet quality standards. The typeface is no longer overly large, photographs and illustrations are outstanding, paper quality does not differ from that used in standard trade books, and many authors have crossed over to this genre from other areas of age-level writing.

The editors would like to commend the many publishing companies that are producing books in the high/low genre and to thank the many authors who have a facility for crafting books that are interesting and right on target for reluctant readers. They are both providing an essential service through supplying transitional materials for teenagers who need to improve their reading skills.

A number of authors write excellent books in the high/low genre that should serve as models of simple vocabulary, short sentence structure, and brief chapter format, many with pagination not exceeding sixty-four pages. In all the books, the writing is fast paced and spiced with good line drawings or photographs, continually engaging the reader in the storyline. Among the outstanding authors whose works are listed in the Core Collection are Tana Reiff, Anne Schraff, and Margo Sorenson.

Tana Reiff, a literacy tutor administrator and pioneering author of high/low books, writes sensitive explorations of the immigrant experience with deeply moving, true-to-life characters who meet the many challenges of life in a new land—for example, *Making Heaven: The Koreans*, about a family adjusting to life in 1970s New York. She also tackles issues in the workplace in titles such as *The Easy Way*, about a nursing home worker who steals drugs. In the series about teens at Bluford High, Anne Schraff (*Someone to Love Me*) writes compassionately about the conflicts that typical contemporary African American teens face in making decisions about family, friendship, trust, and peer pressure. Margo Sorenson tackles school bullies (*The Gotcha Plot*) and survival in the wilderness (*Danger Canyon*) with rhythmic teen dialogue and humor.

Many nonfiction titles deliver information and are enjoyable to read at leisure or for homework assignments. The following are exceptional in subject appeal, writing style, and book design. *Inhalants and Your Nasal Passages: The Incredibly Disgusting Story* by Kerri O'Donnell exceeds anyone's expectations of a "just say no" book that educates teens about the dangers of drugs in a non-preachy voice; *Weight Training* by Gus Gedatus inspires teens to become strong and fit with a good diet and exercise program; and *Odd Jobs: True Stories About Real Work* (John Diconsiglio) portrays individuals who have chosen unusual work environments and includes a brief profile of a window washer at the World Trade Center before his death in the terrorist attacks of September 11, 2001.

For the first time, a small sample of graphic novels has been included in the Core Collection, among them *Harlem Beat* by female manga artist Yuriko Nishiyama, the first in a series that included nine at this writing using pick-up basketball as a metaphor for the experiences of teen life.

In the decade since the last edition of *High/Low Handbook* many publishers have expanded their lists, producing challenging books written at a low reading level to meet the range of interests of an ethnically diverse population that varies in maturity. The topics are well chosen—dealing with loss, historical fiction, and memoirs, to mention just a few—and they will help to combat teen illiteracy.

Many of the twenty-three publishers represented in this volume publish large lists aimed at the reluctant teen reader; others have simply produced happy accidents that fit the genre. There is new and steady growth from the Rosen Publishing Group, Mitchell Lane Publishers, Perfection Learning Corporation, Capstone Press, and the Scholastic Read 180 Program. Librarians wishing to build collections of high/low materials are urged to consult publishers' Web sites (listed at the back of this book), many of which include reviews of titles.

Guidelines for Book Selection

The following guidelines, which were originally developed in 1978 by the American Library Association's Young Adult Services Division's High Interest/Low Reading Level Materials Evaluation Committee, have been adapted as the criteria for selection of titles for the Core Collection in this edition of *High Low Handbook*. These standards make for a book that is appealing to the intended audience—the reluctant teen reader.

- ◆ The appearance of the book must be suitable for teenagers.
- ◆ Photos and illustrations are of teens and accurately reflect the text.
- ◆ Photos and illustrations contribute to the pace and texture of the narrative.
- ◆ The bindings and style of book design should conform to the look of standard YA books.

- The topic must have teen appeal.
- Teens should identify with the premise of the book.
- A title may be included because it is the "first" book on a topic.
- Coverage of the topic in nonfiction has enough depth to stimulate the reader to read further.
- Nonfiction titles are appropriate for curriculum use.
- Fiction titles must compare favorably with other junior novels both in theme and character depiction.
- Difficult words in the text are defined.
- Most important, *is the book readable?*

The goal of the *High/Low Handbook* is, as always, to recommend books that—once placed in the hands of teenagers—will excite them enough that they will gain the satisfaction of having read a whole book.

Anatomy of a Book Entry

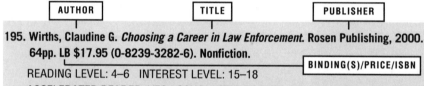

| AUTHOR | TITLE | PUBLISHER |

195. Wirths, Claudine G. *Choosing a Career in Law Enforcement.* Rosen Publishing, 2000. 64pp. LB $17.95 (0-8239-3282-6). Nonfiction.

BINDING(S)/PRICE/ISBN

READING LEVEL: 4–6   INTEREST LEVEL: 15–18
ACCELERATED READER: YES   SCHOLASTIC COUNTS: YES

An overview of the great variety of careers in law enforcement, a field of growing opportunities in this sad era of terrorism. Men and women are pictured in all types of police and security work in both the public and private sector—as police officers, security guards, border patrol guards, and private investigators, to name a few. Testimonials by law enforcement workers about their actual duties and the preparation needed to apply for these positions give teens an accurate image of what daily life in the security field would be like. Black-and-white photos, glossary.

For information on the **ACCELERATED READER PROGRAM,** visit **RENAISSANCE LEARNING** (http://www.renlearn.com/). This field appears only if the book is part of the program.

For information on the **SCHOLASTIC READING COUNTS PROGRAM,** visit **http://src.scholastic.com/ecatalog/readingcounts/index.htm.** This field appears only if the book is part of the program.

High/Low Web Sites

CATHERINE BARR

THE WORLD WIDE WEB offers great advantages—and almost as many disadvantages—for educators and others interested in literacy.

Teens enjoy using the Web for both research and entertainment. A survey by the Kaiser Family Foundation in 2001 (reported in *USA Today*, Dec. 12, 2001) found that about 90 percent of young people aged fifteen to twenty-four had been online.

Reluctant readers are particularly drawn to the Web. Many sites are attractively designed and offer graphics, sound, animation, and interactivity along with the text. Some of the better sites present the same information in a variety of ways, catering to different learning styles and reading abilities.

Unfortunately, the initial surge to publish information on the Web produced a large number of sites of very differing quality. Users must learn to distinguish reliable sites from those that merely use "bells and whistles" to attract visitors and ignore the traditional standards of accuracy maintained by print publishers.

For this reason, it is useful to have a number of sites bookmarked, ready for use by particular populations. The sites presented here have been selected with the reluctant reader in mind. They were chosen for the most part to extend the print titles listed in the front of the book, and to give teens who have found an interest in a subject yet another resource to explore.

Teen Web Use

Kaiser's study of Web use by young people found that health is the main interest: 75 percent of those surveyed had searched for health information, against 72 percent who played games and downloaded music, 67 percent who used the Web to chat, 50 percent who shopped online, and 46 percent who connected to check sports scores.

Teens' interest in health was fairly evenly divided between disorders/diseases and sexually related issues, according to Kaiser (44 percent researched pregnancy, birth control, AIDS, or sexually transmitted diseases online).

Happily, many teens recognized that the Internet is not always a reliable source. Kaiser found that 17 percent trusted health information on the Internet "a lot," while 40 percent trusted it "somewhat."

Another revealing study is *USA Weekend*'s 1998 survey on teens and image (http://www.usaweekend.com/98_issues/980503/980503teen_report_cover.html). An amazing 272,400 teens responded to this self-confessed unscientific survey, and confirmed that self-image and difficulty communicating with parents are high on their list of concerns. Seven out of ten said they had been depressed and nearly one in three had a friend who had discussed or attempted suicide.

Criteria for Web Site Selection

Unfortunately, there are very few Web sites created specifically with the reluctant reader in mind. So our initial search was for sites that would extend the print materials recommended here. We then added sites on additional topics that we believe will be of interest to teens.

All sites were reviewed for the following:

Suitable, age-appropriate content—The range of information that is considered suitable for teens varies from place to place and culture to culture. Web sites can add and subtract content at any time, so we cannot guarantee that sites will not subsequently add material that will be distasteful to some viewers. However, we have made every effort to select sites that are run by reputable organizations and that do not include unmonitored chat rooms.

High-quality content—Sites were carefully reviewed for accuracy. Unfortunately, a lack of editorial care is endemic on the Web. Typographical and other errors can be found on sites created even by well-respected organizations such as PBS, Discovery, the Smithsonian Institution, the BBC, and the Library of Congress. All students should be reminded on a regular basis to check facts with other sources.

Interest level—We have kept teens' strong interests in mind while searching for sites. Precise interest levels are not indicated with the annotations. Many of the sites contain sections that will attract different age groups.

Reading level—Reading levels are often inconsistent across sites; therefore they are not included with the annotations. Some sites include sections of great interest with easily read text and many images, only to follow this with dense passages that would challenge any reader. In some cases we have stated that the help of a tutor or other adult may be necessary.

General appeal—Sites were also reviewed for their overall appeal to teens and for their potential to spur further investigation into a given subject.

The Core Collection

Fiction

CONTEMPORARY FICTION

BOOKS

1. **Allred, Alexandra Powe. *The Code*. Perfection Learning, 2002. 167pp. Paper $5.95 (0-7891-5692-X). Fiction.**

   READING LEVEL: 6   INTEREST LEVEL: 12–18

   Narrated in the first person by a teenager living in "the Hood" in Washington, D.C., with present events alternating with the past, this is a complicated novel, but a great choice for older urban readers and others with the ability to imagine such an environment. It is a gritty tale that portrays realistically the tough choices facing urban teens who live in gang-infested neighborhoods. The narrator is a good student whose single mother works two jobs to support the boy and his grandmother. When his best friend joins the Jags, the narrator is drawn in also. When he decides he wants to leave the gang, he cannot work out how to extricate himself without breaking "The Code" of the streets or bringing harm to his family. The excellent narration brings alive the look and sounds of the narrator's world and reveals his thoughts on what he is learning in school (with a focus on Malcolm X), from his mother, and on the streets.

2. **Anastasio, Dina. *The Band*. Scholastic Read 180, 1999. 27pp. Paper. Sold as part of a set (0-439-05699-3). Fiction.**

   READING LEVEL: 1.5–2.5   INTEREST LEVEL: 12–15

   Many talented teens have to make difficult choices. To play basketball or to choose music is the dilemma facing Jake. He plays drums with a band that shows real potential and does not want to offend his fellow band members,

11

who are also his friends. Jake takes a long hard look at his life and decides to be true to himself—to find a replacement for the band and to devote himself to his true love—basketball! Line drawings, glossary.

3. **Anastasio, Dina, and Stedroy Cleghorn, illus.** *Friends: American Expressions.* **Globe Fearon, 1997. 92pp. Paper $8.95 (0-8359-3352-0). Fiction.**

READING LEVEL: 3–4 INTEREST LEVEL: 12–14

One of a series of readers, for and about teenagers, integrating many kinds of writing (diary entries, letters, poems, plays, folktales, and short stories) around a common theme. This title incorporates sixteen stories about the most fundamental elements of friendship, each between two and ten pages long.

4. **Anaya, Rudolfo A.** *Selected from Bless Me, Ultima.* **New Readers Press, 1989. 64pp. Paper $5.00 (0-929631-06-4). Fiction.**

READING LEVEL: 4–5 INTEREST LEVEL: 7–12

Included here are selected passages from the novel *Bless Me, Ultima* by Rudolfo A. Anaya, who captures the flavor of life in a small New Mexico town and the impact magic has on its residents. Background information includes a brief history of the Chicano in the Southwest. The interplay of Spanish and English throughout the introduction and the excerpts impart the color of the Southwest and warm the soul. Thoughtful questions append the text. This is a title in the Writers' Voices series.

5. **Angelou, Maya.** *Selected from I Know Why the Caged Bird Sings and The Heart of a Woman.* **New Readers Press, 1989. 64pp. Paper $5.00 (0-929631-04-8). Fiction.**

READING LEVEL: 4–5 INTEREST LEVEL: 7–12

Included here are selected excerpts from *I Know Why the Caged Bird Sings* and *The Heart of a Woman.* Maya Angelou's strengths as a woman and her enduring talents as a writer are heard in these excerpts that focus on her early childhood in Stamps, Arkansas, her parenting experiences, and her relationship with her mother. This multifaceted woman speaks about the universalities of life. The writings are preceded by a brief history of the civil rights movement. An appendix lists thoughtful questions for the reader. This is a title in the Writers' Voices series.

6. **Bahlinger, Lisa, and Michael R. Strickland.** *The Club.* **Perfection Learning, 2002. 119pp. Paper $5.95 (0-7891-5542-7). Fiction.**

READING LEVEL: 6 INTEREST LEVEL: 12–18

True Monroe wants to join "The Club." Membership carries many rights and privileges, including a snazzy Club jacket. Entry to the Club involves passing a test. True is arrested while breaking into a house and is sent to a Youth Study Center. Although this center is progressive by contemporary standards, it is not a pleasant experience and True has time to reflect on the events that brought him there. After his release True must weigh the continuing lure of material goods and the hold the members of the Club have over him.

7. **Benchley, Peter.** *Selected from Jaws.* **New Readers Press, 1990. 64pp. Paper $4.75 (0-929631-14-5). Fiction.**

READING LEVEL: 5 INTEREST LEVEL: 12–18

Many readers will already know the story line of *Jaws*. This excerpted version gives the chilling opening scene of the novel—the shark attacking the girl swimmer at night—to set up the big climax in which the policeman and the fisherman finally kill the shark. A great deal of supporting information about sharks, fishing, and nautical terms, and also some excellent questions, should provoke good discussions about this book. This is a title in the Writers' Voices series.

8. **Bette, Nina K.** *Heaven Sent: Janet Dailey's Love Scenes.* **New Readers Press, 1998. 64pp. Paper $3.50 (1-56853-030-7). Fiction.**

READING LEVEL: 5–6 INTEREST LEVEL: 14–18

Galen, a female angel on her first big assignment, tries to help Nancy find romance with Mike. This is not easy, especially when Nancy's former love Jake re-enters the picture. Galen must draw out Nancy's true feelings in order to find the best way to help her.

9. **Casas, Arvin, and Alan Nahigian, illus.** *Struggles: American Expressions.* **Globe Fearon, 1997. 96pp. Paper $8.95 (0-8359-3359-8). Fiction.**

READING LEVEL: 3–4 INTEREST LEVEL: 12–14

One of a series of readers, for and about teenagers, integrating many kinds of writing (diary entries, letters, poems, plays, folktales, and short stories) around a common theme. One of the more notable titles in the series, this includes eleven stories about different kinds of personal and social struggles. The stories are good by themselves, but better in comparison with each other. The stories are between two and twelve pages long.

10. **Clark, Mary Higgins.** *Selected from The Lost Angel.* **New Readers Press, 1990. 63pp. Paper $4.75 (0-929631-13-7). Fiction.**

READING LEVEL: 5 INTEREST LEVEL: 12–18

An excellent selection from a novel that will draw teens to this popular contemporary novelist. This is the tale of a four-year-old girl who is kidnapped by her father. The story alternates between the mother's perspective and the little girl's. The girl is eventually found at the Port Authority Bus Terminal in New York. The police help the mother in her search, but it is her own efforts and intelligence, and those of the child, that bring this narrative to a happy conclusion. Includes a note from the author and an essay on parental kidnapping. This is a title in the Writers' Voices series.

11. **Dailey, Janet. *Riding High: Janet Dailey's Love Scenes*. New Readers Press, 1994. 64pp. Paper $3.50 (1-56420-098-1). Fiction.**
READING LEVEL: 5–6   INTEREST LEVEL: 14–18

Cowboy Deke Flanders must teach spoiled actress Victoria Thornton how to ride for a movie role. Teachers will be reminded of Lady Chatterley and her lover; younger readers may think these two will never get along. Deke finds humor in Victoria's ways, but Victoria decides "the only thing I hate worse than flies and horses is cowboys." Genuinely funny moments and a realistic and interesting male lead make this a good choice for boys and girls.

12. **Haynes, David, and Laura J. Bryant, illus. *Business as Usual: West 7th Street Series*. Perfection Learning, 2001. 111pp. Paper $5.95 (0-7891-5413-7). Fiction.**
READING LEVEL: 3–6   INTEREST LEVEL: 12–15

Another story involving the West 7th Street Wildcats, a group of twelve-year-old boys. African American sixth-grader Bobby Sampson narrates events that take place primarily in school, involving an economics class and the antics of class cut-up Kevin Olsen. The story also develops the character of Jenny Pederson, nemesis of the Wildcats, who winds up with Kevin in her project group and works to turn him against his former mates. The author won't let you root for Jenny, so this is (like the others in the series) very much a boys' book. The economics lesson is handled well, providing more actual instruction than the other reviewed titles in this series.

13. **Haynes, David, and Laura J. Bryant, illus. *The Gumma Wars: West 7th Street Series*. Perfection Learning, 2001. 99pp. Paper $5.95 (0-7891-5414-5). Fiction.**
READING LEVEL: 3–6   INTEREST LEVEL: 12–15

This second book in the series about the adventures of the West 7th Street Wildcats, a group of young boys, is told by Lawrence Underwood, known to his friends as Lu. Though Lu is looking forward to Tony R's 12th birthday party and a Wildcats sleepover, the date conflicts with his grandmother (Gumma) Jackson's birthday. Meanwhile, Gumma Underwood will be looking after Lu for the weekend. The book is something of a homage to strong

African American grandmothers, and both Gumma Jackson and Gumma Underwood are well-drawn characters. Needless to say, the two Gummas do not get along, and some very funny situations evolve from the tension.

14. **Haynes, David, and Laura J. Bryant, illus. *Who's Responsible: West 7th Street Series.* Perfection Learning, 2002. 118pp. Paper $5.95 (0-7891-5694-6). Fiction.**

READING LEVEL: 3–6 INTEREST LEVEL: 12–15

Each book in this series is narrated in the first person by a different member of the West 7th Street Wildcats, a group of twelve-year-old boys who seem wiser than their age. Two of the boys are African American, one is Mexican American, one is white, and two are of Hmong ancestry. This third book of the series, narrated by Tony Rodriguez, tells the story of Max, a homeless boy who is secretly adopted by Bobby Sampson. Bobby hides Max in his basement and sneaks him into school for gym class and lunch. In the meantime, Tony's father pushes him to be more responsible, which will ultimately force Tony to face some difficult choices.

15. **Howe, Quincy. *The Longest Night: Uptown, Downtown.* Globe Fearon, 1995. 60pp. Paper $8.50 (0-8359-1081-4). Fiction.**

READING LEVEL: 2–5 INTEREST LEVEL: 12–18

One of a series of novels told in the first person by New York teenager Vesey McCall. The books are as much about the people he meets as about Vesey himself. In this first book of the series, Vesey decides to spend the night on the streets to mitigate some trouble he is in at school. He sees scenes that will be unfamiliar to many readers and meets some thought-provoking characters. Other titles in the series include *Love on the Subway, Action on the Cape, Wheels of Danger, Hitting the Ice, Broken Chains, Looking for Trouble,* and *The Road South.*

16. **Keller, Roseanne. *Five Dog Night and Other Tales.* New Readers Press, 1979. 32pp. Paper $6.25 (0-88336-320-8). Fiction.**

READING LEVEL: 2–3 INTEREST LEVEL: 10-12

A slim collection of four humorous short stories, all with survival as a theme. Each is illustrated with rather casual black-and-white line drawings. In the story "Bear in the Sky," the Heimlich maneuver saves a life during a plane trip. "Five Dog Night" is about two flyers who survive a crash landing. In "See You in Valdez," a boy must learn to care for his family after his father's departure to work on the Alaska pipeline. The final story, "When I Think of You," is about missing someone you love. A glossary appends the text.

17. **Keller, Roseanne.** *Two for the Road.* **New Readers Press, 1979. 32pp. Paper $6.25 (0-88336-319-4). Fiction.**

READING LEVEL: 1–2 INTEREST LEVEL: 9–12

A slim little volume containing two very short stories. In the first, "Ms. Trucker," Ann is the central character. With humor and skill, a contemporary message is delivered in a very simple format reminiscent of a primary reader (one sentence per line). The saga of Ann, a trucker, and Tom, a mechanic, trying to break out of their traditional roles, is hilarious. Older teenagers will understand the role identification scenario. The other tale, "The Ups and Downs of a Pikes Peak Peanut Pusher" (two and a half pages), is a comical look at a man who pushed a peanut up Pikes Peak. This title, and others in the series, are recommended by the publisher as adult basic education material, but older teenagers will find the books meaningful to their experiences as well. A glossary is included.

18. **Langan, Paul.** *The Gun.* **Townsend Press, 2001. 123pp. Paper $4.95 (0-944210-04-X). Fiction.**

READING LEVEL: 4–6 INTEREST LEVEL: 12–18

The Gun is one of seven titles in the Bluford High School series. This series, set in contemporary urban America, explores the lives of African American students—family, friendship, trust, isolation, violence, and peer pressure. In *The Gun*, a sequel to *The Bully* (also by Paul Langan), Bluford freshman and school bully Tyray Hobbs finds that the tables are turned when the boy he is bullying, Darrell Mercer, finally stands up to him. Tyray, the son of an abusive father, is determined to buy a gun to seek revenge on Darrell. Much of the text is a rich dialogue that will captivate the teen ear. An exceptionally well-written book that teens will read quickly as they see the series characters dealing with many issues relevant to their daily lives.

19. **Lindsay, Jeanne Warren, and Jami Moffett, illus.** *Do I Have a Daddy? A Story About a Single-Parent Child.* **Morning Glory Press, rev. ed. 2000. 46pp. Hardcover. $12.95 (1-885356-62-5). Fiction.**

READING LEVEL: 1–2 INTEREST LEVEL: 12–18

In simple, logical terms, Lindsay offers a read-aloud story for single moms to use as a springboard for discussion and reassurance when asked the often-painful question "Do I have a daddy?" Also included is a thoughtful guide to young single mothers about how to handle the feelings she experiences when telling her child about the father. Attractive color crayon drawings complement the read-aloud text.

20. Logan, Alyssa. *The Magic of Love: Janet Dailey's Love Scenes*. New Readers Press, 1998. 64pp. Paper $3.50 (1-56853-031-5). Fiction.
READING LEVEL: 5–6 INTEREST LEVEL: 14–18

Beth, a single mom and business owner, has no time for romance with professional clown Kevin, even though he is great with kids and Beth's son, Josh, likes him a lot. Beth rejects Kevin's advances until Josh has an accident that makes her re-evaluate her choices.

21. McFall, Karen. *Pat King's Family*. New Readers Press, 1982. 64pp. Paper $6.25 (0-88336-203-1). Fiction.
READING LEVEL: 2–6 INTEREST LEVEL: 7–12

Pat King, married at 18 and now the mother of two young children, is faced with providing for the children and herself after her husband leaves. Teen mothers who are raising their children alone will identify with the emotional and economic support that Pat must seek out while resolving her marital and family difficulties. An excellent book, written with compassion. Pencil drawings; word list.

22. Meier, Jane P., and Larassa Kabel, illus. *Summer Friends*. Perfection Learning, 2000. 55pp. Paper $5.95 (0-7891-2927-2). Fiction.
READING LEVEL: 2–3 INTEREST LEVEL: 12–18
ACCELERATED READER: YES

This book is a real treasure. Told from the perspective of Cassie Foster, it is a nicely focused story of two young people becoming friends during a summer vacation. Joey Ryan is disabled and confined to a wheelchair. His disability is presented in a comfortable and unobtrusive way that teaches acceptance of diversity and tragedy without being heavy-handed. As Cassie and Joey are of an indeterminate age, this is an excellent choice for older students with low reading ability.

23. Miller, Kathryn Ann, and Jami Moffett, illus. *Did My First Mother Love Me? A Story of an Adopted Child*. Morning Glory Press, 1994. 47pp. Paper $5.95 (0-930934-84-9). Fiction.
READING LEVEL: 1–6 INTEREST LEVEL: 12–18

This volume consists of two sections. "Did My First Mother Love Me?" is a read-aloud picture book that adoptive parents can read to the child. It is written at a very easy reading level. The appendix—"Talking to Your Child About Adoption"—is written at a fifth- to sixth-grade reading level. In question-and-answer format, it covers all issues relating to adoption from the perspectives of the adopted child, adoptive parents, and birth parents. Pen-and-ink drawings complement the picture-book portion.

24. **Pollard-Johnson, Lori, and Margaret Sanfilippo, illus.** *The Truth Test*. **Perfection Learning, 2001. 75pp. Paper $5.95 (0-7891-5318-1). Fiction.**

READING LEVEL: 2–3 INTEREST LEVEL: 12–15

Twelve-year-old Jared Springer is not happy in school. He is victimized by bullies, and he's bored much of the time, except in his accelerated chemistry class. Jared rigs up a chemical gimmick that changes color when tested on saliva. He says the color change only occurs when a person has just told a lie. Jared makes a lot of money and enjoys a period of popularity.

25. **Reiff, Tana.** *The Easy Way: Work Tales*. **Globe Fearon, 1991. 60pp. Paper $8.50 (0-8224-7157-4). Fiction.**

READING LEVEL: 3 INTEREST LEVEL: 12–18

One of a series of workplace novels with a non-traditional narrative style with sentences broken into phrases, each printed on its own line of text. All the stories have a moral education component and negative behavior leads to serious consequences. In this book, Jason is a hospital worker who finds that cocaine helps him get through his difficult day and makes him less cranky with patients. When his stash is stolen, he helps himself to pain pills from the hospital supplies and suffers a near-fatal overdose.

26. **Reiff, Tana.** *Handle with Care: Work Tales*. **Globe Fearon, 1991. 60pp. Paper $8.50 (0-8224-7151-5). Fiction.**

READING LEVEL: 3 INTEREST LEVEL: 12–18

Bianca is an immigrant from the Philippines. She is an abandoned single mother who finds work in a nursing home. Although she is very dedicated, her poor literacy skills lead to unfortunate complications.

27. **Reiff, Tana.** *The Rip-Offs: Work Tales*. **Globe Fearon, 1991. 60pp. Paper $8.50 (0-8224-7160-4). Fiction.**

READING LEVEL: 3 INTEREST LEVEL: 12–18

Wendy Kim, a Korean who has been in the United States for three years, enjoys her job in a department store until she realizes many of her fellow employees are stealing. When the store manager encourages Wendy to inform on her coworkers, Wendy faces some difficult choices.

28. **Reiff, Tana.** *The Saw That Talked: Work Tales.* **Globe Fearon, 1991. 60pp. Paper $8.50 (0-8224-7152-3). Fiction.**

READING LEVEL: 3   INTEREST LEVEL: 12–18

Lindy has always enjoyed working with wood and is happy to start a new job at an industrial wood shop when she graduates from high school. But there are difficulties in being the only woman and some safety issues that concern her. When she loses the tip of her finger in an accident, Lindy has to consider whether some issues are more important than being liked by the men in the shop.

29. **Reiff, Tana.** *You Call, We Haul: Working for Myself.* **American Guidance Service, 1994. 75pp. Paper $5.95 (0-7854-1114-3). Fiction.**

READING LEVEL: 4   INTEREST LEVEL: 14–18

One of a series of fiction books designed to provide information on starting a small business. In each book, the protagonist has a particular talent, interest, or ability that is eventually turned into a thriving enterprise. Much of the action of the story involves planning and taking basic steps such as obtaining necessary licenses and permits. Other elements are usually introduced as surprises—unanticipated problems, such as not thinking to ask for directions or a timetable that fails to work—and are solved with more thought and planning. This book tells the story of a single father, down on his luck, who turns his proudest possession (a pick-up truck) into the workhorse of a carting and hauling business. Other titles in the series cover new businesses in daycare, pet care, lawn care, handyman chores, cleaning, craft making, catering, and flower arranging.

30. **Schraff, Anne E.** *Bridge to the Moon: Passages.* **Perfection Learning, 1995. 99pp. Paper $5.95 (1-5631-2396-7). Fiction.**

READING LEVEL: 3–6   INTEREST LEVEL: 12–18
ACCELERATED READER: YES

Although a sequel to *Maitland's Kid* (see below), this book reads like a stand-alone novel. A changed Jonathan returns to his family after his experiences with his biological father. The book details how the new Jonathan interacts with his old environment, spurring changes in other family members and friends. The story is, in one sense, the opposite of the first book about Jonathan. In it, the individual goes to a community and is changed by it. In the sequel, the individual changes the community. Interesting subplots involving school rivalries and romances should make the book as interesting to girls as to boys. This is one of the best titles in a very good series.

31. **Schraff, Anne E.** *Gingerbread Heart: Passages 2000.* **Perfection Learning, 1999. 114pp. Paper $5.95 (0-7891-4926-5). Fiction.**

READING LEVEL: 3–6 INTEREST LEVEL: 12–18
ACCELERATED READER: YES

Jalena Puljic is a survivor of the Bosnian conflict, living in America with her older brother Mirko. Jalena is tortured by flashbacks and memories of her experiences in her native country. Disillusioned by the fact that Muslims and Serbs who she thought were friends had shown themselves to be deadly enemies (responsible for the death of her parents and many others), Jalena finds herself incapable of trusting anyone besides Mirko, and uninterested in making friends. Jalena is a basketball star and gets good grades, but this is all for a purpose—getting into a top college—not for enjoyment. Eventually, Jalena's friends teach her to gain a perspective on her history and current life, a perspective that includes good memories with the bad, and allows her to understand the risks involved in trusting people.

32. **Schraff, Anne E.** *Going for Gold: Passages 2000.* **Perfection Learning, 2001. 124pp. Paper $5.95 (0-7891-5362-9). Fiction.**

READING LEVEL: 3–6 INTEREST LEVEL: 12–18

Keely Wayne is a promising young gymnast with the potential to make the Olympic team. When she gets the chance to study with Wassily Karpov, she takes a leave of absence from school to do gymnastics full time. She befriends another girl, Sandra Ashton, and together they try to stand up to Wassily's relentless pressure to be the best. Weight is an issue for young gymnasts, and both girls start to experience symptoms of eating disorders. An accurate portrayal of eating disorders.

33. **Schraff, Anne E.** *The Hyena Laughs at Night: Passages 2000.* **Perfection Learning, 1999. 114pp. Paper $5.95 (0-7891-4925-7). Fiction.**

READING LEVEL: 3–6 INTEREST LEVEL: 12–18
ACCELERATED READER: YES

Dustin Brand is an aspiring cartoonist who becomes interested in Basma Saad, a bright girl from Iraq who lives with her brother Nazar. Nazar is a traditionalist who wants Basma to obey him, to stay apart from Americans, and to stay away from boys like Dustin, whom he dislikes and derisively calls "the hyena." Although Dustin appears in every scene, the author does a good job of developing the conflict between Basma and Nazar, and Basma is a central character in the book. This title is a good choice for boys or girls.

34. Schraff, Anne E. *Just Another Name for Lonely: Passages 2000*. Perfection Learning, 1999. 107pp. Paper $5.95 (0-7891-4923-0). Fiction.

READING LEVEL: 3–6   INTEREST LEVEL: 12–18
ACCELERATED READER: YES

Tina Hayes returns in this sequel to *Please Don't Ask Me to Love You*. At the start of the book, Tina is comfortable in the home of her former employers, the Lovells, whose dying daughter Tina had befriended. But after receiving a phone call from her mother, who has joined Alcoholics Anonymous and divorced her abusive boyfriend, Tina decides to return home to New Mexico. There she finds that she has acquired quite a reputation. Among the legendary exploits attributed (falsely) to her is a starring role in pornographic movies. She falls in with a "bad boy" who is the only one who will treat her nicely, and unwittingly becomes the driver in a robbery. One of the few Passages titles with an unabashedly happy ending, this is an excellent choice for troubled girls.

35. Schraff, Anne E. *Maitland's Kid: Passages*. Perfection Learning, 1989. 117pp. Paper $5.95 (0-8959-8255-2). Fiction.

READING LEVEL: 3–6   INTEREST LEVEL: 12–18
ACCELERATED READER: YES

Jonathan decides to use his Christmas break to track down the father he has never met. Jonathan's relations with his overachieving adoptive father are strained, and he hopes to form a bond with his biological father. Ed Maitland turns out to be an alcoholic who makes a living doing odd jobs and whose home is a rundown shack in the woods. As Jonathan and his father get to know each other, he realizes that he is taking on a parental role and is caring for his father. This will resonate with many young people who are facing similar situations. *Bridge to the Moon* (see above) is a sequel.

36. Schraff, Anne E. *Memories Are Forever: Passages*. Perfection Learning, 1993. 135pp. Paper $5.95 (0-7891-4924-9). Fiction.

READING LEVEL: 3–6   INTEREST LEVEL: 12–18
ACCELERATED READER: YES

Bien Tran must reconcile her family's Vietnamese culture, her growing interest in American culture, and her desire to be accepted as a normal kid. This is a complicated relationship novel, with friendships pulling the characters in different (and sometimes contradictory) directions. The main issues Bien must cope with are complex teenage romantic machinations and the grandfather of her best friend, a greybearded, long-haired, Harley-riding misanthrope who hates all Vietnamese and still has flashbacks to his experiences in the Vietnam War.

37. **Schraff, Anne E.** *Old Traditions, New Pride: Passages 2000.* Perfection Learning, 2001. 123pp. Paper $5.95 (0-7891-5386-6). Fiction.

READING LEVEL: 3–6   INTEREST LEVEL: 12–18

This book tells the story of Tom Long, a Nez Perce teenager living on an Indian reservation. Tom has two special friends with conflicting ambitions. Eddie wants to be assimilated into white culture, like European immigrants. Paul would prefer to cling to the old ways. When a new teacher, a Ute, comes to town, Tom starts to question his family's values. Although the book makes use of stereotypes, for the sake of brevity, it does provide a fair depiction of the problems faced by Native American youth today, as well as providing some interesting background on the Nez Perce.

38. **Schraff, Anne E.** *The Petition: Passages 2000.* Perfection Learning, 2001. 104pp. Paper $5.95 (0-7891-5359-9). Fiction.

READING LEVEL: 4–5   INTEREST LEVEL: 12–18

Izzy Saenz is a good student. He plans a career in computers but dreams of becoming a writer. His English teacher, Mr. Pedroza, is an experienced instructor with very high standards, so tough that a group of students band together seeking to have him dismissed. Izzy refuses to sign their petition, openly supports Mr. Pedroza, and is ostracized by the other students. A good choice for helping students understand the teacher's side of schools and schoolwork.

39. **Schraff, Anne E.** *Please Don't Ask Me to Love You: Passages.* Perfection Learning, 1978, revised 1989. 116pp. Paper $5.95 (0-8959-8253-6). Fiction.

READING LEVEL: 3–6   INTEREST LEVEL: 12–18
ACCELERATED READER: YES

Tina Hayes flees an alcoholic mother and her mother's abusive boyfriend, hoping to find a new life in Los Angeles. However, this proves difficult. A job as a waitress doesn't last long and Tina turns to shoplifting to make ends meet. A lowlife named Eddie suggests an involved scam: He will provide her with fake references for a domestic position in a wealthy home; in return she will give him information that will help him rob the house. Tina succeeds in finding a job as companion to a dying girl who is preoccupied by the troubled children she cares for. Can she betray this girl's trust? The mature topics and difficult moral challenges Tina faces make this a good choice for older readers and for classroom discussion. Also available in Spanish.

40. **Schraff, Anne E.** *The Price of Friendship: Passages 2000.* **Perfection Learning, 2001. 140pp. Paper $5.95 (0-7891-5375-0). Fiction.**

READING LEVEL: 3–6 INTEREST LEVEL: 12–18

One of several books in the Passages 2000 series geared toward black teenagers, this one tackles the difficult issue of "acting white." Kirk Howell is a capable African American high school senior torn between his dream of being an engineer and his friends, who are less concerned with doing well in school and are attracted by the easy money available on the streets. Kirk must deal with all the usual problems facing today's teens, plus the realization that many white people may fear him and leap to conclusions about his interests and intellectual capabilities. The best of the Passages 2000 titles for boys, this is a good choice for any reader.

41. **Schraff, Anne E.** *Someone to Love Me.* **Townsend Press, 2001. 162pp. Paper $4.95 (0-944210-06-6). Fiction.**

READING LEVEL: 4–6 INTEREST LEVEL: 12–15

Part of the Bluford High School series. Fifteen-year-old Cindy Gibson is a Bluford freshman. She has a stormy relationship with her single-parent mother, who spends all her time with a boyfriend who may be a drug dealer at Bluford High. Although Cindy is selected to draw cartoons for the school paper, she still suffers from low self-esteem because of abusive taunts from her mother's boyfriend. Seeking love in all the wrong places, Cindy gets involved with a physically abusive boyfriend and is fortunately rescued by a sincere and supportive group of friends. By the book's end, Cindy and her mother have forged a close relationship and decide to go it alone, rejecting the men who are wrong for them. An exceptional story that will get teens reading to the end and quickly moving on to other titles in this series, including *Lost and Found, A Matter of Trust, Secrets in the Shadows*, and *Until We Meet Again.*

42. **Schraff, Anne E.** *A Song to Sing: Passages.* **Perfection Learning, 1989. 132pp. Paper $5.95 (0-8959-8257-9). Fiction.**

READING LEVEL: 3–6 INTEREST LEVEL: 12–18
ACCELERATED READER: YES

Reina Valdez and her friend Efren Mora seem to be set to win school elections. However, conflicts at school—and at home—threaten this outcome and make for an exciting read for boys and for girls. Also available in Spanish.

43. **Schraff, Anne E. *Sparrow's Treasure: Passages*. Perfection Learning, 1989. 116pp. Paper $5.95 (0-8959-8258-7). Fiction.**

READING LEVEL: INTEREST LEVEL: 12–18
ACCELERATED READER: YES

Rachel Dorr is a small-town nobody, a little sparrow, hopping and chirping, but getting no attention. She decides she is "tired of being a kid like me." A moody new history teacher offers her a challenge, and Rachel begins to change.

44. **Schraff, Anne E. *To Be Somebody: Passages 2000*. Perfection Learning, 2001. 120pp. Paper $5.95 (0-7891-5366-1). Fiction.**

READING LEVEL: INTEREST LEVEL: 12–18

Nondescript Marcus Platt wants to become the kind of person others look up to. A lucky family connection provides Marcus with tickets to a hot concert, which he parlays into a date with a popular cheerleader, Sheryl Williams. More light-hearted than the other Passages 2001 titles, this book is largely concerned with Marcus's streetwise ways of endearing himself to the popular girl and using his success with her to raise his stature among his peers. The reader should see through Marcus's foolishness long before Marcus does, making this a fun book for boys or girls.

45. **Seward, Angela, and Donna Ferreiro, illus. *Goodnight, Daddy*. Morning Glory Press, 2001. 48pp. Paper $7.95 (1-885356-72-2). Fiction.**

READING LEVEL: 2–4   INTEREST LEVEL: 14–18

Eight-year-old Phoebe looks forward to a visit from her absent father and must deal with her disappointment when he postpones his visit. This is a story that a teen mom can read to her child when the father's missed visits cause anxiety. Guidelines that append the text are written at a higher level but would help a young mother understand how to reassure a child that he or she is not neglected, that many other people in the child's life show care and concern. Crayon drawings throughout.

46. **Sorenson, Margo. *Danger Canyon*. Perfection Learning, 1996. 80pp. Paper $5.95 (0-7891-0227-7). Fiction.**

READING LEVEL: 2–3   INTEREST LEVEL: 12–14
ACCELERATED READER: YES

Calvin and Rob are bored with everyday life in the city. They yearn for adventure. So when Calvin's sister moves to a subdivision near a state park, the boys plan a leisurely one-day hiking trip. With extra sandwiches and sodas in their backpacks and armed with a flashlight for emergencies, the two hikers take off before sunup. Arriving too early to check into the ranger station, they forge ahead, confident that as long as they follow the green trail they will have no trouble finding their way back. But a mountain lion, two escaped prisoners, and an attempt to take a shortcut before darkness leave the boys trapped by waterfalls in a narrow gorge as darkness descends. A fast-paced Gary Paulsen-style tale for reluctant readers.

47. **Sorenson, Margo, and Michael Aspengren, illus.** *Don't Bug Me.* **Perfection Learning, 1996. 79pp. LB $11.95 (0-7891-0232-3). Fiction.**

READING LEVEL: 2–3 INTEREST LEVEL: 12–14
ACCELERATED READER: YES

Zack Washington has enough trouble starting out in a new junior high school without being nicknamed Bug Boy. Zack is so named because he's dropped off by his dad's pest control van, which has a big ant on top. His chances to make friends are limited by his responsibilities: he has to help his dad after school and babysit his younger sisters at weekends. Zack's attitude about his rotten luck makes for a light, humorous read for boys or girls.

48. **Sorenson, Margo, and Michael Aspengren, illus.** *The Gotcha Plot.* **Perfection Learning, 1996. 79pp. Paper $5.95 (0-7891-0234-X). Fiction.**

READING LEVEL: 2–3 INTEREST LEVEL: 12–14
ACCELERATED READER: YES

Cecil and Carlos are the target of a pair of persistent bullies. But thanks to the custodian, Mr. O'Malley (whose mission is to "clean up the school"), and his special invisibility fluid, the boys are able to turn the tables on their persecutors. The bullies are unlikable, and readers will enjoy seeing them learn a lesson. A good choice for boys who are bullies or bullied.

49. **Taylor, Bonnie H., and Christine McNamara, illus.** *Joker.* **Perfection Learning, 1999. 64pp. Paper $5.95 (0-7891-2931-0). Fiction.**

READING LEVEL: 2–3 INTEREST LEVEL: 12–15
ACCELERATED READER: YES

Twelve-year-old Scott loves his horse, Joker. But Joker keeps getting in trouble, doesn't train well, and might be more trouble than he is worth. An amusing book for any boy or girl who likes horses and other animals.

50. **Widener, Sandra, and Jose Miralles, illus.** *The Quest: American Expressions.* **Globe Fearon, 1997. 96pp. Paper $8.95 (0-8359-3355-5). Fiction.**

READING LEVEL: 3–4 INTEREST LEVEL: 8–12

One of a series of readers, for and about teenagers, integrating many kinds of writing (diary entries, letters, poems, plays, folktales, and short stories) around a common theme. Notes help the reader conceptualize the issues under discussion. Possibly the best of the eight titles in the series, these sixteen stories about different kinds of quests highlight the idea that a quest is special, something beyond an ordinary struggle or challenge. The stories are between two and twelve pages long.

HISTORICAL FICTION

BOOKS

51. Baxter, Linda, and Sue F. Cornelison, illus. *River of Amber*. Perfection Learning, 2001. 111pp. Paper $5.95 (0-7891-5395-7). Fiction.
READING LEVEL: 3–5   INTEREST LEVEL: 12–16
ACCELERATED READER: YES

In this novel about agonizing choices, it is 1938 and Sasha Victorovich is finishing the equivalent of high school in Latvia. He lives with his sister in Riga. Sasha specializes in chemistry and track, and is good enough to qualify for the 1949 Olympic team. But his Jewish friend Ralph encourages him to emigrate to the United States, to escape the impending war. The political and military complexities of life in the Baltic region at this time are brought out in discussions between the characters. The second novel in a trilogy that includes *River of Ice* and *River of Freedom*.

52. Baxter, Linda, and Sue F. Cornelison, illus. *River of Freedom*. Perfection Learning, 2002. 96pp. Paper $5.95 (0-7891-5537-0). Fiction.
READING LEVEL: 3–5   INTEREST LEVEL: 12–16

In this third and last volume of a trilogy, Sasha Victorovich is attending Yale University during World War II and carefully monitoring events in Latvia, where his sister still lives. He agonizes about his decision not to join the armed forces and worries about his mother in the Soviet Union. Against this backdrop of tension, he develops suspicions about his mathematics professor's activities and decides the professor must be a spy. The novel is sweetened by a long-awaited reunion. Readers will enjoy this novel more if they have read the previous volumes, *River of Ice* and *River of Amber*.

53. **Baxter, Linda, and Sue F. Cornelison, illus.** *River of Ice.* **Perfection Learning, 2001. 103pp. Paper $5.95 (0-7891-5392-0). Fiction.**

READING LEVEL: 3–5 INTEREST LEVEL: 12–16
ACCELERATED READER: YES

Sasha Victorovich, a boy of 15, lives with his mother and grandmother in Moscow after the Bolshevik Revolution. Sasha's mother is a doctor but the Soviet government will not allow her to emigrate to her native Latvia to be with her ailing husband. The novel does a good job of using representative types (like the stern bureaucrat Carina Mikalonova) to create a realistic sense of living under early Russian communism, and gives a good view of the philosophy behind the movement, while building toward a dramatic conclusion. Sequels are *River of Amber* and *River of Freedom.*

54. **Grohmann, Susan.** *The Shining Prince.* **Perfection Learning, 2002. 148pp. Paper $5.95 (0-7891-5533-8). Fiction.**

READING LEVEL: 4–7 INTEREST LEVEL: 12–18

One of the first novels in a new YA imprint from Perfection Learning, this book is a nicely crafted mix of modern and ancient Japanese cultural history. Fifteen-year-old Michael Tsukamoto lives in San Francisco. An elderly uncle, a professor of Japanese literature, is visiting his family when they are forcibly moved to a desert relocation camp, soon after Pearl Harbor. The uncle tells stories from a Japanese folklore collection about a "shining prince" of ancient Japan; Michael strives to relate the tales of his heritage with the circumstances of his present.

55. **Hagen, Alice M.** *Jack Sloan in Tin Star Promise.* **New Readers Press, 2001. 64pp. Paper. Sold as part of a set (1-56853-048-X). Fiction.**

READING LEVEL: 2–3 INTEREST LEVEL: 8–13

The first of a four-book series about Sheriff Jack Sloan and the various supporting characters who help him solve crimes. Sloan is a Civil War veteran who returns to his Texas home to find his wife and son missing. He sets out to find them with the help of the town sheriff. The boy is rescued and the outlaws captured, but the wife is not found. Later the sheriff is murdered and Jack leads the posse to catch the perpetrator. The series makes extensive use of stereotypes, for the sake of brevity, but handles this well. The portrayal of Native Americans is particularly good. Chief Gray Hawk is one of the good guys, and the stories include genuine elements of Native American culture. The books do a good job of setting a tone consistent with the historical American West; they do not take place in the mythical, romantic land of the Western genre. Sequels are *Jack Sloan in Justice on Horseback, Jack Sloan in Shotgun Revenge,* and *Jack Sloan in Mississippi Stranger.*

56. Haley, Alex. *Selected from A Different Kind of Christmas.* **New Readers Press, 1991. 62pp. Paper $4.75 (0-929631-26-9). Fiction.**

READING LEVEL: 5   INTEREST LEVEL: 12–18

This excerpted version of a classic tells the tale of the son of a North Carolina plantation-owner who attends school in the North, becomes involved with Quaker Abolitionists, and changes his views about the institution of slavery. He is challenged to prove his loyalty to his new ideals by helping twelve slaves to escape from his home county (including six from his home) via the Underground Railroad. The plot is further complicated when it is discovered that a slave escape is planned, forcing the conspirators to use Christmas Eve as a diversion. The characters are realistically drawn. A good choice for those who read and enjoyed *Nightjohn* by Gary Paulsen. This is a title in the Writers' Voices series.

57. Kenna, Gail Wilson. *Along the Gold Rush Trail.* **New Readers Press, 1982. 96pp. Paper $5.00 (0-88336-203-1). Fiction.**

READING LEVEL: 3   INTEREST LEVEL: 9–12

Yearning for fortune and adventure, Eugene heads for California during the 1849 Gold Rush. Undaunted by the hardships of prairie life and the dangers of the Santa Fe Trail, he is determined to become a miner. Weary, hungry, and penniless, Eugene survives thanks to the help of a doctor he befriends along the way. Together they make the journey west, crossing mountains and deserts. At journey's end, Eugene has matured considerably, manifesting courage, humanity, and an indomitable spirit. Drawings.

58. Mattern, Joanne. *Coming to America: The Story of Immigration.* **Perfection Learning, 2001. 64pp. Paper $8.95 (0-7891-2851-9). Fiction.**

READING LEVEL: 4–5   INTEREST LEVEL: 12–15
ACCELERATED READER: YES

Twenty million people came to the United States between 1892 and 1920. This book takes us through the experiences of the Martini family as they voyaged across the sea to Ellis Island, settling on New York's Lower East Side. Photos of the teeming neighborhoods of 1920s New York re-create life as it was for millions of settlers who rode trolleys for the first time, moved into crowded tenement houses, learned English, and visited settlement houses to further their education. A warm look at the life of the author's immigrant grandmother's voyage to America. Glossary.

59. **Mercati, Cynthia, and Dan Hatala, illus. *A Light in the Sky*. Perfection Learning, 2000. 72pp. Paper $5.95 (0-7891-5094-8). Fiction.**

READING LEVEL: 2–5   INTEREST LEVEL: 12–15

It's 1941 in German-occupied France and fourteen-year-old Jeanne Legrande dreams of joining the French Resistance, to avenge the brother she saw murdered by Nazis. One night, she sees an RAF fighter shot down. She finds the pilot—an American volunteer named Tom Murphy—and hides him in her family's woodshed. Her friend Andre turns out to be a Resistance fighter and helps Tom to escape. The tense plot, the romance between Jeanne and Andre, and a discussion of the reasons why the United States joined the Allies make this a fine choice for boys or girls.

60. **Mercati, Cynthia, and Paul Micich, illus. *The Secret Room*. Perfection Learning, 2000. 72pp. Paper $5.95 (0-7891-5108-1). Fiction.**

READING LEVEL: 2–5   INTEREST LEVEL: 12–18
ACCELERATED READER: YES

Annie Van Vries is the daughter of a Dutch minister, living in a small town under Nazi occupation in World War II. Annie's father decides to shelter a Jewish family in a secret room above the church and enlists her help in caring for them. When he is arrested on unrelated charges, he gives Annie responsibility for the family, instructing her not to tell her older sister or her mother. The story covers a great deal of ground in a short time, and the character of brave little Annie should provide inspiration to girls of any age.

61. **Olson, Tod. *Donner Party: A Diary of a Survivor*. Scholastic READ Program, 1999. 28pp. Paper. Sold as part of a set (0-439-05700-0). Fiction.**

READING LEVEL: 1.5–2.5   INTEREST LEVEL: 12–14

In 1846, many families set out for a new start in California. In this fictionalized diary, twelve-year-old Virginia Reed describes her family's struggle to survive in the midst of widespread starvation and the family's miraculous rescue and reunion. Drawings follow the easy-reading text. Glossary.

62. **Reiff, Tana. *Boat People: Hopes and Dreams: The Vietnamese*. Globe Fearon, 1989. 76pp. Paper $12.10 (0-8224-3685-X). Fiction.**

READING LEVEL: 2–3   INTEREST LEVEL: 7–12

After a treacherous voyage that involves robbery aboard ship, sailing through storms, and several near sinkings, the Nguyen family finally arrives in Malaysia, where for three months they live safely while making repairs to their boat. Forced to leave Malaysia, the boat people make their way to Indonesia, where the youngest Nguyen boy dies. From Indonesia, they are flown to San Francisco and a new life. The Nguyens are told that because they are fishermen, they should settle on the Gulf Coast of Texas. But life there is not easy as cultures collide over fishing grounds. It takes much compromise on both sides before the Nguyen family finds peace. Part of a historical fiction series with an unusual presentation involving sentences broken into phrases, each on its own line of text. The simple narrative style allows very moving stories to sneak up on the reader. The books are primarily about adults.

63. Reiff, Tana. *Fair Fields: The Filipinos: Hopes and Dreams 2*. Globe Fearon, 1993. 76pp. Paper $8.50 (0-8224-3808-9). Fiction.
READING LEVEL: 3   INTEREST LEVEL: 12–18

Fabian Beltram, an elderly, very ill man, recounts his life story to a young nurse, Trini. Both are of Filipino descent, and it's important to Fabian that Trini understand the difficulties of earlier generations of Filipinos, particularly migrant agricultural workers.

64. Reiff, Tana. *Here and There: The Puerto Ricans: Hopes and Dreams 2*. Globe Fearon, 1993. 76pp. Paper $8.50 (0-8224-3807-0). Fiction.
READING LEVEL: 3   INTEREST LEVEL: 12–18

In 1965, Hector and Gloria Martinez leave their home and children in Puerto Rico to find a better life in the United States. They settle in crowded Spanish Harlem, where drugs, violence, crime, and gangs make living conditions difficult. But Hector finally lands a good job, the family is reunited, and they continue to struggle to improve their lives and at the same time retain their Latin identity.

65. Reiff, Tana. *Little Italy: Hopes and Dreams: The Italians*. Globe Fearon, 1989. 76pp. Paper $11.30 (0-8224-3677-9). Fiction.
READING LEVEL: 2–3   INTEREST LEVEL: 7–12

The Trella family comes to the United States from Italy, landing at Ellis Island in the 1920s. Dominick Trella soon finds work in construction and the family lives quite nicely, although in crowded conditions, on New York's Lower East Side. As the children grow (as does the family, swelling to nine), the parents continue to live in the small rooms in the congested tenement. The Trella children spread out from their home, but the parents remain in Little Italy.

66. Reiff, Tana. *Making Heaven: The Koreans: Hopes and Dreams 2*. Globe Fearon, 1993. 76pp. Paper $8.50 (0-8224-3801-1). Fiction.

READING LEVEL: 3   INTEREST LEVEL: 12–18

Newlyweds Song and Jae migrate from Korea to the United States in 1970, using combined family savings to start a vegetable stand in Harlem, New York. Building the business is difficult but rewarding—until protestors picket the store and then burn it down.

67. Reiff, Tana. *Many Miles: The Arabs: Hopes and Dreams 2*. Globe Fearon, 1993. 76pp. Paper $8.50 (0-8224-3804-6). Fiction.

READING LEVEL: 3   INTEREST LEVEL: 12–18

In 1902, Habib Malouf leaves his small village in Syria with a group going to the United States. After his arrival, he heads west from New York and starts selling housewares in remote locations. He eventually achieves enough success to become involved in charity work.

68. Reiff, Tana. *Never So Good: The Jamaicans: Hopes and Dreams 2*. Globe Fearon, 1993. 76pp. Paper $8.50 (0-8224-3806-2). Fiction.

READING LEVEL: 3   INTEREST LEVEL: 12–18

In 1978, Roz Nash leaves his home and friends in Jamaica to look for work in the United States, hoping eventually to reunite his family in New York City. Although he succeeds in this goal, he and his family are surprised to meet discrimination, even from other people of color, that makes their life difficult.

69. Reiff, Tana. *The Next Life: The Indians: Hopes and Dreams 2*. Globe Fearon, 1993. 74pp. Paper $8.50 (0-8224-3802-X). Fiction.

READING LEVEL: 3   INTEREST LEVEL: 12–18

This book is set in the early 1980s and features Indian immigrant Saura Patel, a dental student who is determined not to fall into the same trap as her female relatives and end up dependent on a man for support. When she meets and falls in love with Ravi Mehta, she feels the strain of living between two worlds.

70. Reiff, Tana. *Nobody Knows: Hopes and Dreams: The Africans*. Globe Fearon, 1989. 76pp. Paper $11.30 (0-8224-3683-3). Fiction.

READING LEVEL: 2–3   INTEREST LEVEL: 7–12

The year is 1902, and life for many young black people in the South is one of endless farmwork and housework. Mattie and Nate decide that a move to a big city will offer them a new and better life. But their migration to Chicago is not easy. They fight segregation and difficult working conditions. Nate becomes an activist, joining the black union, and life improves for this growing family. But tragedy strikes when Nate cuts his hand. Lacking sufficient medical care, Nate develops an infection and dies. Mattie is left alone with five children to support and struggles through the Depression working as a maid. We rejoice when, at the conclusion of the book, Mattie returns to the South to challenge segregation at a lunch counter.

71. **Reiff, Tana.** *Sent Away: The Japanese: Hopes and Dreams 2.* **Globe Fearon, 1993. 75pp. Paper $8.50 (0-8224-3800-3). Fiction.**

READING LEVEL: 3 INTEREST LEVEL: 12–18

The Higashi family is happy and prosperous at the beginning of World War II. However, their lives change dramatically after Pearl Harbor, when, as Japanese Americans, they are relocated to a desert camp. There are many stories like this in print, but something about the simple narration—in the typical Hopes and Dreams series style—makes this one particularly powerful.

72. **Reiff, Tana.** *Ties to the Past: The Poles: Hopes and Dreams 2.* **Globe Fearon, 1993. 74pp. Paper $8.50 (0-8224-3803-8). Fiction.**

READING LEVEL: 3 INTEREST LEVEL: 12–18

Kassia Loloski and her Polish immigrant parents have quite different ideas about how to be a good American citizen. Kassia must work to support the family, and, although her father doesn't value education for women, she succeeds in obtaining a diploma in early twentieth-century Buffalo, N.Y.

73. **Reiff, Tana.** *Two Hearts: The Greeks: Hopes and Dreams 2.* **Globe Fearon, 1993. 76pp. Paper $8.50 (0-8224-3805-4). Fiction.**

READING LEVEL: 3 INTEREST LEVEL: 12–18

In 1911, George Stavros leaves his small mountain village in Greece. He plans to move to the United States to earn money for his sister's dowry. When he meets his padrone, who promises to help him, George thinks he's in luck. However, he soon sees unanticipated pitfalls and decides he must make a success on his own.

74. **Reiff, Tana.** *Who Is My Neighbor? The Salvadorans: Hopes and Dreams 2.* **Globe Fearon, 1993. 76pp. Paper $8.50 (0-8224-3809-7). Fiction.**

READING LEVEL: 3 INTEREST LEVEL: 12–18

Ramon Saymoya leaves his coffee plantation in war-torn El Salvador in 1980 and travels north, hoping to be granted political asylum in the United States. Events in El Salvador and Ramon's travels through Central America constitute most of the novel. The action/adventure elements make this an excellent choice for boys.

75. **Schraff, Anne E.** *The Bloody Wake of the Infamy: Passages to History.* **Perfection Learning, 2000. 128 pp. Paper $5.95 (0-7891-5240-1). Fiction.**

READING LEVEL: 4–5 INTEREST LEVEL: 12–18

It is 1760, and sixteen-year-old Peter McCall is headed to England to attend medical school. But Riley Oliver, an enemy of Peter's father, has plotted with pirates to kidnap Peter and hold him for ransom. Peter and Riley eventually are left alone on a deserted island, Riley shot and dying and the aspiring physician trying to save his new friend's life. The book makes a clear comparison between the lives of the McCalls and of the Olivers, who struggle to make ends meet. Packed with action scenes, this title is a better choice for boys.

76. **Schraff, Anne E.** *Darkness: Passages to History.* **Perfection Learning, 2000. 120pp. Paper $5.95 (0-7891-5183-9). Fiction.**

READING LEVEL: 4–5 INTEREST LEVEL: 12–18
ACCELERATED READER: YES

It is 1939 in rural Ohio and seventeen-year-old Karl Schmidt has a crush on pretty Rebecca Silverman. Karl is part of a large community of descendents of German immigrants. Rebecca is Jewish. Mr. Wagner, the history teacher, spouts Aryan propaganda, often humiliating Rebecca. Karl finds himself confused by the different information he receives from the news media, his teachers, his family, and Rebecca—whose Jewish information sources seem to be totally in conflict with what Mr. Wagner is teaching. The star-crossed romance of Karl and Rebecca makes this a good choice for boys or girls. The theme of evaluating conflicting/contradictory information resources make this a good choice for librarians interested in novel ways of teaching about information literacy.

77. **Schraff, Anne E.** *Freedom Knows No Color: Passages to History.* **Perfection Learning, 2000. 120pp. Paper $5.95 (0-7891-5183-9). Fiction.**

READING LEVEL: 4 INTEREST LEVEL: 12–18
ACCELERATED READER: YES

It is 1858 in rural Louisiana and eighteen-year-old Julian Holland, a black slave, fears that the death of the kind plantation owner bodes ill for him. When Julian is sold to the mean Cyrus Cannon, he and another slave, Daniel, decide to run away. Luckily they get help from the Underground Railroad and escape to the North. However, once free, the two men find their difficulties are not over, because they cannot find work. The book does a good job of using Julian as a vehicle to present the different arguments about the moral dilemma of slavery in pre-Civil War America. Julian was possibly better off under the benign plantation owner than as a legally free wage slave in the North; but the horror of slavery under a greedy owner is sharply portrayed.

78. Schraff, Anne E. *The Greatest Heroes: Passages to History.* Perfection Learning, 2000. 143pp. Paper $5.95 (0-7891-5133-2). Fiction.

READING LEVEL: 3–6 INTEREST LEVEL: 12–18

It is January 1968, and Ken Sutton is about to turn 18 and register for the draft. Ken's dad fought on the D-Day beaches and has little patience with Ken's doubts about whether he wants to fight in Vietnam. Ken's friends David and Bryan also differ on this conflict and Ken finds himself in the middle. David soon volunteers but Bryan flees to Canada. A final note that indicates that the stories of David and Ken are based on real Vietnam casualties will give this novel a powerful impact, especially for boys.

79. Schraff, Anne E. *Hear That Whistle Blow: Passages to History.* Perfection Learning, 1999. 120pp. Paper $5.95 (0-7891-4946-X). Fiction.

READING LEVEL: 3–6 INTEREST LEVEL: 12–18
ACCELERATED READER: YES

It is 1930s Depression America, and Hank Proctor wants to study to be a doctor. But Hank's friends don't see the sense in Hank's dream, when the whole community is struggling just to scrape together enough coins to stay one step ahead of starvation. Hank's dad sets off to look for work in California and Hank has to work to support the family, neglecting his studies. When a moral crisis causes Hank to lose his after-school job, it seems he must abandon his dream and follow his father. The book does a nice job of helping readers understand the different choices faced by the average person in the Depression era, using minor characters to illustrate their dilemmas.

80. Schraff, Anne E. *Strawberry Autumn: Passages to History.* Perfection Learning, 1999. 136pp. Paper $5.95 (0-7891-4940-0). Fiction.

READING LEVEL: 4 INTEREST LEVEL: 12–18
ACCELERATED READER: YES

It is 1956 in a small town in Alabama. Grace Foster has a crush on Jimmie Burke but fears that Jimmie's ambition to improve the lot of his fellow blacks may backfire. Jimmie has set his sights on Mr. Waite's drugstore, angered by the different levels of service—the owner reserves strawberry ice cream for whites only. But many feel that Mr. Waite is good to black people, serving them at the same counter as whites and contributing to a scholarship fund. At first Grace is determined to dissuade Jimmie from making waves. But as she begins to notice other racial injustices, Grace comes to realize that Jimmie is right. A nice depiction of the main issues in the Martin Luther King boycott era of the civil rights movement.

81. **Stadelhofen, Marcie Miller.** *The Freedom Side.* **New Readers Press, 1989. 64pp. Paper $5.00 (0-88336-204-X). Fiction.**

READING LEVEL: 3 INTEREST LEVEL: 7–12

When Becky Horn, a young black slave, hears that her mistress is planning to sell her, she risks her life to escape to Canada. As a runaway, Becky relies on the help of a white man sent by her father to escort her to the free state of Ohio. Pursued by her former owner, Becky almost gets caught along the way. Her strong will and courage to fight for freedom are an inspiration to all. Drawings.

82. **Stuart, Dee.** *Mission Sabotage.* **Perfection Learning, 2002. 72pp. Paper $5.95 (0-7891-5605-9). Fiction.**

READING LEVEL: 2–5 INTEREST LEVEL: 12–15

It is a night in 1942, and fifteen-year-old William Colvin is walking with his dog on a beach in Florida when he comes across a group of men who have just been landed by submarine and are burying something in the sand. They claim to be fishermen, but William realizes they are Nazi spies and informs the authorities, who find uniforms and explosives buried on the beach. This sets off a race against time. William is the only person who can identify the men; can he lead the authorities to the Nazis before the Nazis find him? This is primarily a boys' book, with an educational component that teaches about wartime blackouts, beach patrols, the Coast Guard, and anti-submarine tactics including the use of airships.

SCIENCE FICTION AND FANTASY

BOOKS

83. **Gresh, Lois, and Danny Gresh.** *Chuck Farris and the Tower of Darkness.* **ECW Press, 2001. 255pp. Paper $6.95 (1-55022-440-9). Fiction.**

READING LEVEL: 5–6 INTEREST LEVEL: 12–15

Chuck is an ordinary thirteen-year-old new millennium teen until he finds himself possessing extraordinary powers that enable him to use the wizardry of a video game superhero to battle his nemesis. When Chuck and his friends become the target of school bully Digger McGraw's taunts and physical abuse, Chuck enters a virtual world fortified with new powers learned from his mastery of many Playstation2 video games. As Chuck wages battle with Digger, his new powers get him into big trouble with his mom, teachers, and basketball coach. This is the first book in a series of novels based on Playstation 2 video games that reluctant readers craving fantasy will find difficult to put down.

84. **Kluepfel, Brian, and David Sell, illus. *Anatoly of the Gomdars*. Perfection Learning, 2002. 120pp. Paper $5.95 (0-7891-5516-8). Fiction.**

READING LEVEL: 4–7 INTEREST LEVEL: 12–18

The Gomdars, a traveling band of performers, are entertaining the Hurs when a group of bandits attacks the village. The rampaging Razoots use loud trombones, tubas, and trumpets to distract the villagers, driving the Gomdars and the Hurs in separate directions. In the confusion, Anatoly, the son of a Hur breadmaker, is mistaken for a wrapped loaf of bread and is snatched up by a Gomdar woman. (Bread was the form of payment for the Gomdars' performance.) Twelve years pass before the two tribes meet up again and must decide the fate of the child. The colorful characters of the Gomdar tribe are the real heroes, particularly the beekeeper and his clever bees. A good choice for older boys and girls and for adults.

WEB SITES

85. **Lord of the Rings**

http://www.lordoftherings.net/

Fans will find much of interest here: ads and posters, information on the cast and the making of the film of *The Lord of the Rings*, a gallery of images, an interactive map of Middle Earth. Anyone who enjoyed the fantasy Narnia stories by C. S. Lewis will love the beautifully presented and illustrated Narnia site (http://www.narnia.com/), where you can meet the characters and explore the lands.

MYSTERY, SUSPENSE, AND HORROR

BOOKS

86. **Hagen, Alice M.** *Tony Jefferson in Double Back.* **New Readers Press, 2001. 64pp. Paper $8.00 (1-56420-276-3). Fiction.**
READING LEVEL: 3–4 INTEREST LEVEL: 12–14

The first in a four-book series about Private Investigator Tony Jefferson and the various supporting characters who help him solve crimes. Jefferson is a crusty, tough former homicide detective with a soft inner core, assisted by stock characters who are well defined and whose small roles are important to advancing the plot. This first novel does little more than develop the premise of the series, although there is a mystery to solve. The opening scene grips the reader right away, describing the death of Jefferson's police partner in Baltimore. This prompts Jefferson to take a break in his grandparents' quiet hometown in Virginia. However, the local police soon seek his help in finding a missing girl and, assisted by his new partner, a former police dog named Chance, Jefferson solves the mystery. Along the way, he meets characters who will assist him in future cases. Fast-paced and interesting, with many twists and turns. The later books in the series are even better: *Broken Trust, Beyond a Doubt,* and *Burning Question.*

87. **King, Stephen.** *Selected from Carrie.* **New Readers Press, 1992. 63pp. Paper $4.75 (0-929631-24-2). Fiction.**
READING LEVEL: 5 INTEREST LEVEL: 12–18

Many readers will already know the storyline of *Carrie* (King's first novel, subsequently made into a movie). This excerpted version sets up the big climax with two short scenes: the "menstruation in the girls' shower" and one with Carrie's mother. The bulk of the narrative details the conclusion, in which the entire town is destroyed. An interesting focus on the differences between the novel and the low-budget film ends the book. This is a title in the Writers' Voices series.

88. **Kudalis, Eric.** *Dracula and Other Vampire Stories.* **Capstone Press, 1994. 48pp. LB $15.95 (1-56065-212-8). Fiction.**
READING LEVEL: 4–6 INTEREST LEVEL: 12–18
ACCELERATED READER: YES

Teenagers love the story behind Count Dracula. This is a very abbreviated retelling of the classic myth that also includes a brief biography of Bram Stoker, references to films and books about Dracula, and an overview of vampire bats with photos so bloodcurdling and revolting to the eyes that even the most resistant of teens to reading will pick up this book! This is a series of books that includes *Frankenstein and the Other Stories of Man-made Monsters, Stories of Mummies and the Living Dead,* and *Werewolves and Stories About Them.*

89. Schraff, Anne E. *An Alien from Cyberspace: Passages to Suspense.* Perfection Learning, 2002. 117pp. Paper $5.95 (0-7891-5494-3). Fiction.

READING LEVEL: 3–6   INTEREST LEVEL: 12–18

One of an extensive series of coming of age novels published for the school market by Perfection Learning. The titles in the Passages to Suspense sequence are simpler in thematic content than any of the other Passages imprints. Passages to Suspense are clearly designed to give more mature readers a case of Goosebumps. Joshua Madison, 17, is a UFO buff who shares his interest in extraterrestrials with far-flung friends on the Internet. Orson and Silver Girl are two such friends, keeping in touch by email and instant messaging. Joshua receives a strange message from Orson's account, claiming to be from a space alien being held captive by Orson. Joshua and Silver Girl go to check out the possibility that there might really be an alien. Readers will be satisfied that the alien exists, and that Joshua and Rina (Silver Girl) are able to rescue the extra-terrestrial. This is a good reading choice for readers who may be reluctant to get off their computers and read a book.

90. Schraff, Anne E. *An Alien Spring: Passages.* Perfection Learning, 1978, revised 1989. 113pp. Paper $5.95 (0-8959-8256-0). Fiction.

READING LEVEL: 3–6   INTEREST LEVEL: 12–18
ACCELERATED READER: YES

The little town of Marnard is experiencing a rash of bad luck: a terrible torna-do and suspicious fires. Could they have been caused by a UFO? A strange, deaf teenager appears, and rumors spread that he is an alien, responsible for spreading disease. *Summer of Shame* is a sequel.

91. Schraff, Anne E. *The Chain: Passages to Suspense.* Perfection Learning, 2002. 120pp. Paper $5.95 (0-7891-5510-9). Fiction.

READING LEVEL: 3–6   INTEREST LEVEL: 12–18

High school junior Catie Rezo receives a chain letter and decides not to for-ward it—she doesn't believe in bad luck. But bad things start to happen to her, like finding a tarantula in her purse and having her tires slashed. Luckily she has her new friend Marty to help her through the crises . . . but Marty is not what she seems.

92. **Schraff, Anne E.** *The Dangerous Breakup: Passages to Suspense.* **Perfection Learning, 2002. 118pp. Paper $5.95 (0-7891-5502-8). Fiction.**

READING LEVEL: 3–6   INTEREST LEVEL: 12–18

Star senior quarterback Reece Riley recently broke up with Natalie Carr, but she is still in his life. Not only is she now his supervisor at work, she is stalking him and interfering in his relationship with his new girlfriend, Leah. Reece quits his job to get away from Natalie, but Natalie succeeds in breaking up his new romance and persists in trying to win him back. She is determined that if she can't have Reece, nobody else will either. This is a nice switch on the usual stalker formula, with a female stalker and male victim, and is a good choice for boys or girls.

93. **Schraff, Anne E.** *The Darkest Secret: Passages.* **Perfection Learning, 1993. 115pp. Paper $5.95 (1-5631-2150-6). Fiction.**

READING LEVEL: 3–6   INTEREST LEVEL: 12–18
ACCELERATED READER: YES

When Brian Lewis's family moves to his father's boyhood home, Brian accidentally digs up an old diary buried in the yard. Although Brian's father quickly burns the diary, the few entries Brian reads before the diary is confiscated lead him into solving a family mystery and reuniting his father with an estranged brother.

94. **Schraff, Anne E.** *Don't Blame the Children: Passages.* **Perfection Learning, 1978, revised 1989. 113pp. Paper $5.95 (0-8959-8252-8). Fiction.**

READING LEVEL: 3–6   INTEREST LEVEL: 12–18
ACCELERATED READER: YES

Teen couple Kathy Benedict and Todd Macon are the main characters in this book, in which mischievous troublemaker Alec Ross vanishes. Kathy begins to suspect that Todd may be involved in Alex's disappearance. Todd is indeed involved, but in trying to solve the mystery. When a popular teacher is seriously injured, Todd takes matters into his own hands. This title is a good choice for boys and girls. Also available in Spanish.

95. **Schraff, Anne E.** *The Ghost Boy: Passages.* **Perfection Learning, 1978, revised 1989. 117pp. Paper $5.95 (0-8959-8251-X). Fiction.**

READING LEVEL: 3–6   INTEREST LEVEL: 12–18
ACCELERATED READER: YES

Told in the first person by Trisha, this book features Michael, an emotionally disturbed runaway living in a cave whom Trisha initially mistakes as a ghost. It turns out that Michael is in danger from the townspeople, who are afraid of him. In a parallel plot, Trish is at odds with her stepfather; she finds him a poor replacement for her genetic father and wonders what her mother sees in him. Trish eventually discovers that there are many kinds of bravery and develops a new understanding for and relationship with her stepfather.

96. **Schraff, Anne E.** *The Ghost of Mangrove Manor: Passages to Suspense.* **Perfection Learning, 2002. 120pp. Paper $5.95 (0-7891-5460-9). Fiction.**

READING LEVEL: 3–6 INTEREST LEVEL: 12–18

A very basic ghost story, without complications, that would be a good introduction to the genre. Sixteen-year-old Aaron Hayes's family moves into a spooky old mansion, left to them by Aaron's great uncle. A fairly predictable plot quickly unfolds, involving the ghost of a murdered woman, the legacy of the great uncle, and the most detested teacher in Aaron's school.

97. **Schraff, Anne E.** *The Haunting of Hawthorne: Passages.* **Perfection Learning, 1978, revised 1989. 126pp. Paper $5.95 (0-8959-8249-8). Fiction.**

READING LEVEL: 3–6 INTEREST LEVEL: 12–18
ACCELERATED READER: YES

Valerie Moran narrates this haunting tale of the ghost of a private school's first principal. Basil Harris is the handsomest boy Valerie has ever seen. Basil is new in school, but seems to have a deeper maturity to go with his haunting good looks—giving Valerie a feeling of confidence and trust that grows quickly into deeper feelings. Does Basil have strange powers including precognition and telekinesis, or is Val seeing only coincidences? Whether supernatural or not, Basil has a big impact on the school and a bigger impact on the narrator. In the end, the legends of the school and the events of the novel are tied together in a powerful and emotional climax, when Valerie finds out that Basil and the first principal of Hawthorne High have uncanny traits in common.

98. **Schraff, Anne E.** *The Monster in the Mountains: Passages to Suspense.* **Perfection Learning, 2002. 118pp. Paper $5.95 (0-7891-5517-6). Fiction.**

READING LEVEL: 3–6 INTEREST LEVEL: 12–18

Recently graduated from high school, eighteen-year-old Carmela Masters is working as a counselor at a summer camp. She uses a monster costume to scare the young campers during ghost stories. But soon there is more than one monster. When a counselor goes missing, the mystery deepens, but Carmela is not afraid to try to solve it.

99. Schraff, Anne E. *The Shadow Man: Passages.* **Perfection Learning, 1993. 134pp. Paper $5.95 (1-5631-2149-2). Fiction.**

READING LEVEL: 3–6   INTEREST LEVEL: 12–18
ACCELERATED READER: YES

This is one of the numerous Passages titles that focuses on the lives of urban black teenagers. Fifteen-year-old Damien Blair's father has been killed by a hit-and-run driver. Damien seeks to unravel all the mysteries that surround his father's death and begins to suspect he is being shadowed by someone who was involved.

100. Schraff, Anne E. *The Shining Mark: Passages.* **Perfection Learning, 1995. 110pp. Paper $5.95 (1-5631-2398-3). Fiction.**

READING LEVEL: 3–6   INTEREST LEVEL: 14–18
ACCELERATED READER: YES

In this sequel to *When a Hero Dies*, Tony Gibbs has another mystery to solve. His friend Soroya has been injured in a hit-and-run car accident. Much of the novel is concerned with Soroya's recovery from a head injury. The rest involves following clues and bringing the perpetrator to justice. The mature topic and difficult moral choices Tony faces make this a good choice for older readers.

101. Schraff, Anne E. *Summer of Shame: Passages.* **Perfection Learning, 1995. 111pp. Paper $5.95 (1-5631-2397-5). Fiction.**

READING LEVEL: 3   INTEREST LEVEL: 12–18
ACCELERATED READER: YES

In this sequel to *An Alien Spring*, we find that the mysterious Thomas brothers—Edward and Jules—are not in fact extraterrestrials. A tabloid newspaper journalist comes to town to investigate reports of these strange boys and their extraordinary size and strength, stirring up rumors about Bigfoot and Yeti. Mark Scott and his father set out to find Edward and Jules before the hysteria and fear of the townspeople puts them in danger again.

102. Schraff, Anne E. *To Slay the Dragon: Passages.* **Perfection Learning, 1995. 106pp. Paper $5.95 (1-5631-2394-0). Fiction.**

READING LEVEL: 3   INTEREST LEVEL: 12–18
ACCELERATED READER: YES

All the characters from *Don't Blame the Children* return in this tale of a peaceful summer under threat. Kathy Benedict and Todd Macon are in their first year of junior college. Kathy meets a handsome boy named Zuma, but soon realizes that Zuma is dangerous. The story involves Zuma's stalking endeavors, Todd's detective work, and the advancement of the Todd/Kathy romance. Readers will enjoy this more if they have read the previous book. This title is a good choice for both boys and girls.

103. Schraff, Anne E. *The Vandal: Passages.* Perfection Learning, 1978, revised 1989. 133pp. Paper $5.95 (0-8959-8250-1). Fiction.

READING LEVEL: 3–6 INTEREST LEVEL: 12–18
ACCELERATED READER: YES

An action-packed title in the Passages series. A vandal breaks into school and ruins Michelle Dennis's artwork. Michelle is involved romantically with Randy, but she makes an effort also to befriend lonely Damon. She comes to regret this kindness as she discovers that Damon is deeply disturbed and suspects him of committing the act of vandalism. She's afraid he may be stalking her. A perfect day on the beach with Randy is quickly followed by despair when she is kidnapped by Damon. Though Michelle is rescued, Damon is still on the loose when a teacher is shot. A surprise ending makes this a very busy book, but a good choice for girls seeking romance and adventure. Also available in Spanish.

104. Schraff, Anne E. *When a Hero Dies: Passages.* Perfection Learning, 1993. 115pp. Paper $5.95 (1-5631-2150-6). Fiction.

READING LEVEL: 3–6 INTEREST LEVEL: 12–18
ACCELERATED READER: YES

Tony Gibbs, an aspiring young black track-and-field star, loses his mentor, store-owner Hiram Jefferson, when Jefferson is killed in a robbery. Alternating between past and present, the novel relates Tony's investigation of the murder and his concurrent struggles in English class and in sports. The novel does an excellent job of capturing the flavor of the inner city, with realistic and fully drawn supporting characters on both sides of the law. This is a particularly strong title, evidenced by very high sales figures, and a nice choice for readers who may not be quite ready for Chris Crutcher's novels. Also available in Spanish.

GRAPHIC NOVELS

BOOKS

105. Doran, Colleen. *A Distant Soil: Vol. 1: The Gathering*. Image Comics, 1997. 240pp. Paper $19.95 (1-887279-51-2). Graphic novel/Fiction.

READING LEVEL: 4–6   INTEREST LEVEL: 13–18

Colleen Doran was 12 when she conceived this epic novel that grew into three volumes. It features Liana and her older brother, Jason, who break out of a mental health institute only to encounter a warship sent by their father's people to assassinate her. The reading level in this graphic novel varies considerably from scene to scene, but reluctant readers will be pulled into this story full of adventure, intrigue, and political and religious undertones. The illustrations follow the text perfectly and will surely inspire teens who enjoy drawing to consider creating their own graphic novels. More than 500,000 copies have been sold.

106. Nishiyama, Yuriko. *Harlem Beat #1*. Tokyopop Press, 1999. 198pp. Paper $9.95 (1-892213-04-4). Graphic novel/Fiction.

READING LEVEL: 3–6   INTEREST LEVEL: 14–18

This is the first in a series that was originally published in Japan. Nate is a failure at organized basketball in his school. Feeling terribly embarrassed and suffering from a lack of confidence, he meets beautiful Mizz who introduces him to street basketball. Learning the ins and out of street hoops, he finds more than just a pick-up game: here he learns the real value of teamwork and finds true glory in winning. Wonderful appealing teen characters who speak in brief phrases but convey all the grittiness of the city sidewalk game to the reader. No teen can put this book down. Any reluctant teen reader will not only finish the book, but will devour additional titles in the series.

107. Shanower, Eric. *Age of Bronze, Vol. 1: A Thousand Ships*. Image Comics, 2001. 223pp. Paper $19.95 (1-58240-200-0). Graphic novel/Fiction.

READING LEVEL: 4–6   INTEREST LEVEL: 12–18

Reluctant readers cannot tackle many assigned readings. Even attempting to read *The Iliad* will only bring frustration. But here, in the form of a graphic novel, is the complete story of the Trojan War, from Paris's days herding cattle on the slopes of Mount Ida through the end of the war and the heroes' departures for home. Although the reading level varies in complexity from balloon to balloon, there is real feeling here for the story and its inherent danger, romance, familial tragedy, and hope. Freshly retold for the 21st century, this book is essential for any collection of books to inspire the reluctant reader. This is Volume 1 of a projected seven volumes. Maps, glossary, geographic atlas, and historical notes complement the graphic novel text.

108. Talbot, Bryan. *The Tale of One Bad Rat.* Dark Horse, 1995. 136pp. Paper $14.95 (1-565971-077-5). Graphic novel/Fiction.

READING LEVEL: 4–6   INTEREST LEVEL: 12–18

An extraordinary tale of Helen Potter (whose only source of affection is her pet rat) before and after suffering sexual abuse by her father. This is more than a story of a child who has endured sexual abuse, a runaway experience, emotional deprivation, and loss of self-esteem. Through Bryan Talbot's beautiful drawings and elegant prose, which always establishes the same mood as the drawing, we see Helen emerge victorious as a mature young woman and a burgeoning artist. Helen's rise from misery is inspired by her namesake, Beatrix Potter, who serves as both a personal and artistic inspiration for our young heroine. The illustrations incorporate many classic Beatrix Potter touches. Winner of the U.K. Comic Art New Publication Award. This book is used as a resource in many child abuse centers.

WEB SITES

109. Marvel.com

http://www.marvel.com/

Don't know Asgard from your elbow? Mystified by Mystique? Go to the Bios section of the Marvel Comics site and all will be revealed (real name, occupation, base of operations, first appearance, height, weight, powers, weapons, etc.). There are also spotlights on current issues, previews of forthcoming issues, plot summaries, polls, and downloadable screensavers. For Batman, Superman, and other DC Comics characters, visit http://www.dccomics.com/.

Poetry and Drama

BOOKS

110. Abdullah, Omanii. *I Wanna Be the Kinda Father My Mother Was.* **New Readers Press, 1993. Paper $7.75 (0-88336-033-0). Nonfiction.**

READING LEVEL: 4   INTEREST LEVEL: 12–18

Light, free-verse poetry with a streetwise tang and appropriate topics for teenagers. Most of the poems are brief but thought provoking. References to current sports stars and pop music will help keep boys and girls interested. Africa-inspired artwork.

111. Shepard, Elizabeth. *Just Talk: A Play.* **Scholastic Read 180, 1999. 20pp. Paper. Sold as part of a set (0-439-05695-0). Fiction.**

READING LEVEL: 1.5–2.5   INTEREST LEVEL: 12–15

The author has packed in a lot of information about how the hearing impaired communicate through sign language and how important it is for the family and friends of the deaf to learn to sign. The play is fictionalized, but is based on the true story of a fifteen-year-old girl who took her father to court because he refused to learn sign language. It explores the loneliness and isolation that the deaf feel when they cannot make themselves understood. The judge's ruling that the deaf teen live with her sign language teacher—and therefore in an environment in which she could communicate—sends a powerful message to the hearing world about the needs of people with disabilities. Teens will enjoy acting out this brief play. Includes Chart of Dictionary of American Sign symbols. Web sites on American Sign language are listed under the heading Reference below.

Folklore and Mythology

BOOKS

112. Reiff, Tana, and Bill Baylis, illus. *Tall Tales: Timeless Tales.* **New Readers Press, 1993. 48pp. Paper $8.50 (0-88336-463-8).**

READING LEVEL: 2–3   INTEREST LEVEL: 10-16

Seven tall tales, five to eight pages in length, adapted from folklore: Paul Bunyan, the Lumberjack; Pecos Bill, the Cowboy; John Henry, the Natural Man; Stormalong, the Sailor; The Tall-Tale Tellers; Oona and the Giants; Nothing But Lies.

113. Reiff, Tana, and Cheri Bladholm, illus. *Folktales: Timeless Tales.* **New Readers Press, 1993. 48pp. Paper $8.00 (0-88336-271-6).**

READING LEVEL: 2–3   INTEREST LEVEL: 12–16

Nine legends from mythology and folklore, four to seven pages long: The Man in the Moon, Lazy Jack, Money or Mind, The Shoes of Jewels, Aladdin's Lamp, Making Rain, The Happy Man's Shirt, The Tar Baby, and Stone Soup.

114. Reiff, Tana, and Cheri Bladholm, illus. *Love Stories: Timeless Tales.* **New Readers Press, 1993. 48pp. Paper $8.00 (0-88336-462-X).**

READING LEVEL: 2–3   INTEREST LEVEL: 10-16

Six familiar love stories (Cupid and Psyche, Test of Fire, Rhodopis and the Golden Shoes, Beauty and the Beast, Deer Hunter and Corn Maiden, and Romeo and Juliet), each five to nine pages in length, are adapted from mythology, folklore, and Shakespeare.

115. Reiff, Tana, and Holly J. Dobbs, illus. *Tales of Wonder: Timeless Tales.* **New Readers Press, 1993. 48pp. Paper $8.00 (0-88336-459-X).**

READING LEVEL: 2–3   INTEREST LEVEL: 12–16

Ten familiar folktales, two to six pages long, adapted from mythology and folklore: The Firebird, The Three Wishes, The Fountain of Youth, The Elephant From Heaven, The Magic Eagle, A Strange Place to Visit, Talk, The Mirror, Why the Sea Is Salty, and The Thunderbird.

116. Reiff, Tana, and Bob Doucet, illus. *Adventures: Timeless Tales.* **New Readers Press, 1993. 48pp. Paper $8.00 (0-88336-458-1).**

READING LEVEL: 2–3   INTEREST LEVEL: 12–16

Five familiar adventure tales, six to eight pages long, adapted from mythology and folklore: Gilgamesh, Tom Thumb, Sinbad the Sailor, The Twin Brothers, The Quest for the Golden Fleece.

117. Reiff, Tana, and Sherry Kruggel, illus. *Myths: Timeless Tales.* **New Readers Press, 1993. 48pp. Paper $8.00 (0-88336-272-4).**

READING LEVEL: 2–3   INTEREST LEVEL: 10–16

Five familiar tales from Greek mythology (including Pandora's Box) and three from the *Iliad* (including the Trojan War), four to six pages in length, are well selected and retold for this audience.

Biography and Memoir

GENERAL: COLLECTIVE BIOGRAPHIES

BOOKS

118. Chipman, Dawn, and Mari Florence. *Cool Women: The Thinking Girl's Guide to the Hippest Women in History.* **Girl Press, 2001. 104pp. Paper $19.95 (1-931497-02-8). Nonfiction.**

READING LEVEL: 6 AND UP   INTEREST LEVEL: 12–18

A collection of short biographies of strong and independent women who rose above society's oppression of women to achieve unique fame and fortune and excel in their chosen endeavors. Guaranteed to raise the self-esteem of any teenaged girl. Essentially a browsing book, written in a talkie hip style, with sidebars that zero in on the unique aspects of how each subject deviated from the norms of her time to change the course of women's history. The reader is immediately pulled into the text and is quickly immersed in unconventionalities that make for interesting biographical reading. Each profile is told in one or two pages. The women include such disparate figures as Josephine Baker, Rosie the Riveter, Jane Goodall, and Annie Oakley. Even Nancy Drew is there. The text is embellished with lush color and black-and-white drawings and photos throughout. Foreword by Lisa Ling. A great book, which should not be reserved just for Women's History Month reading.

119. Taylor, Bonnie Highsmith. *Women With Grit.* **Perfection Learning, 2000. 62pp. Paper $8.95 (0-7891-5045-X). Nonfiction.**

READING LEVEL: 4–5   INTEREST LEVEL: 12–18
ACCELERATED READER: YES

Brief biographical sketches of eight women, some of whom had to overcome sex bias and racial bigotry to become pioneers in professions including medicine, photography, aviation, and astronomy that were not previously open to women. Black-and-white photographs enhance the easy-reading text as we read about Maria Mitchell, Marion Anderson, Margaret Bourke White, Jackie Cochran, and others whose contributions to women's history are both inspirational and key to the advancement of the role women play in society. Although many of these women are featured in the colorful and exciting book Cool Women (Girl Press), this is an easier read—but when a reluctant reader is presented with both titles, a rich reading and browsing experience awaits. Glossary.

WEB SITES

120. Academy of Achievement

http://www.achievement.org/

This is a good place to start in any search for biographical material. The Gallery of Achievement is divided into Halls of Arts, Business, Public Service, Science and Exploration, and Sports. Each hall contains a good mix of achievers and presents information in three ways: a profile, a biography, and an interview. Many readers will find the interview the most rewarding source of material and will want to refer to the profile or biography for dates and other basic facts. Audio and video clips are scattered throughout the site. A sixth hall (The American Dream) consists of quotes from notable figures, with audio and video. Opposite the Gallery of Achievers you'll find Steps to Success: Halls of Passion, Vision, Preparation, Courage, Perseverance, and Integrity. All are full of quotes from people demonstrating these qualities. There is a search function on the site, but users will find browsing through the individual halls far more appealing.

121. Astronaut Quiz

http://www2.worldbook.com/students/just_fun_index.asp

Select Apollo Astronauts from the list of quizzes on this page, and a new window will open. This World Book site gives users a chance to test their knowledge by identifying nine astronauts. Photos and a short biographical sketch are clues. A sidebar gives background information, including an interesting article on how astronauts are selected and trained today.

122. Inventors Online Museum

http://www.inventorsmuseum.com/

Inventors are listed under various subject headings—African American, Colonial, Communications, Fun and Games, Medical, and so forth. The individual articles are written by different authors and vary considerably in reading level. Students should verify facts with another print or Web source and should be alert for grammatical and typographical errors. However, with these caveats, this can be a useful site.

123. Terrorists, Spies, and Assassins

http://www.crimelibrary.com/terrorists-spies-assassins.htm

A collection of articles on famous villains, including John Wilkes Booth and James Earl Ray, Mata Hari and the Rosenbergs, and Timothy McVeigh, Carlos the Jackal, and Osama bin Laden. The standard of writing on this site is very uneven and the reading levels vary. However, the subject matter is compelling.

124. Women of the Century: One Hundred Years of American Heroes

http://school.discovery.com/schooladventures/womenofthecentury/

A great place for students to start investigating women of achievement. It gives brief information on "phenomenal women" in all walks of life. You can also access a timeline, organized by decade, that places these women in historical context. Links take the reader to more detailed information on other sites. Note the Quote is a game in which you have to match the words with the woman who spoke them.

ACTORS, MUSICIANS, AND WRITERS

CURTIS, CHRISTOPHER PAUL

BOOKS

125. Gaines, Ann G. *Christopher Paul Curtis: A Real-Life Reader Biography.* Mitchell Lane Publishers, 2002. 32pp. LB $15.95 (1-58415-076-9). Nonfiction.
READING LEVEL: 4–5 INTEREST LEVEL: 12–15
ACCELERATED READER: YES

Many teens will enjoy reading about this award-winning author and how he hated the monotony of working on an automobile assembly line. To make time for writing, Curtis arranged with his coworker to alternate their work (hanging doors on car bodies) in half-hour intervals so that he could record his thoughts in a journal. When his short stories about work in the automobile industry started winning writing contests offered by the University of Michigan, he knew it was time to turn his attention to a novel. His first book, *The Watsons Go to Birmingham*, won a Newbery Honor from the American Library Association. Curtis realized his dream of becoming a fulltime writer, earning substantial royalties from his craft. A warm, inspiring portrait of a contemporary children's novelist. Black-and-white photos, chronology.

WEB SITES

126. Christopher Paul Curtis

http://www.randomhouse.com/teachers/authors/curt.html

Biographical details are followed by brief Fun Facts and by audio and text versions of a message from Curtis describing the reasons he became a writer and giving advice for young authors.

DESTINY'S CHILD

BOOKS

127. Kenyatta, Kelly. *Destiny's Child: The Complete Story*. Busta Books, 2001. 114pp. Paper $12.95 (0-9702224-4-0). Nonfiction.

READING LEVEL: 4–6   INTEREST LEVEL: 12–18

A lovely biography of one of the most popular girl groups (there were four members when the book was written). A very attractive 20+-page photo album of the original group and the group as it is today (Michelle, Kelly, and Beyonce) is a charming insert, sure to appeal to all teens. Written in a breezy style, the book captures the down-home values of the beautiful girls who have won almost every musical award. The book is an informative companion piece for all teens who collect Destiny's Child CDs, with touches of gossip about the singers' lives on and off the road. Includes a list of the group's musical awards.

EDMONDS, KENNY

BOOKS

128. Roberts, Jack. *Babyface: In Love with Love.* **Scholastic READ 180, 1999. 19pp. Paper. Sold as part of a set (0-439-05698-5). Nonfiction.**

READING LEVEL: 1.5–2.5   INTEREST LEVEL: 12–18

For Babyface, aka Kenny Edmonds, life is full of love and as delicately balanced as his voice. But life was not always like this for the singer, who was painfully shy as a teenager. He wrote love letters and poems for his friends' girlfriends rather than risk approaching a girl himself. Babyface kept a diary of his most intimate feelings. Losing his father to lung cancer when he was in the eighth grade made him determined to succeed as a songwriter and performer. His first big break came in 1987, with the song "RockSteady," which reached No. 1 hit on Billboard's rhythm-and-blues chart. Working with top stars Sheena Easton, Whitney Houston, and Madonna pushed Babyface to superstardom. With more than 100 top-ten hits to his credit, this happy family man now devotes time and money to the Boarder Baby Project and the United Negro College Fund. Photos, album list, glossary.

GELLAR, SARAH MICHELLE

BOOKS

129. Powell, Phelan. Sarah Michelle Gellar: A Real-Life Reader Biography. Mitchell Lane Publishers, 2001. 32pp. LB $15.95 (1-58415-034-3). Nonfiction.

READING LEVEL: 4–5   INTEREST LEVEL: 12–15
ACCELERATED READER: YES

Child actress Sarah Michelle Gellar is a familiar face on television as the star of *Buffy the Vampire Slayer* and has millions of fans. Earlier in her career, at the age of 5, she appeared in a Burger King commercial followed by roles in the film *Invasion of Privacy* and as Erica Kane's daughter on the soap opera *All My Children*. Aspiring actors will want to follow the rise of this talented young star. Photos, filmography, chronology.

HILL, FAITH

BOOKS

130. Gaines, Ann. *Faith Hill: A Real-Life Reader Biography.* Mitchell Lane Publishers, 2002. 32pp. LB $15.95 (1-58415-091-2). Nonfiction.

READING LEVEL: 4–5 INTEREST LEVEL: 12–18
ACCELERATED READER: YES

This 2001 Grammy winner is a literacy hero. Along with Time Warner and Warner Brothers Records, Faith Hill established the Faith Hill Literacy Project in honor of her stepfather, who never learned to read. Hill, a devoted wife and mother, takes the whole family on the road to gigs and signings. While she is on tour, her literacy project takes top billing and she has contributed 25,000 books to schools and libraries. An enchanting story of one of today's top performers. Black-and-white photos, chronology.

INGLESIAS, ENRIQUE

BOOKS

131. Granados, Christine. *Enrique Inglesias: A Real-Life Reader Biography.* Mitchell Lane Publishers, 2001. 32pp. LB $15.95 (1-58415-045-9). Nonfiction.

READING LEVEL: 4–5 INTEREST LEVEL: 12–18
ACCELERATED READER: YES

As the son of one of the world's most famous performers, Enrique Inglesias knew many record producers but he decided to break into the music world using an assumed name. He auditioned as Enrique Martinez while he was a business student at the University of Miami but initially failed to land a record contract. His first break came when he was signed by Fonovisa, a small company specializing in Mexican music. His debut record sold more than 5 million copies and his career was launched. Additional information about Enrique's childhood and his parents' divorce will show teens the personal struggles that this superstar has had to overcome. Discography, chronology.

LOPEZ, JENNIFER

BOOKS

132. Menard, Valerie. *Jennifer Lopez: A Real-Life Reader Biography*. **Mitchell Lane Publishers, 2001. 32pp. LB $15.95 (1-58415-025-4). Nonfiction.**

READING LEVEL: 4–5 INTEREST LEVEL: 12–18
ACCELERATED READER: YES

A brief biography of J.Lo, who has become the highest-paid Latina film star and is also an award-winning singer and dancer. The book was prepared before Jennifer's second marriage—it takes us up to her life with boyfriend Sean "Puffy" Combs. Growing up in the Bronx, the daughter of Puerto Rico-born parents who wanted her to study law, Jennifer's drive to act landed her small parts in television commercials until her big break on the Fox television show, *In Living Color*, in which she danced as one of the Fly Girls. Film roles soon followed and in 1997 she played the role of the murdered Tejano performer Selena. Photos, filmography, chronology.

MARTIN, RICKY

BOOKS

133. Menard, Valerie. *Ricky Martin: A Real-Life Reader Biography*. **Mitchell Lane Publishers, 2000. 32pp. LB $15.95 (1-58415-059-9). Nonfiction.**

READING LEVEL: 4–5 INTEREST LEVEL: 12–18
ACCELERATED READER: YES

Ricky Martin started singing with the teen group, Menudo, at the age of 12, becoming a millionaire before leaving the group at age 17. Moving on to become an actor on the popular soap opera General Hospital, Ricky captivated millions of people who watch daytime television. Teens who have followed Ricky's career since he started singing at the age of 7 will enjoy reading this brief biography of the Puerto Rico-born talent who had to overcome his shyness and the emotional stress of long tours away from his divorced parents. A charming glimpse into the world of this entertainer who looks forward to performing in films and on Broadway. Photos, discography, and chronology.

PAULSEN, GARY

BOOKS

134. Gaines, Ann. *Gary Paulsen: A Real-Life Reader Biography*. Mitchell Lane Publishers, 2002. 32pp. LB $15.95 (1-58415-077-7). Nonfiction.

READING LEVEL: 4–5   INTEREST LEVEL: 12–16
ACCELERATED READER: YES

Many reluctant readers may have seen the film version of Gary Paulsen's book *Nightjohn* and indeed many will be familiar with the themes of his classic novels *Hatchet* and *Brian's Return*. This brief biography focuses on the difficult periods in Paulsen's life as a child of alcoholic parents, divorce, and incredible loneliness. A kindly librarian who offered him a library card turned his life around. Becoming a reader enabled Gary to acquire the confidence to leave home at 15, becoming a migrant worker. It would be many years later that Gary would discover his love for dogs and the harsh Minnesota winter and go on to write lovingly about his dogsled team and the many Iditarod races they would run together. Gary's books are an inspiration to all teens, and the background material on his life presented here may make reluctant readers curious about reading his award-winning books. Photos, booklist, chronology.

WEB SITES

135. Gary Paulsen

http://www.ipl.org/youth/AskAuthor/paulsen.html

Gary Paulsen's story should inspire any reluctant reader. In this interview he tells how a trip into a library to warm up on a cold night turned his life around. This is only one of several interviews in the Internet Public Library's Youth area. Among others of interest are talks with Daniel Pinkwater (notable for the brevity and humor of his answers), Matt Christopher, and Jane Yolen.

ROWLING, J. K.

BOOKS

136. Gaines, Ann. *J. K. Rowling: A Real-Life Reader Biography*. Mitchell Lane Publishers, 2002. 32pp. LB $15.95 (1-58415-078-5). Nonfiction.

READING LEVEL: 4–5   INTEREST LEVEL: 12–15
ACCELERATED READER: YES

Reluctant readers who tackle the Harry Potter books, and the many who have seen the film *Harry Potter and the Sorcerers' Stone*, will enjoy the behind-the-scenes scoop on the genius behind the series. This brief biography of Harry Potter's creator can introduce students to the origins of the best-selling books and Rowling's life can serve as inspiration to many young people who feel their financial circumstances could be improved. Pre-Potter, Rowling was a single parent on welfare clinging to the hope that her Potter yarn would enchant a publisher as much as she enjoyed creating the fantasy. As luck would have it, the manuscript caught the eye of Bloomsbury Press and now Harry and his creator are household names! Photos, chronology of Rowling's life.

WEB SITES

137. Harry Potter

http://www.kidsreads.com/harrypotter/jkrowling.html

Teens who want to know more about Potter can read the transcript of an interview with the author here. Questions include "How did you get the idea for Harry Potter?" and "How long did it take to write the first book?" and "What are your hobbies."

SELENA

BOOKS

138. Marvis, Barbara. *Selena: A Real-Life Reader Biography.* Mitchell Lane Publishers, 1998. 24pp. LB $15.95 (1-883845-47-5). Nonfiction.

READING LEVEL: 4–5   INTEREST LEVEL: 12–18
ACCELERATED READER: YES

A sensitive portrait of the rise to fame and tragic death of the Texas-born Tejano singer. It is as much a story of Selena's father, who believed his daughter would succeed and risked everything for her musical career. The family coped with homelessness and a tough life as they moved around Texas playing at dances, weddings, and festivals, hoping to be recognized. In 1987, Selena won the Tejano Music Awards for female vocalist and the band prospered thereafter. However, in 1995, Selena was murdered by her fan club manager, a tragic end to the life of this beautiful and talented young performer who was an inspiration to many young Latina girls. Photos, chronology.

139. Seshan, Sandhya, and Elvira Ortiz. *Selena!* **Scholastic READ 180, 1999. 25pp. Paper. Sold as part of a set (0-439-05680-2). Nonfiction.**

READING LEVEL: 1.5–2.5   INTEREST LEVEL: 12–14

Bursting upon the Tejano music scene when she was 12, this young woman destined to have a long and successful career tragically died at the age of 24. As her career skyrocketed, the "Latina Madonna" started a clothing line, married, and began to perform worldwide. She was eventually murdered by Yolanda Saldivar, the president of her fan club. A moving portrait of a very talented young singer that includes photos and a glossary.

WEB SITES

140. Dreaming of You: A Tribute to Selena

http://www.texmexqueen.com/index2.htm

Selena Quintanilla Perez is the subject of many Web sites; key her name into any browser and you'll get numerous hits in a number of languages. This site is one of the more attractive and includes a detailed biography with many images. Another site worth a visit is Selena, an article from the *Houston Chronicle*, copyrighted in 1995 (http://www.chron.com/content/chronicle/metropolitan/selena/95/05/21/legend.html).

SEUSS, DR.

BOOKS

141. Gaines, Ann Graham. *Dr. Seuss: A Real-Life Reader Biography.* **Mitchell Lane Publishers, 2002. 32pp. LB $15.95 (1-58415-074-2). Nonfiction.**

READING LEVEL: 3–4   INTEREST LEVEL: 12–15
ACCELERATED READER: YES

Is there a teen out there who is not nostalgic about all the Dr. Seuss books read as a child? This is a fact-filled, brief biography of the award-winning writer and illustrator (born Theodor Seuss Geisel). He loved humor and was the editor of the Dartmouth College humor magazine, pursuing his goal of becoming a cartoonist. His early jobs, at *Life* magazine and at *The Judge*, led to freelance work in advertising and in drawing cartoon strips for newspapers. On a bet with Bennett Cerf, he composed one of his most popular books *Green Eggs and Ham*, written with just fifty short, easy words. When Dr. Seuss became the president of Random House children's beginner book division, he was able to influence the course of books for young readers. Black-and-white photos, bibliography, chronology.

HISTORICAL FIGURES

CHAVEZ, CESAR

BOOKS

142. Falstein, Mark. *Cesar Chavez: Freedom Fighters*. Globe Fearon, 1994. 73pp. Paper $8.95 (0-8224-3223-4). Nonfiction.

READING LEVEL: 3–4   INTEREST LEVEL: 12–16

One of a series of biographies designed to interest the reader in finding out more about freedom fighters. The content is substantially meatier than other biographies at this reading level. This volume concentrates on Chavez's youth, when his grandfather lost a large farm, and his subsequent efforts to help migrant workers, culminating in the grape boycott of the late 1960s. Black-and-white photos.

WEB SITES

143. Cesar Chavez

http://www.americaslibrary.gov/cgi-bin/page.cgi/aa/chavez

A wonderful illustrated biography of Chavez covering his early life as the child of migrant workers and his later efforts to gain better working conditions for grape pickers and other farm workers through the formation of a union. Be sure to click through every page of these stories and to watch for signposts to additional stories.

FRANK, ANNE

WEB SITES

144. Anne Frank: Her Life and Times

http://www.annefrank.com/site/af_life/1_life.htm

An easy introduction to Anne and her life and times. The Timeline gives quick access to the important dates and puts them in historical context. The

Scrapbook includes photos and artifacts. There is also a section with a few excerpts from her diary. Students should watch for typographical and other errors, which may be due to translation into English. Scholastic also provides a timeline and information at the site called Anne Frank and Her Diary (http://teacher.scholastic.com/frank/diary.htm). Terms such as deportation are defined in a glossary. Links take you to additional Stories of Courage and profiles of Anne's childhood friend Hanneli Pick-Goslar and of Miep Gies, who hid the Frank family.

HAMER, FANNIE LOU

BOOKS

145. Falstein, Mark. *Fannie Lou Hamer: Freedom Fighters*. Globe Fearon, 1994. 71pp. Paper $8.95 (0-8224-3222-6). Nonfiction.

READING LEVEL: 3–4 INTEREST LEVEL: 12–16

One of a series of biographies designed to interest the reader in finding out more about freedom fighters. This volume focuses on Hamer's struggles to gain voting rights for black Mississippians. The book links Hamer's religious background and her love of gospel music to her civil rights efforts. Black-and-white photos.

KING, MARTIN LUTHER, JR.

BOOKS

146. Falstein, Mark. *Martin Luther King, Jr.: Freedom Fighters*. Globe Fearon, 1994. 73pp. Paper $8.95 (0-8224-3220-X). Nonfiction.

READING LEVEL: 3–4 INTEREST LEVEL: 12–16

One of a series of biographies designed to interest the reader in finding out more about freedom fighters. This volume concentrates on King's boycotts and the March on Washington, doing a very good job of mixing quotations from King into the text. Black-and-white photos.

WEB SITES

147. Martin Luther King, Jr.

http://seattletimes.nwsource.com/mlk/

This *Seattle Times* site offers a winning combination of text and other media. Two timelines (of King's life and of the civil rights movement as a whole), combined with the photo gallery, will give an easy introduction. There are audio files of important King speeches and text and audio comments from people inspired by King. Among these are brief statements by members of the Sonics basketball team, available in both text and audio. An interesting but more challenging feature chronicles some of the American roads that have been named for Martin Luther King. Powerful Days in Black and White (http://www.kodak.com/US/en/corp/features/moore/mooreIndex.shtml) is a fine collection of well-annotated photographs by Charles Moore depicting stirring moments in the civil rights struggle. This will appeal to students who prefer visual resources. (Navigate by clicking on the words around the screen or the arrows beside each photo.)

MALCOLM X

BOOKS

148. Falstein, Mark. *Malcolm X: Freedom Fighters*. Globe Fearon, 1994. 71pp. Paper $8.95 (0-8224-3222-6). Nonfiction.

READING LEVEL: 3–4   INTEREST LEVEL: 12–16

One of a series of biographies designed to interest the reader in finding out more about freedom fighters. Almost half the book focuses on Malcolm's life before he was released from prison at age 28. From that point on it offers a quick glance at most of the important events in Malcolm's live, without going into great depth about complex political issues involving the Nation of Islam. Black-and-white photos.

MANDELA, NELSON

BOOKS

149. Falstein, Mark. *Nelson Mandela: Freedom Fighters*. Globe Fearon, 1994. 73pp. Paper $8.95 (0-8224-3221-8). Nonfiction.

READING LEVEL: 3–4   INTEREST LEVEL: 12–16

The author concentrates on the early period of Mandela's life, before his long stint in prison, which may not be as familiar to contemporary readers. Black-and-white photos.

WEB SITES

150. Nelson Rolihlahla Mandela

http://www.anc.org.za/people/mandela.html

Students looking for basic information on Mandela should scroll down to the Brief Biography at the bottom of the page. Higher up are a useful Profile, which includes details of his favorite foods, and in-depth biographical information. A link takes you to additional sites about Mandela, including the extensive PBS site The Long Walk of Nelson Mandela: An Intimate Portrait of One of the 20th Century's Greatest Leaders (http://www.pbs.org/wgbh/pages/frontline/shows/mandela/). The Chronology and Map may be the most useful parts for reluctant readers.

TAMMEN, GERTRUD SCHAKAT

BOOKS

151. Helmer, Diana Star. *Diary of a War Child: The Memoir of Gertrud Schakat Tammen as Told to Diana Star Helmer*. Perfection Learning, 2001. 71pp. Paper $8.95 (0-7891-5436-6). Nonfiction.

READING LEVEL: 4   INTEREST LEVEL: 12–18
ACCELERATED READER: YES

This book continues the biography of Gertrud Schakat Tammen (started in *Once Upon a War*) as she moves into her teens, covering the years 1944 to 1946. Gertrud and her mother and sister move to Annenberg, sharing one room while war rages around them. Gertrud begins her diary on May 21, 1945, recording the harshness of daily life—hair lice, the constant search for food, tattered old clothing that hangs on her thinning body. From July 1945 until the end of the war the family moves from town to town, hoping to return to Tilsit once again. The book ends on an upbeat note—the family united and Gertrud falling in love with a young boy named Frank. Frank would soon leave for America; he would call for his young bride, who would settle with him in Iowa and become a nurse. Photos, glossary.

152. Helmer, Diana Star. *Once Upon a War: The Memoir of Gertrud Schakat Tammen as told to Diana Star Helmer*. Perfection Learning, 2001. 56pp. Paper $8.95 (0-7891-5357-2). Nonfiction.

READING LEVEL: 3   INTEREST LEVEL: 12–18
ACCELERATED READER: YES

The first of two books about the life of Gertrud Schakat Tammen, who was born in 1931 in Nazi Germany. This first volume covers her life as a child, beginning in 1941 with warplanes flying over her hometown of Tilsit as Germany begins bombing Russia (Tilsit is a small town, just a few miles from Russia). The book chronicles the routines in the everyday life of a normal child living amid the devastating political and social events taking place in Germany at the time. At the book's end the family is separated when all women and children are forced to leave Tilsit; Gertrud and her mother board a train to an unknown destination. Photos and glossary. German words are defined in the text.

SPORTS: COLLECTIVE BIOGRAPHIES

BOOKS

153. Mattern, Joanne, and James Mattern. *Breaking Barriers: Athletes Who Led the Way.* Perfection Learning, 2002. 64pp. Paper $8.95 (0-7891-5534-6). Nonfiction.

READING LEVEL: 5–6   INTEREST LEVEL: 12–18
ACCELERATED READER: YES

Some athletes found themselves in pioneering roles in breaking racial and sexual barriers. Six such athletes' stories are told in short biographical sketches with an emphasis on how they were able to achieve a place in sports history. From Jackie Robinson's role in breaking the color barrier in baseball to Billie Jean King's plight against sex discrimination, teens will see how prejudice was as significant a hurdle for athletes as for other historical figures. Also includes information on Jim Abbot, Janet Guthrie, Lee Elder, Manon Rheaume, and the WNBA. Photos and glossary.

154. Mattern, Joanne, and James Mattern. *Courageous Comebacks: Athletes Who Defied the Odds.* Perfection Learning, 2002. 59pp. Paper $8.95 (0-7891-5483-8). Nonfiction.

READING LEVEL: 5–6   INTEREST LEVEL: 12–18
ACCELERATED READER: YES

Nine athletes who met the difficult challenge of emotional and physical illness, defied the odds, and came back winners. Among those featured are: Lance Armstrong, winner of the Tour de France after cancer; Gail Devers (Graves' disease) who won the Olympic Gold for the 100-meter dash; and Jim Eisenreich, who conquered Tourette's syndrome to become a champion baseball player. Glossary and photos.

155. **Mattern, Joanne, and James Mattern.** *Record Breakers: Incredible Sports Achieve-ments.* **Perfection Learning, 2002. 67pp. Paper $8.95 (0-7891-5522-2). Nonfiction.**
READING LEVEL: 5–6 INTEREST LEVEL: 12–18
ACCELERATED READER: YES

Eight stories of record-breaking achievements in a wide variety of sports are told in an exciting, fast-paced manner that will engage all teens who are interested in the behind-the-scenes facts about famous champions. Included in this collection are Mark Maguire, Wilt Chamberlain, Florence Griffith Joyner, Tiger Woods, Wayne Gretsky, Jerry Rice, Nadia Comaneci, and Secretariat, the best-known horse of the twentieth century. Glossary and photos.

156. **Sandler, Michael.** *Winning Against All Odds.* **Scholastic READ 180, 2001. 39pp. Paper Order as part of a set (0-439-31291-4). Nonfiction.**
READING LEVEL: 2.5–4 INTEREST LEVEL: 12–14

Short biographies of five young athletes, all of whom have triumphed over illness or other adversity. Lance Armstrong overcame cancer to win the Tour de France again and again. Gail Devers became the fastest woman in the world despite suffering from Graves' disease. Sang Lang, who suffered an injury during vault practice, has learned to apply the discipline of her sport to physical therapy and to her new goal of earning a college degree. Orlando Hernandez (El Duque) escaped from Cuba in a small wooden boat so that he would be free to pitch with a professional baseball team. Tyrone "Muggsy" Bogues, an aspiring basketball player despite his 5-foot-3-inch height, outran other players to become his college team's MVP. Glossary and color photos.

157. **Sullivan, George.** *Power Football: The Greatest Running Backs.* **Atheneum, 2001. 60pp. Hardcover. $18.00 (0-689-82432-7). Nonfiction.**
READING LEVEL: 5–6 INTEREST LEVEL: 12–18

Running backs have football's toughest job. Carrying and advancing the ball are vital. This book profiles, with photos, running back specialists from past to present. Among them are Jim Thorpe, saluted by the *New York Times* as the greatest player of all; O. J. Simpson, the most talented running back the game has ever known; and Franco Harris, known not only for speed but also powerful enough to get the tough yards between tackles. Each player featured was the top runner of his time. The short bios are packed with facts about each man's championship plays, awards, and games.

WEB SITES

158. Crossing the Color Barrier: Jackie Robinson and the Men Who Integrated Major League Baseball

http://www.aafla.org/9arr/JackieRobinson/aafbb.htm

Click on the baseball cards for biographical information on Robinson, Larry Doby, Henry Thompson, Willard Brown, and Dan Bankhead. The *Sporting News* also has a Jackie Robinson page that features an interesting timeline (http://www.sportingnews.com/features/jackie/) and a gallery of photos with captions, among other items.

159. Sports Century

http://www.espn.go.com/sportscentury/athletes.html

ESPN profiles the top 100 athletes of the twentieth century.

SPORTS: INDIVIDUALS

ANDRE THE GIANT

BOOKS

160. Davies, Ross. *Andre the Giant*. Rosen Publishing, 2001. 112pp. LB $14.95 (0-8239-3430-6). Nonfiction.

READING LEVEL: 4–6   INTEREST LEVEL: 12–18
ACCELERATED READER: YES

A gentle giant standing 7 feet 4 inches tall and weighing in at 440 pounds, World Wrestling Federation champion and star of *The Princess Bride* Andre the Giant had a life of adventure and wealth. But Andre suffered from a rare glandular disease that would bring a premature death, before the age of 50. His affliction, giantism or acromegaly, gave him abnormally large and strong extremities. Capitalizing on his unusual strength, Andre began wrestling in Japan and soon moved on to the International Wrestling Association. Named Jean Ferre, "The Eighth Wonder of the World," he became a kind of superman of wrestling. The book is filled with Andre's most famous matches as well as his feats in WrestlingMania I and II. A sure favorite with any teen fascinated with the history of the sport of wrestling. Photos of Andre in his bouts with other heroes of the sport, including Hulk Hogan, and a glossary of wrestling terms enhance the easy-reading, fast-paced text.

WEB SITES

161. Professional Wrestling Online Museum: Andre the Giant
http://www.wrestlingmuseum.com/

Click on Photos and Bios, then select Andre the Giant under Males—Modern to find a brief profile of Andre and a link to a more in-depth "Spotlight" with a brief fact sheet and accompanying photos. The Photos and Bios include both contemporary and legendary male and female wrestlers as well as managers and announcers. There is also a special section featuring topics from Women in Wrestling and Tag Team Greats to Legendary Families and the Von Erichs. The message boards on the site are not monitored, but a student would have to delve quite deep before reaching offensive comments.

BRAZIL, BOBO

BOOKS

162. Davies, Ross. *Bobo Brazil*. Rosen Publishing, 2001. 112pp. LB $14.95 (0-8239-3431-4). Nonfiction.
READING LEVEL: 4–6   INTEREST LEVEL: 12–18
ACCELERATED READER: YES

As a young boy growing up on a farm in Arkansas, Bobo (born Houston Harris) was strong and fit, and on a good day, he earned $2 picking fruit. His goal was to play professional baseball, like his idol Jackie Robinson. Chosen to play on the House of David baseball team, he was very happy. But then along came wrestler Joe Savoldi, who coaxed him into considering a new career as a wrestler; with the name change to Bobo Brazil, a champion wrestler was born. Bobo was soon able to break blocks of plywood with his head, and in developing the abdominal stretch, he was able to subdue many of his opponents. Bobo led a life full of travel and achievement. He was inducted into the World Wrestling Foundation Hall of Fame in 1994. A warm tale of how one man used his physical and mental strength to overcome poverty.

CALHOUN, HAYSTACKS

BOOKS

163. Davies, Ross. *Haystacks Calhoun*. Rosen Publishing, 2001. 97pp. LB $14.95 (0-8239-3435-7). Nonfiction.

READING LEVEL: 4–6   INTEREST LEVEL: 12–18
ACCELERATED READER: YES

At 6 feet 4 inches and 601 pounds wearing size 12 EEEEE shoes, wrestling great Haystacks was also literally three times the size of most people. This is the story of a lonely man whose size eclipsed his gentle demeanor. The star of the wrestling circuits in the 1960s and 1970s married three times, fought all over the world, and won the respect of thousands of wrestling fans. Wearing custom-made overalls, needing two airplane seats, Calhoun is a likable fellow who will win over the hearts of teens who see size as an impediment to success. Glossary of wrestling terms, list of magazines on the sport, and further reading about wrestling.

EARNHARDT, DALE

WEB SITES

164. Remembering Dale Earnhardt 1951-2001

http://tsn.sportingnews.com/archives/earnhardt/

Compiled from the archives of the *Sporting News*, a tribute to racecar driver Dale Earnhardt with links to stories filed at the time of his fatal crash, career statistics, a timeline of his career, and farewell messages from fans.

FLAIR, RIC

BOOKS

165. Davies, Ross. *Ric Flair*. Rosen Publishing, 2001. 112pp. LB $18.95 (0-8239-3436-5). Nonfiction.

READING LEVEL: 4–6   INTEREST LEVEL: 12–18
ACCELERATED READER: YES

A biography of the wrestling great that traces his ascent to stardom. From his athletic high school career in Minnesota to the Four Horsemen of the Apocalypse, one of wrestling's most formidable teams, the book shows how Flair combined athleticism and showmanship. Photos and glossary.

FOLEY, MICK

BOOKS

166. Molzahn, Arlene Bourgeois. *Mankind: Pro Wrestler Mick Foley*. Capstone Press, 2002. 49pp. LB $15.95 (0-7368-0919-8). Nonfiction.

READING LEVEL: 3–4   INTEREST LEVEL: 12–18
ACCELERATED READER: YES

Mick Foley made an indelible mark in pro wrestling, winning many World Wrestling Federation championship bouts. Mick, who is now retired, devotes his time to his children and to raising money to help children who are ill. Full-color photos of Mick in and out of the ring, lists of major matches won, career highlights, and a glossary make this a very manageable and breezy title for reluctant readers. Other recommended titles in the Pro Wrestlers series include *The Rock, Goldberg,* and *Stone Cold.*

FUNK, DORY, DORY JR., AND TERRY

BOOKS

167. Davies, Ross. *The Funk Family*. Rosen Publishing, 2001. 112pp. LB $14.95 (0-8239-3437-3). Nonfiction.

READING LEVEL: 4–6   INTEREST LEVEL: 12–18
ACCELERATED READER: YES

An exciting story of Dory Funk Sr. and his two sons, Dory Jr. and Terry, as they flourish as world wrestling champs in the 1960s and 1970s. All three Funks were to capture championship status in the ring. With the death of Dory Funk Sr. in 1973 and Dory Jr.'s loss of the National Wrestling Alliance title the same year, it was up to Terry to recapture the NWA title. He defeated Jack Brisco on Dec. 10, 1975, and brought the NWA world championship back to the family. To this day, no other two brothers have won the title. An inspiring tale of two men, who continued to succeed after leaving the ring, opening a wrestling training school and appearing in many big-box-office films such as *Rambo*. A glossary of wrestling terms appends the text.

JETER, DEREK

BOOKS

168. Covert, Kim. *Derek Jeter.* Capstone Press, 2001. 48pp. LB $15.95 (0-7368-0777-2). Nonfiction.

READING LEVEL: 3–4 INTEREST LEVEL: 12–18
ACCELERATED READER: YES

Action photos and career statistics are included in this life of the shortstop for the New York Yankees, from his early career in the minor leagues in Florida to his rise to become one of the most important players in professional ball. The author highlights his family life, childhood athletic awards, and his decision to forgo college and at the age of 20 become the youngest player in the American League. In 1996 he founded the Turn2 Foundation, which raises money for programs to help prevent teenage drug and alcohol abuse. Glossary.

MONSOON, GORILLA

BOOKS

169. Davies, Ross. *Gorilla Monsoon.* Rosen Publishing, 2001. 112pp. LB $14.05 (0-8239-3434-9). Nonfiction.

READING LEVEL: 4–6 INTEREST LEVEL: 12–18
ACCELERATED READER: YES

The life story of Robert James Marella, born in 1937 in Rochester, New York, to Italian immigrant parents, is a touching tale of a gentle giant who chose a sport where strength can kill. Robert grew into a big teenager who, at 6 feet 5 inches, weighed 250 pounds. A star wrestler in high school, he also achieved athletic fame in college as a defensive and offensive player on the Ithaca Colleges' Bomber Division III football team. After college, he joined the U.S. wrestling team but failed to secure a spot on the U.S. Olympic Team in 1960. A problem with his knees forced him to pursue a teaching career. But although he enjoyed teaching, he felt a strong pull to the ring. He became a pro, and was an instant success, winning many matches in less a minute and establishing great popularity with the crowds. He acquired the name Gorilla Monsoon when he joined the World Wrestling Federation. After his championship wrestling career, he became the announcer on WrestleMania's closed-circuit TV broadcasts. A heartwarming tale of a man who succeeded in many careers. Photos and glossary.

RUTH, BABE

WEB SITES

170. BabeRuth.com: The Official Web Site of the Sultan of Swat
http://www.baberuth.com/

"It's hard to beat a person who never gives up." "To understand him you had to understand this: he wasn't human." These quotes from and about Babe Ruth are just two of those collected on this site devoted to the baseball great. The Did You Know? section will also make good reading. Students may need help with the fairly extensive biography and some of the news articles.

SAMMARTINO, BRUNO

BOOKS

171. Davies, Ross. *Bruno Sammartino*. Rosen Publishing, 2001. 112pp. LB $14.95 (0-8239-3432-2). Nonfiction.

READING LEVEL: 5–6   INTEREST LEVEL: 12–18
ACCELERATED READER: YES

This vivid biography of professional wrestling's Living Legend traces Sammartino's life from his humble beginnings in war-torn Italy during the 1940s, his teen years in Pittsburgh, and his early wrestling competitions in the air force. Before Bruno attempted to wrestle professionally, while working as a carpenter's apprentice, he won the North American power-lifting contest. At the age of 23, 6 feet tall and weighing in at 265 pounds, Bruno began his pro wrestling career. Thanks to his skill and size, he won 192 of his first 193 matches. Billed as the world's strongest man, Bruno became the Worldwide Wrestling Federation world champion at age 26. A fan favorite from wrestling history will delight twenty-first-century teens. Bruno's son follows in his father's footsteps. Black-and-white photos.

SWOOPES, SHERYL

BOOKS

172. Wallner, Rosemary. *Sheryl Swoopes.* **Capstone Press, 2001. 48pp. LB $15.95 (0-7368-0780-2). Nonfiction.**

READING LEVEL: 3–4   INTEREST LEVEL: 12–18
ACCELERATED READER: YES

Sheryl began playing basketball with her brothers when she was eight years old. She went on to become Texas High School Player of the year and later led Texas Tech to victory in the Southwest Conference. Sheryl's goal was to play in the Olympics, and she succeeded as a member of the 1996 gold-medal-winning U.S. Women's Basketball Team. A very uplifting biography detailing a young woman's tough road to stardom, her career choices, and some tidbits about her personal life as a mother and supporter of the battle against respiratory syncytial virus, which she believes afflicted her son Jordan as a baby. Photos and glossary.

WEB SITES

173. Player File: 22 Sheryl Swoopes

http://www.wnba.com/playerfile/sheryl_swoopes.html

This site presents concise biographical and career information on Swoopes and will be useful for students who need up-to-date details. Note that a Printable Player File is available that consolidates the important facts that are found on various parts of the site.

Careers

BOOKS

174. Aaseng, Nathan. *The Marine Corps in Action.* Enslow Publishers, 2001. 128pp. LB $18.85 (0-7660-1637-4). Nonfiction.

READING LEVEL: 5–6   INTEREST LEVEL: 15–18
ACCELERATED READER: YES   SCHOLASTIC COUNTS: YES

Semper Fidelis/Always Faithful is the motto of the Marine Corps, the tough, elite fighting force that is always ready to deploy to any location in the world when the nation's freedom is challenged. Black-and-white prints and photos show the marines in action in various wars and conflicts from the American Revolution to the Bosnian conflict. A wide range of career opportunities is presented, from recruiting to playing in the Marine Corps band. "The Few, the Proud, the Marines" is an inspiring portrait of one of America's armed service sectors that offers special appeal to young men and women right out of high school. Glossary.

175. Burgan, Michael. *U.S. Navy Special Forces: Seal Teams.* Capstone Press, 2000. 48pp. LB $15.95 (0-7368-0340-8). Nonfiction.

READING LEVEL: 3–4   INTEREST LEVEL: 14–18

Color photos of Navy Seals in training and at war in World War II, Grenada, and other U.S. military actions draw the reader to a text that is easy to read, yet informative about the mission and weapons used in peacekeeping and wartime efforts. This book also can serve as an introduction for teens interested in serving in the military. Timeline, glossary, and bibliography.

176. Clinton, Susan. *Tractor-Trailer-Truck Driver.* Capstone Press, 1998. 48pp. LB $15.95 (1-56065-710-3). Nonfiction.

READING LEVEL: 3–4   INTEREST LEVEL: 12–18
ACCELERATED READER: YES

An exciting and challenging career for those considering a career without college. Both long-haul and local driving careers are presented along with the training needed to pursue a career that presents opportunities for travel, job security, and interaction with people. Knowledge of geography, the ability to maintain a travel log, and some mechanical know-how are essential skills for drivers. Glossary and truck driving skills appended to text.

177. Diconsiglio, John. *Odd Jobs: True Stories About Real Work*. Scholastic, 1999. 27pp. Paper. Sold as part of a set (0-439-05712-4). Nonfiction.

READING LEVEL: 1.5–2.5   INTEREST LEVEL: 12–14

Choosing a career that is considered non-traditional can bring great joy and this book will generate creative employment ideas for young people to explore as they ponder how they will earn a living. The author presents brief portraits of people who have chosen unusual work in such areas as alligator wrestling, sumo wrestling, acting as a sports mascot, air traffic control, and washing windows at the World Trade Center. Roko Camaj, a window washer at the World Trade Center for twenty-five years, is interviewed about the high points of his job, which involved being strapped in a basket (pictured) as high as 1,400 feet (110 stories) above New York City. He is quoted as saying "Sometimes planes fly beneath me, other times it's snowing up here and raining down on the ground." Sadly, he died in the attacks on September 11, 2001. Photos, glossary.

178. Draper, Allison Stark. *Fighter Pilots: Life at Mach Speed*. Rosen Publishing, 2001. 64pp. LB $19.95 (0-8239-3366-0). Nonfiction.

READING LEVEL: 4–7   INTEREST LEVEL: 12–15
ACCELERATED READER: YES

This title explores the high-flying high-tech world of today's men and women who have the stamina to endure the intense physical and educational training necessary to join the ranks of this military elite. Aviation history and the rapidly changing world of aviation are presented, as well as a portrait of today's air-to-air combat. Although this book contains many passages written at the seventh-grade level, teens who follow modern-day war on television will enjoy reviewing the facts that make life at mach speed not only an extreme career choice but also an exciting informational topic to explore. Color photos, glossary.

179. Gaffney, Timothy R. *Hurricane Hunters*. Enslow Publishers, 2001. 48pp. LB $17.05 (0-7660-1569-6). Nonfiction.

READING LEVEL: 4–5   INTEREST LEVEL: 12–18

An average of five hurricanes hit the U.S. coastline during every three-year period. Hurricanes form at sea and are tracked by satellite, but the true measure of a storm's strength, size, and movement is determined by the U.S. Air Force Reserve's 53rd Weather Reconnaissance Squadron, whose teams fly WC-130 Hercules aircraft through the eye of the storm. These life-or-death missions are essential for the protection of the people on land and at sea whose lives are at risk. Terrific color photos showing the actual eye of a storm and planes in flight on hurricane watch heighten the reader's interest in a truly exciting and risky occupation. Glossary included.

180. **Giacobello, John.** *Choosing a Career in the Toy Industry.* **Rosen Publishing, 2001. 64pp. LB $17.95 (0-8239-3438-1). Nonfiction.**
READING LEVEL: 4–6 INTEREST LEVEL: 15–18
ACCELERATED READER: YES

Teens who still love and are fascinated by scooters, action figures, and computer games may want to consider a career in the growing toy industry. Jobs in drafting engineering, design, sales and marketing, computer animation, and advertising all show promise as the Harry Potter generation moves on to new trends. Even computer boy wonders like Steve Wozniak and Nolan Bushnell have joined forces to develop electronic toys for children. As the chain stores enlarge their toy departments, there is a bright future for creative young people in toy design. Color photos, index, and glossary.

181. **Green, Michael.** *Bicycle Patrol Officers.* **Capstone Press, 1999. 48pp. LB $15.95 (0-7368-0186-3). Nonfiction.**
READING LEVEL: 3–4 INTEREST LEVEL: 12–18
ACCELERATED READER: YES

An introduction to law enforcement officers who use mountain bicycles to patrol and to track down criminals. The history of bicycle police dates back to 1895, when Theodore Roosevelt, then in charge of the New York Police Department, suggested that bicycles would enable officers to navigate the city's serious traffic problems. More than 100 years later, police are now using mountain bikes to cut through cities with heavy construction blockages and to gain a better vantage point for locating and arresting drug dealers and other criminals on city streets. An exciting career for any teen who is interested in combining sports and police work. Photos and glossary.

182. **Higman, Anita.** *Lights, Camera, Action! A Fun Look at the Movies.* **Perfection Learning, 1999. 56pp. Paper $8.95 (0-7891-2866-7). Nonfiction.**
READING LEVEL: 3–4 INTEREST LEVEL: 12–15
ACCELERATED READER: YES

Careers in film are dream careers. Higman presents a number of alternative opportunities for teens interested in working in the movie industry. Darlene Koldenhoven sings and acts in films and commercials. Gordon Williams is a successful movie extra who has performed in 90 stage productions. One chapter is devoted to using unusual extras; Tom Townsend describes his business that provides everything from military vehicles to mythical beasts for films and commercials. The book gives many alternative ideas for a film industry career beyond the competitive and traditional acting and directing jobs. Photos and glossary.

183. Higman, Anita. *Lights, Camera, Action! 2: Another Fun Look at Movies.* **Perfection Learning, 1999. 55pp. Paper $8.95 (0-7891-2870-5). Nonfiction.**

READING LEVEL: 4 INTEREST LEVEL: 12–15
ACCELERATED READER: YES

The author continues to present unusual careers in the film industry for teens with an interest in film. Stunt men and women are interviewed about the fine points of their craft; additionally there is a crash course on creating your own film and script with tips on animation and special effects. Glossary and color photos.

184. Hopkins, Ellen. *The Thunderbirds: The U.S. Air Force Aerial Demonstration Squadron.* **Capstone Press, 2001. 48pp. LB $15.95 (0-7368-0776-4). Nonfiction.**

READING LEVEL: 3–4 INTEREST LEVEL: 12–18
ACCELERATED READER: YES

A brief overview of the U.S. Air Force Thunderbirds, their history, mission, aircraft maneuvers, and the roles the team members play in maintaining the squadron and in executing their demonstration performances. The Thunderbirds have performed before 50 million people in all fifty states and sixty foreign countries. They attend as many as sixty air shows a year, flying in exciting formations lasting an hour. Sharp color photos give the reader a good look at the bravery and skill needed to fly planes that can reach speeds of 1,500 miles per hour. Includes information on the tragic diamond crash. As the Thunderbirds are used as a promotional tool to draw 30,000 recruits to the air force each year, this tightly constructed title will engage even the most reluctant teen reader. A glossary appends the text.

185. Langley, Wanda. *The Air Force in Action.* **Enslow Publishers, 2001. 128pp. LB $18.85 (0-7660-1636-6). Nonfiction.**

READING LEVEL: 5–6 INTEREST LEVEL: 15–18
ACCELERATED READER: YES SCHOLASTIC COUNTS: YES

This is an overview of the history of the Air Force, including information on the Women Air Force Service pilots, the Tuskegee airmen, and others who set records as pilots and as defenders of democracy. Once a branch of the army, now a separate branch of the military, the Air Force seeks personnel with scientific and technical expertise. With an emphasis on the many exciting and varied career opportunities available (cooks, mechanics, painters, musicians, etc.), the author reviews the roles of air force personnel in the last few wars as well as giving a glimpse of daily life during basic training and career options that lie ahead. Black-and-white photos, glossary.

186. Manley, Claudia. *Secret Agents: Life as a Professional Spy.* **Rosen Publishing, 2001. 64pp. LB $19.95 (0-8239-3369-5). Nonfiction.**
READING LEVEL: 4–7 INTEREST LEVEL: 12–14
ACCELERATED READER: YES

Written at a slightly higher reading level than many high/lows, this title is included because of its relevance to our contemporary world. Teens get a glimpse of the top spies in history: Mata Hari, the Rosenbergs, Aldrich Ames, Morris "Moe" Berg, and others who worked for and against the goals of their governments. There are details of the activities of spies and double agents and of the training involved in working for agencies like the FBI and CIA. The idea of a career in intelligence work will interest teens who love watching spy films (many of which are mentioned in the book), reading books on spies, and following developments in the world around them. Black-and-white and color photos, glossary.

187. Maupin, Melissa, and Curt R. Brown. *Landscape Contractor.* **Capstone Press, 2001. 48pp. LB $15.95 (0-7368-0490-0). Nonfiction.**
READING LEVEL: 3–4 INTEREST LEVEL: 12–18
ACCELERATED READER: YES

The job outlook for all levels of work in the landscape contracting business is projected to grow in the United States. Residential and commercial demand for the attractive grounds that raise property values have spurred a need for workers to plan and design outdoor environments; operate heavy equipment; maintain shrubs, grass, and plants; and install decks and patios. This is an especially appealing career for young people with an interest in the outdoors; some knowledge of horticulture, chemistry, and biology; and a love of plants. Photos and glossary.

188. Oleksy, Walter. *Choosing a Career as a Firefighter.* **Rosen Publishing, 2000. 64pp. LB $17.95 (0-8239-3245-1). Nonfiction.**
READING LEVEL: 4–6 INTEREST LEVEL: 15–18
ACCELERATED READER: YES

The horrific terrorist attack of September 11, 2001, gave the world a clear view of how very dangerous and vital a career as a firefighter can be. From the first permanent fire company, organized in Philadelphia by Ben Franklin in 1736, to the typical day of a modern firefighter, we see how these individuals prepare to meet emergencies. Readers will find an overview of the education and training needed, brief biographies of men and women who have selected firefighting as a career, and a list of less traditional opportunities to work as a firefighter—in private industry, as part of the forest service, as a nautical fire-fighter, and so forth. Black-and-white photos, glossary.

189. Quinlan, Kathryn. *Make-Up Artists*. Capstone Press, 1999. 48pp. LB $14.95 (0-7368-0175-8). Nonfiction.

READING LEVEL: 5–6   INTEREST LEVEL: 15–18
ACCELERATED READER: YES

Describes the work of a makeup artist, including education, training, and licensing requirements. Teens interested in the theatrical industry may want to consider this high-salary career that does not require a college degree. Makeup is exciting, and the proper application enhances the image of TV and film newscasters and actors. A skilled makeup artist can remove wrinkles, lighten or darken skin, and create contours. Theatrical makeup artists can create exotic appearances for stage and screen. Photos, glossary.

190. Sawyer, Susan. *The Army in Action*. Enslow Publishers, 2001. 128pp. LB $18.85 (0-7660-1635-8). Nonfiction.

READING LEVEL: 5–6   INTEREST LEVEL: 14–18
ACCELERATED READER: YES   SCHOLASTIC COUNTS: YES

There are many career paths to follow if one chooses to join the Army, and many educational opportunities await the young recruits. An overview of the Army's history shows young people how varied life in the military can be. Profiles of women, minorities, and historical figures give a solid picture of how military life can offer world travel, good benefits, and career advance-ment. Black-and-white photos, glossary.

191. Schwartz, Stuart, and Craig Conley. *Interviewing for a Job*. Capstone Press, 1998. 32pp. LB $14.95 (1-56065-714-6). Nonfiction.

READING LEVEL: 5–6   INTEREST LEVEL: 15–18
ACCELERATED READER: YES

It's never too early to start preparing a resume and interviewing for a job. Many teens apply for first jobs in the fast food industry and need to know how to write a resume, fill in a job application, choose an appropriate outfit, and conduct themselves professionally while ·they and their prospective employer discuss the content of an advertised position during an interview. This bare-bones guide will give teens all the essentials needed to master the interview process and to secure that first job. Glossary.

192. Schwartz, Stuart, and Craig Conley. *Writing a Resume.* **Capstone Press, 1999. 32pp. LB $15.95 (0-7368-0181-2). Nonfiction.**

READING LEVEL: 3–4 INTEREST LEVEL: 15–18
ACCELERATED READER: YES

This book examines the purpose of a resume, the first step in securing a job, and provides great model resumes for teens to emulate in preparing for their job search. There is an overview of the different styles of resume writing. Chronological and functional approaches are shown with typical skill sets that teens can use in creating their own resumes. Includes tips on filing your resume electronically and advice on keeping it up to date. Glossary.

193. Tetrick, Byron. *Choosing a Career as a Pilot.* **Rosen Publishing, 2002. 64pp. LB $17.95 (0-8239-3271-X). Nonfiction.**

READING LEVEL: 4–6 INTEREST LEVEL: 14–18
ACCELERATED READER: YES

The author discusses a variety of piloting jobs, from military helicopters to commercial jets, and explains their educational requirements, the qualifications necessary, the duties, salaries, and employment outlook. This is an extremely attractive book with exquisite all-color photos of men and women pilots in the air, behind the controls, reading maps, researching, and training for flight. The last chapter is devoted to the wealth of information that teens can find about careers in aviation on the Web, from chat rooms to Web sites. Color photos, glossary.

194. Tobey, Cheryl L. *Choosing a Career as a Model.* **Rosen Publishing, 2001. 64pp. LB $17.95 (0-8239-3243-5). Nonfiction.**

READING LEVEL: 4–6 INTEREST LEVEL: 12–15
ACCELERATED READER: YES

Many teenage girls dream of a career as a model. This book takes an unbiased look at a career that is often associated with drugs, alcohol, bulimia, and anorexia, but also offers attractive opportunities as a full-time runway model, part-time catalog model, or the newly popular plus-size model. Gives information on everything from putting together a portfolio to what to expect during a photo shoot, developing a look, and handling the all-important test shoot. A profile of teen model Tonya gives a good overview of the life of a part-time catalog model. Color photos. Glossary.

195. Wirths, Claudine G. *Choosing a Career in Law Enforcement.* **Rosen Publishing, 2000. 64pp. LB $17.95 (0-8239-3282-6). Nonfiction.**

READING LEVEL: 4–6 INTEREST LEVEL: 15–18
ACCELERATED READER: YES SCHOLASTIC COUNTS: YES

An overview of the great variety of careers in law enforcement, a field of growing opportunities in this sad era of terrorism. Men and women are pictured in all types of police and security work in both the public and private sector—as police officers, security guards, border patrol guards, and private investigators, to name a few. Testimonials by law enforcement workers about their actual duties and the preparation needed to apply for these positions give teens an accurate image of what daily life in the security field would be like. Black-and-white photos, glossary.

WEB SITES

196. America's Career InfoNet

http://www.acinet.org/

Perhaps the best place to start looking at this large site is the Career Tools section, which features videos (with text subtitles) for nearly 300 occupations that will allow students a brief glimpse of each career. Next, an Employability Checkup will show the student's readiness for a selected career and the prospects for continuing in such a position. (Students who have held a regular part-time job will also find this useful.)

197. The Career Key

http://www.ncsu.edu/careerkey/index.html

A wonderful site for teens trying to work out what they want to do when they grow up. Select the "you" section of the site to start. The site will then assess your personality and the kinds of jobs to which you are suited. Once all these variables have been narrowed down, the site will take you to the appropriate part of the Occupational Outlook Handbook. Here students may need guidance. However, the site's prime role will be in helping teens to analyze their own talents and ambitions without having to interact with adults.

198. CareerZone

http://www.nycareerzone.org/

If you have Flash software, this site will be even more enjoyable, but the graphic and text versions work fine. Among archived Featured Careers are athletic trainers, chefs and cooks, graphic designers, and U.S. marshal. If you wish to assess your interests, you will have to choose whether you are investigative, artistic, social, enterprising, conventional, or realistic. Students may need help with this site, which will be challenging in terms of reading level, but nonetheless a cool and popular destination.

199. Fire Call: A Wildland Firefighter Speaks

http://www.nationalgeographic.com/firecall/

The men and women who fight wildfires across the United States each year face very difficult conditions that are well described in this excellent presentation that makes good use of the Internet's interactivity. Note that you can pause the sequence if the text is moving too fast for you. List of related Web sites with links.

200. Firefighting Occupations

http://www.bls.gov/oco/ocos158.htm

The Occupational Outlook Handbook gives an overview of firefighters' working conditions and employment opportunities and describes the qualifications needed for such a career.

201. The Hurricane Hunters

http://www.hurricanehunters.com/

Feeling brave? Will you need a "burp bag"? The 53rd Weather Reconnaissance Squadron has been flying into tropical storms and hurricanes since 1941. Now you have the opportunity to take a cyberflight into Hurricane Opal. This adventure is presented in text and photos, but is surprisingly suspenseful. There is also information on the flying jobs involved in this kind of research, a history of the squadron, and a gallery of images.

202. ISeek: Internet System for Education and Employment Knowledge

http://www.iseek.org/

The Career Planning area of this Minnesota site is excellent, and although some of the information may be specific to that state, most of it applies generally to the whole country. Links to various online skills assessment tools are followed by information on growing careers and industries, self-employment, and opportunities in the military. Two sections are of particular interest:

Descriptions of Specific Careers and Descriptions of Specific Industries. Encourage students to scroll down the descriptions. The early paragraphs may consist of dense text but are followed by bulleted lists of such interesting items as Work Activities, Working Conditions, Physical Demands, Skills and Abilities, and Knowledge. These can give a very clear idea of what workers in these fields actually do each day. For example, from the Printing and Publishing overview: "Press operators may work in noisy environments. Prepress workers usually in work in quiet, clean, air-conditioned offices. Most printing work involves working with fine detail, which may be mentally and physically tiring. Some workers work nights, weekends, and holidays."

203. Life of a Firefighter

http://www.pbs.org/itvs/testofcourage/life.html

An interesting description of a firefighter's day is interspersed with quotes, photos, and sidebars. Aspiring firefighters can test their aptitude in areas including math, physical agility, ability to understand oral information, and ability to get on with others in a community situation.

204. MyFuture.com

http://www.myfuture.com/

A very teen-friendly site on opportunities in the military. The Career Toolbox has a section called "Ace the Interview" that will be useful for all job candidates, as will the information on creating resumes and cover letters. Other features include personality and work quizzes (you may have to pay to get a full report, but the test itself and the summary results will prove interesting) and a mini-site that describes how military jobs parallel civilian jobs. Created by the Department of Defense. (You can explore the site without filling in the form that appears under the heading How to Get Started.)

205. U.S. Air Force

http://www.airforce.com/index_fr.htm

This Air Force site explains what's involved in a large number of available careers. You can access these by mission (humanitarian, healthcare, flight, aerospace, and scientific research) or by career fields (administrative, avionics, base operation, and so forth). Air Force Life includes a gallery of images of on-base amenities. This is an attractive, high-tech site and may not be easy to use if you have an older computer.

Celebrities and Entertainment
(see also Biography and Memoir)

BOOKS

206. Lamm, Spencer, ed. *The Art of The Matrix*. Newmarket Press, 2001. 488pp. hardcover. $60.00 (1-55704-405-8). Nonfiction.

READING LEVEL: 4–6 INTEREST LEVEL: 12–18

This is a big book (500 pages), based on the art of the very popular film, *The Matrix*. These 600 storyboards, essentially a giant comic strip including 219 scenes of the script and commentary in the artists' own voices, are a delight for movie buffs, science fiction fans, and budding comic artists. The core of the book is the shooting script by Larry and Andy Wachowski, who comment about their work on the film. With two sequels on the drawing board, this browsing book will be devoured by all reluctant readers. Color and black-and-white illustrations.

WEB SITES

207. Academy of Motion Picture Arts and Sciences

http://www.oscars.org/

Click on Academy Awards to find a history of the Oscars and of the ceremony, details of past winners, and a great display of picture posters. But perhaps the most attention-getting areas of the site are the Oscar Trivia quiz and Red Carpet Retro, a survey of the dramatic fashions of Academy Awards nights of the past.

208. Hollywood.com

http://www.hollywood.com/

News, features, interviews, horoscopes, filmographies, weekend box office results—everything you would expect from a site with this name.

209. Internet Movie Database

http://www.imdb.com/

This is the best place for research on contemporary and popular movies. But in addition to helping you choose the movie you want to see, the site also offers movie news, biographical information on stars and directors, photo galleries, and fun with quotes, goofs, and movie trivia. Other sites that may be useful include Film.com (http://www.film.com/) and All Movie Guide (http://www.allmovie.com/index.html).

210. Motion-Picture Industry: Behind the Scenes
http://library.thinkquest.org/10015/

Just what do grips and gaffers do, anyway? Learn the intricacies of movie making—who does what, the elements of pre- and post-production, how special effects are made, how sets are constructed, and how sneak previews, publicity, and film festival awards play an important part in the ultimate success of a movie. Other areas of this site are more ambitious and time consuming.

211. TeenPeople
http://www.teenpeople.com/teenpeople/

Brought to you by *People* magazine, this is the place for teens to keep up with celebrities, the latest fashions, horoscopes, polls, predictions for the next year (and the outcome of the previous year's predictions), trivia, chats with stars . . . in short, everything that appeals to consumers of the adult magazine. The site is light on real content, but is attractively presented. One of the most rewarding areas is the Health section (under Style).

Disasters

BOOKS

212. Ballard, Robert. *Finding the Titanic*. Scholastic Read 180, 1993. 48pp. Paper. Sold as part of a set (0-439-86428-1). Nonfiction.
READING LEVEL: 1.5–2.5 INTEREST LEVEL: 12–15

Using a fictionalized family boarding the *Titanic* for a luxurious crossing, Robert Ballard sets the scene for the April 15, 1912, sinking. He describes how he found the remains of the ship and how he was humbled by the magnitude of the tragedy, feeling as if he was visiting a huge underwater museum. Ballard and his crew used a special underwater sled to locate the ship and a small three-man submarine to explore the wreckage. He identified the staircase, the huge chandelier, and many personal artifacts from the passengers. An in-depth look at one of the twentieth century's greatest tragedies. Color photos, glossary.

213. Bondar, Barbara. *Fire! Raging Destruction.* Perfection Learning, 1997. 56pp. Paper $8.95 (0-7891-1952-8). Nonfiction.

READING LEVEL: 4 INTEREST LEVEL: 12–18
ACCELERATED READER: YES

Fire! is classified by the publisher as an informational book. Filled with facts about forest fires, there is also a fictional story about an eleven-year-old boy whose mother sends from his city home to stay with his older sister, Julie, who is studying to be a forest ranger. The book starts off on a light note as brother and sister collect and classify flora and fauna in the forest to gauge their moisture content and fire danger. The summer job adventure takes on a serious tone when Julie takes a short cut back to the ranger station only to find a forest fire in progress. Trapped in the forest, Julie and her brother use the fire safety skills that Julie has learned in the classroom to save their lives. Building a deep trench, the two spend the night while fire burns all around them, happy to be rescued by a helicopter in the morning. Good factual information about the life-threatening turn that a fire can take. Photos, charts, glossary.

214. Coe, Michael D. *The Titanic: Disaster at Sea.* Enslow Publishers, 2001. 48pp. LB $18.95 (0-7660-1557-2). Nonfiction.

READING LEVEL: 4–5 INTEREST LEVEL: 12–15

A concise overview of the 1912 loss of the *Titanic* (1,503 dead), from the moment the ship hits the iceberg to the sinking two hours later. In the recounting of the legendary tragedy, teens will read about many of the people seen in the motion picture: Captain Smith, the unsinkable Mollie Brown, etc. Issues such as inadequate lifeboats, attempts to send flares to the ship, the *Californian* passing close by the *Titanic* as it was sinking, and the role of the rescue ship, the *Carpathia*, are addressed as well. There is also a chapter with photos of Ballard's explorations to retrieve the remains of the ship, lying 12,500 feet below the surface. Glossary, black-and-white and color photos.

215. Jenkins, Alyce Mitchem. *Lost in a Blizzard: The Towner Bus Tragedy.* Perfection Learning, 2001. 76pp. Paper $8.95 (0-7891-5448-X). Nonfiction.

READING LEVEL: 3–4 INTEREST LEVEL: 12–18
ACCELERATED READER: YES

March 26, 1931, started out as an unusually warm day in eastern Colorado as children and teenagers got ready for the bus to Pleasant Hill School. However, by the time the bus arrived at the school, the weather was changing and the driver was told to take the nineteen students home. The driver soon found himself caught in a fast-moving blizzard and became lost while trying to take a short cut back to the school. Raging winds, snow, ice, and a temperature of

20 degrees below zero trapped the students and driver. As snow began to cover the unheated bus, the driver went for help, telling the children to keep moving. The children endured thirty hours of almost unbearable cold before being rescued by anguished parents. It was miraculous that most of the children survived the severe exposure and frostbite. The story is told in a hang-on-to-your-seat style and the author has integrated information about prairie life and many facts about blizzard conditions into a photo-filled text. Glossary.

WEB SITES

216. The Donner Party: Route to Hell

http://www.pbs.org/wgbh/amex/donner/route2hell2.html

Follow the route (from east to west) of the doomed travelers. Students who are interested in the fates of individuals in the party should visit The Survivors and Casualties of the Donner Party (http://members.aol.com/DanMRosen/donner/survivor.htm), where they will find amazing detail, with photos and even a reconstruction of the kind of shed the victims of this tragedy sheltered in. The page ends with the puzzle: Why did so many more women survive than men?

217. Escape!

http://www.pbs.org/wgbh/nova/escape/

Explore how scientists have profited from past accidents and disasters to make our lives safer: in burning buildings, on the road, in the air, and at sea. Beautifully illustrated and presented, as are all Nova sites, with a high interest level. Be sure to try the dive from a balloon in the stratosphere, reenacting a 1960 experiment. Don't be tempted to skip the climb the first time; the accompanying text enhances the suspense. Survivor stories are followed by strategies for coping with emergencies.

218. Tour *Titanic*

http://www.discovery.com/stories/science/titanic/tour.html

"Then" and "now" photos show the *Titanic* before its maiden voyage and the remains as they lie on the seafloor today. Additional features of this fascinating Discovery Channel site include an audio file of the *Titanic*'s whistle, a timeline of the tragedy, a photo gallery, and a photo-mosaic of how the ship would look if pieced together today. Some of the text will challenge readers, but the accompanying videos and photos will stimulate interest. A well-constructed exhibit at the National Postal Museum entitled "Posted Aboard R.M.S.

Titanic" (http://www.si.edu/postal/titanic/titanic.html) tells the heroic story of postal workers who lost their lives on the ship.

Health and Fitness

BOOKS

219. Gedatus, Gustav Mark. *Weight Training*. Capstone Press, 2001. 64pp. LB $17.95 (0-7368-0708-X). Nonfiction.

READING LEVEL: 4–6 INTEREST LEVEL: 12–18
ACCELERATED READER: YES

An easy-to-follow, easy-to-read book designed to help teens achieve health and wellness through a fitness plan that includes weight training and diet. Weight training focuses on using light weights to improve performance and prevent injury in a prescribed program developed by a coach. Essential information includes a section on the serious side effects of anabolic supplements and warnings that visible bodily changes come slowly. Inspiring advice and color photos of young people engaged in weight training programs will encourage teens to read and to become fit! Glossary.

220. Lindsay, Jeanne Warren, and Jean Brunnelli. *Nurturing Your Newborn*. Morning Glory Press, 1999, 2000. 92pp. Paper $7.95 (1-885356-58-7). Nonfiction.

READING LEVEL: 4–6 INTEREST LEVEL: 13–18

With quotes from teen mothers and fathers about parenting problems they experience every day, the authors present, in a supportive question-and-answer style, information on bonding with your baby, breastfeeding, belly button care, bathing, the first visit to the doctor, dad's rights and responsibilities, and other issues such as filing for child support and help from extended family members. Solid health information for both mother and baby will reassure the birth mother that she is not alone in the care of her infant. Black-and-white photos of caring young people and their babies complement the text.

221. Madaras, Lynda, and Area Madaras. *The "What's Happening to My Body?" Book for Boys: A Growing-Up Guide for Parents and Sons*. Newmarket Press, 2000. 238pp. Paper $12.95 (1-55704-443-0). Nonfiction.

READING LEVEL: 5–6 INTEREST LEVEL: 12–15

The third edition of the classic puberty education book, now written for boys who are experiencing puberty at a younger age, answers all questions related to sex and growing up that pre-teens and teens hesitate to ask. Written in age-appropriate language, coverage includes the body's changing size and shape, hair, voice changes, perspiration, pimples, the reproductive organs, sexuality, and puberty in girls, and adds new sections on diet, exercise, and health. Line drawings complement a text that is written in a reassuring and conversational tone. The workbook *My Body Myself for Boys* is available for schools and the consumer market.

222. **Madaras, Lynda, and Area Madaras.** *The "What's Happening to My Body?" Book for Girls: A Growing-Up Guide for Parents and Daughters.* **Newmarket Press, 2000. 262pp. Paper $12.95 (1-55704-444-9). Nonfiction.**

READING LEVEL: 5–6 INTEREST LEVEL: 12–15

The third edition of the classic puberty education book, now written for girls who are experiencing puberty at a younger age, answers all questions related to sex and growing up that pre-teens and teens hesitate to ask. Written in age-appropriate language, it covers the body's changing size and shape, breasts, the reproductive organs, the menstrual cycle, pubic hair, puberty in boys, diet, exercise, and health. Line drawings complement a text that is written in a reassuring and conversational tone. The workbook *My Body Myself for Girls* is available for schools and the consumer market.

223. **Mayer, Gloria, R.N., and Ann Kuklierus, R.N.** *What to Do When Your Child Gets Sick.* **IHA/Institute for Healthcare Advancement, 2001. 180pp. Paper $12.95 (0-9701245-0-3). Nonfiction.**

READING LEVEL: 4–5 INTEREST LEVEL: 12–18

This book is designed as a medical guide for parents of young children. It is especially useful for teen parents who are reluctant readers. The information about common childhood illnesses, such as fevers, colic, toothache, diaper rash, hives, sunburn, and burns, is delivered in a straightforward and clear manner that can be used as a first aid resource for young parents. It should be a part of every home library. Glossary.

224. **Monroe, Judy.** *Lyme Disease.* **Capstone Press, 2001. 64 pp. LB $17.95 (0-7368-0751-9). Nonfiction.**

READING LEVEL: 4–6 INTEREST LEVEL: 12–18
ACCELERATED READER: YES

Statements by teens who have contracted Lyme disease or those who have been in danger of infection amplify the need to educate all teens about this very serious illness. Because so many teens spend so much time outdoors, it is essential that all teens learn about the symptoms and the ways to avoid and treat Lyme disease. Treatment is explained in a non-threatening manner. Photos of the rash, the tick, and the treatment (including first aid) are explained in a very easy-to-read style that makes this a "must" read. Glossary.

225. O'Donnell, Kerri. *Inhalants and Your Nasal Passages: The Incredibly Disgusting Story.* **Rosen Publishing, 2001. 48pp. LB $18.95 (0-8239-3392-X). Nonfiction.**
READING LEVEL: 5–6   INTEREST LEVEL: 12–18
ACCELERATED READER: YES

Common household items are often used as inhalants—everything from hairspray and cooking spray to spray paint and paint thinner. More than 1,000 legal substances have been misused in this way, making people feel drunk or high. Many teens are unaware of the dangerous effects inhalants can have on the brain, kidneys, liver, and bone marrow. They do not realize, in fact, that inhalants can kill you. This book is a fascinating look at how inhalants damage internal organs, skin, neurons, and nasal passages. Gruesome color photos and diagrams show what inhaling vapors can do to the human body, giving teens a frightening forecast of their own possible futures if they become habitual inhalant abusers. Glossary.

226. Peacock, Judith. *Bipolar Disorder: A Roller Coaster of Emotions.* **Capstone Press, 2000. 64pp. LB $17.95 (0-7368-0434-X). Nonfiction.**
READING LEVEL: 5–6   INTEREST LEVEL: 12–18
ACCELERATED READER: YES

All teens may be depressed from time to time, and this is part of the normal ups and downs of life, but chronic depression followed by an episode of elation (mania) signals bipolar disorder. The period of mania may be marked by an episode of reckless behavior—and delusions and hallucinations may occur. In manic depression, teens may feel sad and empty, experiencing extreme emotional pain. Bipolar disorder has four categories that range from mild to serious. Diagnosis and treatment by a medical doctor are essential. Teens who are taking medication must comply with the prescribed treatment to ensure their survival. The book contains some very difficult words and phrases, but the author has made every effort to define terms and phrases in the body of the text. Teens with low reading levels are just as likely to suffer from manic depression; therefore, this title may need introduction and assistance by tutor, teacher, or librarian to be most effective in reaching teens who may be suffering from this illness. Glossary.

227. Reybold, Laura. *The Dangers of Tattooing and Body Piercing.* Rosen Publishing, 2001. 61pp. LB $17.95 (0-8239-3469-1). Nonfiction.

READING LEVEL: 5–6   INTEREST LEVEL: 12–18
ACCELERATED READER: YES

Body piercing can be dangerous if the needle used is not cleaned in an autoclave. Both tattooing and body piercing are popular teen interests. This book explains the procedures and tells the reader to beware of the risks of HIV, hepatitis B and C, tuberculosis, syphilis, tetanus, and other blood-borne diseases. The photographs show the finished results of body tattooing and the hideous effects that removal can cause. Body piercing with unclean instruments can also lead to very serious and unsightly infections. Let the buyer beware is the motto for both puncturing and permanent body marking. Glossary.

WEB SITES

228. ADA.org: Teens

http://www.ada.org/public/topics/teens/teens.html

In addition to giving advice on dental hygiene and diet, the American Dental Association covers issues important to teens: bad breath, oral piercing, cosmetic dentistry, and whitening. The Frequently Asked Questions often include the most easily understood information. Two young adults tell why they chose dental hygiene in the Career section; there are also good Fact Sheets here.

229. The AIDS Handbook: Written for Middle School Kids, By Middle School Kids

http://www.westnet.com/~rickd/AIDS/AIDS1.html

"HIV is spreading like wild fire among adolescents because they don't believe it can happen to them," this site says. Prevention, transmission, symptoms, and treatment are all explained in clear terms, as is the way the immune system fights the disease. There are grammatical and typographical errors on these pages, but the presentation is designed to appeal to this age group. Students should check facts in print sources or on more authoritative sites.

230. Anatomy of an Epidemic

http://library.thinkquest.org/11170/

AIDS, mad cow disease, Ebola, smallpox: They're all in the news these days. The interactive maps on this site are a good place to start, as they show the spread of individual diseases. Smallpox, for instance, started in Europe and eventually was found worldwide; typhoid has flared up in various places over the last few hundred years and is still found in Latin America, the Middle East, and Asia. The Epidemics page discusses the causes of these outbreaks, the role of transportation in spreading the illness, and means of prevention. You can also look up information on the individual diseases.

231. Cool Nurse

http://www.coolnurse.com/

First Aid, Looking Good, Mental Health, Sex Stuff, Substance Abuse, Teen Health Topics, Fitness and Nutrition, Female Forum, Gyn Stuff, Male Health, Your Social Life, and Teen Reporter are some of the main sections on this site that is intended to help teens make intelligent, informed decisions. Founded by a registered nurse, writer, and educator. Quizzes on birth control, depression, STDs, and rape and abuse are good starting places.

232. Doctor Over Time: You Try It

http://www.pbs.org/wgbh/aso/tryit/doctor/#

A truly cool activity in which you visit a doctor at three different periods in time: 1900, 1950, and 1998. Choose your symptom and the doctor will examine you and proceed to diagnose the problem and describe the treatment and prognosis. It's best to start with 1900 and then move forward in time until you are finished with each of the symptoms, although you must remember to click back to the examination section when you change years. The doctor in 1900 is quite prepared to visit you at home, but has less success actually curing you. Interestingly, the 1950 doctor has a sense of humor that is lacking in both his predecessor and successor.

233. The Eating Disorders Association

http://www.edauk.com/

Teens who are wondering if they have an eating disorder will find an easy self-test on this British site (click on Young People). Are You Worried About a Friend? Athletes and Over Exercising, and How Can I Help? follow the similar format, the latter answering such difficult questions as Should I tell their parents? and Will it help if I cover up for my friend? Various eating disorders are defined and discussed. A useful and attractive site. Readers wanting to know more and to identify resources (print and Web) available in the United States should turn to Eating Disorders: Anorexia and Bulimia on the Teens-Health site (http://kidshealth.org/teen/nutrition/menu/eat_disorder.html).

234. First 9 Months

http://www.first9months.com/

A documentary that takes quite a long time to load. Nevertheless, it's worth the wait. Each stage of pregnancy is carefully but simply documented, with text presented in small enough chunks to be non-threatening.

235. The Fitness Jumpsite

http://primusweb.com/fitnesspartner/

Plain-spoken, sensible advice on everything from getting and staying active to good nutrition, weight management, exercise equipment, and maintaining a healthy focus on life. A calculator lets you work out how many calories you'll burn in many activities.

236. FreeVibe: Heads Up

http://www.freevibe.com/headsup/

A totally cool site. The How to Say No section includes interviews with celebrities who have learned to resist temptation. Did You Know? presents easily digested facts and the Anti-Drug section merits exploration. Unfortunately, some other parts of the site will challenge readers who are defeated by large chunks of text. However, the overall presentation should translate into an eagerness to spend time on the site and consult a tutor when the language becomes too complex. Information on Ecstasy, marijuana, and cocaine is provided in By Girls, For Girls (http://www.windvoice.com/ohof/home.html), along with two stories. A more basic approach, but with some useful information for a teen merely seeking facts, can be found at Tips for Teens: The Truth About Club Drugs (http://www.health.org/govpubs/phd852/).

237. How Dieting Works

http://www.howstuffworks.com/diet.htm

Why is it so easy to gain weight and so hard to lose it? The people at How Stuff Works tackle this issue with their usual skill at presenting scientific material in an easy-to-understand way, well illustrated with photos and graphics. The Table of Contents is displayed on each page, so that a student who is discouraged by one chunk of text can easily move on to a section that will be more helpful. Related articles are flagged as are the temptations of Gadget of the Day, Question of the Day, and Article of the Day.

238. How Lou Got the Flu

http://www.amnh.org/nationalcenter/infection/

How can a virus travel around the world? A humorous and informative answer is provided in this cartoon-like account.

239. Is Your Teacher ADD-Friendly or ADD-Toxic?

http://www.add.org/content/teens/help4.htm

A sympathetic article that discusses the particular stresses that high school places on young people with attention deficit disorder. The author suggests that these teens choose their courses and teachers with care, pinpointing in particular teachers who are likely to exacerbate the problem. The Teens area of this ADD site (http://www.add.org/content/teens1.htm) also features a story titled "Go Take Your Ritalin," which encourages students not to joke about classmates who suffer from this disorder. There's also a Teenagers Guide to ADHD, but this will probably require the presence of a tutor. The vocabulary is more complex and the presentation is poor enough to defeat even skilled readers.

240. Just One Night

http://www.pbs.org/justone/

Tom had a few drinks with friends. Then a few more with strangers. . . . Tom wasn't a teenager, rather a "family man and successful businessman." Yet he ended up in jail for manslaughter after one evening's drinking. Read the background to this PBS program, and then turn to the Drinking and Driving section, which gives statistics, shatters myths, advises on how to stop friends from driving drunk, and lists results of teen studies.

241. Kick the Habit: For a Healthier You

http://www.bbc.co.uk/health/kth/stop.shtml

"How to Stop" and "Cravings and Breakthroughs" give sensible advice for those who still smoke and are thinking of giving up. This BBC site points to practical motivations as well as personal health issues—how much is your smoke hurting your favorite pooch; how much money will you save when you succeed in quitting? A general practitioner rebuts smokers' common excuses in "Don't Give Me That." If all this doesn't provide enough motivation, readers should visit the "cool tool" called the Body Tour, a "little trip through the layers of your body" to "explore the effects of smoking, alcohol, and drugs."

242. Lance Armstrong Foundation

http://www.laf.org/

Lance Armstrong established this foundation to help people manage and survive cancer. In addition to the biographical information on Armstrong, teens will be interested in the story of Cara Dunne-Yates, who lost both eyes before the age of six to retinoblastoma but went on to become an athlete, winning silver and bronze medals at the 1996 Paralympic Games.

243. Oxygen Health

http://www.oxygen.com/topic/health/

Formerly Thrive Online, this is a popular general health and wellness site with information organized under six main headings: Medical, Fitness, Sexuality, Nutrition, Serenity, and Weight. The Health Care Center gives easy access to a variety of overall topics and specific conditions. Tools linked to each of the six main headings allow you to perform many tasks online, for example, assess your health status, check your body mass and target heart rate, plan a fitness regimen, and choose the right contraceptive. An excellent, user-friendly site.

244. Quit Smoking

http://health.discovery.com/centers/quit_smoking/quit_smoking.html

Smoking kills nearly 420,000 people each year. How much would you save if you quit smoking? How do addictions work? Is it tougher for women to give the habit up? All this and more is presented in attractive, often-interactive formats on the Discovery Health site, along with tips from the pros (former smokers) and advice on avoiding weight gain when you quit.

245. Ravages: An Anorexic's Tale

http://www.lifetimetv.com/shows/specials/changingface/ravages.html

Excerpts from a thirteen-year-old girl's diary are accompanied by video highlights and comments by her therapist. As is frequently the case, the reading level varies from page to page of the diary, but the video highlights will serve to maintain interest if the text becomes too difficult. Part of Lifetime Online's site called The Changing Face of Beauty. The Gallery contains fascinating images of women undergoing treatments aimed at enhancing their attributes, each with an informative caption.

246. The Reconstructors

http://reconstructors.rice.edu/

A winning combination of cartoon-style high-tech interactivity and thought-provoking information. You are on Earth in the year 2252, ten years after a

Great Plague that killed millions and caused the collapse of civilization. Much knowledge has been lost. Your particular task is to try to find how they used to make "painkillers." The program is slow to load, but well worth the wait. There's an excellent glossary, and the text is clearly written and presented. You do have to be alert to follow some of the moves from screen to screen. Supported by an award from the National Institute on Drug Abuse, National Institutes of Health.

247. Skin Care for Teenagers: Battling Blemishes and Beyond

http://health.discovery.com/centers/skincare/teens/teen.html

Acne myths, acne success stories, acne medications, "how to pop a pimple," and "how to wash your face" are all addressed on this site. Everything a teen wants to know about skin care.

248. The Surgeon General's Report for Kids About Smoking

http://www.cdc.gov/tobacco/sgr/sgr4kids/sgrmenu.htm

Despite its dry title, this is one of the most appealing anti-tobacco sites. It gives the usual list of facts, destroys some favorite myths, and discusses the seductive nature of tobacco advertising. Lots of photos and graphics make this surprisingly attractive. Links lead to other features including How to Quit and Celebrities Against Smoking. The Campaign for Tobacco-Free Kids has an excellent page called the ABCs of Tobacco (http://tobaccofreekids.org/abc/), which enumerates problems from A to Z, including gingivitis, halitosis, wrinkles, and many more serious side effects. For some light relief, this organization has an irresistible e-movie at http://tobaccofreekids.org/philmo/. Other areas of the site that will be of interest are the Ad Gallery and some of the archived Special Reports—particularly the ABCs of Tobacco. Unfortunately, the Youth Action section is not very user-friendly.

249. Talking to Your Doctor

http://www.kidshealth.org/teen/body_basics/talk_doctor.html

Teens facing difficult choices are often embarrassed to discuss them with their parents. So where should they turn for advice? Friends are often the first option, but they may often lack relevant knowledge and experience. This article emphasizes that you should feel able to discuss any subject with your doctor and that a doctor's role is to help, not to scold or punish.

250. Teen Health Centre: Mental Health: The Road to Recovery

http://www.teenhealthcentre.com/teens/mentalhealth/index.htm

This Canadian site is designed specifically for teens; American students should be reminded that the help-line numbers given are not valid in the United States and that some of the services offered may not be available here. (Other areas of the site may be equally helpful but Canadian laws may differ from those in the United States; for example, the advice regarding birth control may be more liberal than American teens would normally find.) Nevertheless, this is a useful site that is organized in an attractive way. The Mental Health area covers depression, anxiety, stress management, suicide, self-injury, handling grief, and obsessive compulsive disorder. Other areas of similar interest deal with self-esteem (http://www.teenhealthcentre.com/teens/selfesteem/index. htm; including information on abstinence and peer pressure) and controlling one's temper (http://www.teenhealthcentre.com/teens/temper/index.htm; including information on road rage). The reading level differs from section to section but in many cases consists of bulleted lists that are not too challenging.

251. TeensHealth: Depression

http://www.kidshealth.org/teen/your_mind /mental_health/depression.html

Lately Lindsay hasn't felt like herself. Her friends have noticed it, too. This site—created by the Nemours Foundation—catches teens' attention with a short story about Lindsay's behavior before moving on to discuss what depression is, its symptoms, the reasons people become depressed, and, importantly, how people respond to friends who are depressed. Bipolar disorder is covered in similar fashion at http://www.kidshealth.org/teen/your_mind/mental_health/bipolar.html.

252. Unspeakable: The Naked Truth About Sexually Transmitted Diseases

http://www.unspeakable.com/

Four million people are infected with chlamydia each year; the disease is particularly common among teens and young adults. This site calls itself "a frank, accurate, and unembarrassed guide to the prevention and treatment of sexually transmitted diseases." It gives basic information on chlamydia, genital warts, gonorrhea, hepatitis B, herpes, HIV/AIDS, pubic lice and scabies, syphilis, and trichomoniasis. Teenagers will enjoy the Risk Profiler, which assesses their risk of contracting an STD. Note that explanations of each question pop up at the top of the screen; a speedometer-like display shows relative risk when the assessment has been made. The STD Quiz is well thought out and provides good information, as do the Frequently Asked Questions. Perhaps the most useful section is called Unspeakable. This lists some of the problems people have in addressing the issue of STDs with their partners and with their doctors. Appropriate responses/overtures are suggested. Pfizer created this site as an educational service; there is no commercial advertising.

253. The Visible Embryo

http://www.visembryo.com/baby/index.html

Watch the development of an embryo over the forty weeks of pregnancy. The earlier stages involve more complex vocabulary than the latter stages, but students should try to proceed in a chronological direction. Even if comprehension is lacking, this site will generate interest.

254. WebMd

http://webmd.com/

One of the main attractions of this health site is the range of interactive tools. You can keep your own health record, track calories and exercise, and create an ovulation calendar. You can allergy-proof your house room by room, assess the nutrition in your fast food, examine the contents of a "healthy" refrigerator, and watch slide shows on a number of topics and animated illustrations of spinal problems such as scoliosis. The site has good health information, but there is no specific area reserved for teens.

255. whatudo.org: HIV/AIDS facts, opinion, and action

http://www.whatudo.org/

The site is divided into three distinct sections: learn, talk, and do. The first provides FAQs, factsheets, statistics, information on sexuality aimed specifically at teens, and a Thrive Guide—a "survival manual for young people living with HIV." Students may need help with the Thrive Guide, which is clearly written but presented in a dense, text-heavy format. The "talk" section will appeal to teens who have HIV/AIDS or know someone who does. It presents scenarios and asks for input (publishing the best answers on the Web), tells the stories of young people affected by HIV/AIDS, and runs polls such as "Do you think condoms should be available in schools?" The "do" section covers efforts to fight HIV. An extremely frank site; the factual information is written by experts.

256. Your Gross and Cool Body

http://yucky.kids.discovery.com/flash/index.html

"Poop, gas, dandruff, sweat, zits, ear wax, digestion, circulation, and more" is the subtitle to this hilarious and surprisingly informative site, part of the famous Yuckiest Site on the Internet. Pick a body function (ranging from ankle sprain to eye gunk and pee to zits) or a body system, and investigate.

History

BOOKS

257. Jones, Steven. *The Red Tails: World War II's Tuskegee Airmen.* **Perfection Learning, 2001. 64pp. Paper $8.95 (0-7891-5487-0). Nonfiction.**

READING LEVEL: 5   INTEREST LEVEL: 14–18
ACCELERATED READER: YES

An exceptional contribution to high/low literature. The author has chosen to focus on the experimental training plan for African American aviators begun in 1941 at Tuskegee, Alabama, later called the 99th Pursuit Squadron. These pilots became known as the Red Tails and flew bombing and rescue missions all over Europe, earning a reputation for bravery and outstanding flying. Individual chapters focus on the lives of some of the aviators and their contribution to the war effort. A section on segregation and President Truman's executive order to integrate the U.S. military in 1948 completes this very important chapter of military history. Black-and-white photos, glossary.

258. Jordan, Shirley. *The Civil War: Moments in History.* **Perfection Learning, 1999. 56pp. Paper $8.95 (0-7891-2903-5). Nonfiction.**

READING LEVEL: 4   INTEREST LEVEL: 15–18
ACCELERATED READER: YES

A brief history of the Civil War, including a timeline of events, short biographies of significant figures—including Mary Todd Lincoln, Abraham Lincoln, Harriet Tubman, Sojourner Truth, and key generals from the North and the South—and a glimpse of the naval war. There is a wonderfully inspiring section on the life of the slave, life in the South, and the Battle of Gettysburg. Maps, photos, and letters that serve as primary sources.

259. Jordan, Shirley. *World War II: Moments in History.* **Perfection Learning, 1999. 64pp. Paper $8.95 (0-7891-2907-8). Nonfiction.**

READING LEVEL: 4–5   INTEREST LEVEL: 12–18
ACCELERATED READER: YES

Summing up World War II in sixty-four pages is not an easy task, but the author has included timelines, maps, and photos in brief chapters that cover the important events in Europe and the United States. It's all there: battleships, aircraft, the role of women in the armed forces (the WACs, the WAVES, the WASPs, and the nurses), the Navajo code breakers, the death camps, Rosie the Riveter, with an emphasis on the role that each group played in the war effort. Glossary.

260. Owens, L. L. *American Justice II: Six Trials That Captivated the Nation.* Perfection Learning, 2001. 56pp. Paper $8.95 (0-7891-5450-1). Nonfiction.

READING LEVEL: 5–6   INTEREST LEVEL: 12–18

ACCELERATED READER: YES

This book covers six cases that captivated the nation and changed the course of American history: the trials of Scopes, Alger Hiss, Dr. Sam Sheppard, Patricia Hearst, Rodney King, and Timothy McVeigh. Photos, timelines, excerpts from letters, and quotes will give teens a better understanding of the context of these trials that took place in the last century.

261. Robbins, Trina. *The Underground Railroad.* Scholastic READ 180, 2001. 23pp. Paper. Sold as part of a set (0-439-32189-2). Nonfiction.

READING LEVEL: 2–3   INTEREST LEVEL: 12–15

The story of Harriet Tubman's escape from slavery to the North by way of the Underground Railroad is told in a charming, classic comic-book format. The large color drawings and the easy-reading dialog in the balloons capture the ever-present danger during the passage. Teens will find much joy in the life of the woman who led more than 300 slaves to freedom. An essential title for any high/low reading collection.

WEB SITES

262. Air Mail Pioneers

http://www.airmailpioneers.org/

Personal stories are mixed with photos, maps, information about the planes, and an article on Airline Safety First that includes the "Pilot's Code." There is a link to the Smithsonian's National Postal Museum (http://www.si.edu/postal/), home to several fascinating online exhibits. Of particular interest will be Forwarding Address Required, the story of a California librarian's efforts to stay in touch with interned Japanese children during World War II, and an exhibit in English and Spanish on Roberto Clemente, honored twice on postage stamps.

263. American Home Front

http://teacher.scholastic.com/activities/wwii/ahf/index.htm

Explore life on the home front in World War II at this attractively presented site. You'll meet Betty, who graduates from high school and goes to work as a shipbuilder, and ten-year-old Norman Mineta, who must start a new life in an internment camp. You will also investigate the average American's living room and kitchen in an interactive display that details rationing and other hardships.

264. Ancient Greece: Athens

http://www.bbc.co.uk/schools/landmarks/ancientgreece/athens/citya.shtml

This BBC Online Cartoon Classic uses photos of present-day Athens and cartoon illustrations to introduce the city and the differences between democracy, tyranny, oligarchy, and monarchy. Sidebars offer tidbits of information on items such as water clocks; students can explore further in the Research Room, where they'll find articles on topics including how to run an Athenian household, a gallery of images, and a couple of sound extracts from Elektra. Links take you to similar sections on Olympia and Corinth and to a glossary and timeline. Thespis and Melinna also show visitors around the Greek theater (http://www.bbc.co.uk/schools/landmarks/ancientgreece/classics/theatre/intro.shtml). This is not quite so easy to follow; users need to watch for questions that change without the illustration changing. However, it is still a user-friendly basic introduction to Greek drama. See also Ancient Greece: The Olympics under Sports.

265. Australian Canned Food

http://www.cannedfood.org

OK, food canning doesn't sound like an appealing topic, but this Web site is surprisingly rewarding. The History of Canning shows unappetizing artifacts such as a can of roast veal taken on Parry's arctic voyage in 1824 and presents a comic-book account of the invention of cans by Frenchman Nicolas Appert in the 1790s. You can also learn how the cans are manufactured, many of the basic facts about good nutrition, and the economies of cooking in commercial quantities. Good use of graphics and diagrams. An Australian site with Australian spellings and measurements (tonne for metric ton, for example).

266. Become a Spice Trader

http://www.learner.org/exhibits/renaissance/spicetrade/begintrip.php3

Your vessel is a 500-ton, fully rigged galleon and you plan to set sail to trade cloth, copper, and iron for exotic spices and cotton. Your first decision: to travel armed or unarmed. Each decision will take you on a different path and have its own result. Your choices are not easy, as the information supplied covers many important aspects of your voyage.

267. Bodies of Cultures: A World Tour of Body Modification

http://www.upenn.edu/museum/Exhibits/bodmodintro.html

The University of Pennsylvania Museum of Archaeology and Anthropology takes you on a virtual tour of body piercing and tattooing, showing that while this may be trendy now it's nothing new. Eskimos used to wear lip plugs; nose piercing was popular in ancient Mexico and India; men had pierced ears in ninth-century B.C. Iraq. And tattooing and body painting go back to prehistory. Wonderful illustrations—with frequent juxtapositions of ancient and modern—will make up for some complex text passages.

268. Celebrate Hispanic Heritage

http://teacher.scholastic.com/hispanic/

An interactive map that connects with timelines provides an introduction to Hispanic influences in the Americas. Interviews with Hispanic Americans including author Pam Munoz Ryan and astronaut Ellen Ochoa highlight their Hispanic heritage (the transcripts tend to be at a lower reading level than the accompanying biographies). History Makers presents brief profiles of important Hispanic individuals, with links to more detailed information. Hispanic students who are particularly interested in how people capitalize on their ability to speak two languages and understand two cultures should start with the section called What Does My Heritage Mean to Me?

269. Cleopatra of Egypt: From History to Myth

http://www.fmnh.org/cleopatra/cleoexhib.html

Was she beautiful? What language did she speak? Did she really die from the bite of a snake? These are among the questions answered in this beautifully presented overview of Cleopatra's life. Macromedia Flash Player is required to participate in helping the Field Museum's archaeologists search Alexandria for fragments of a portrait of the mysterious queen (collect the twelve pieces by clicking on the city grids). This is a satisfying task. You can explore this site easily by following the links at the bottom of each page. The related site Inside Ancient Egypt at the Field Museum (http://www.fmnh.org/cleopatra/egypt2. html) gives a quick virtual tour of the exhibit.

270. "Dad" Rarey's Sketchbook Journals of the 379th Fighter Squadron

http://www.rareybird.com/

George Rarey was a young cartoonist and commercial artist who served as a pilot in World War II. He kept a cartoon journal of his experiences, which ended with his death shortly after D-Day. His son shares these journals with us, adding comments by Rarey's fellow pilots and letters from Rarey to his wife. There are five volumes of journals, plus photos and originals of the paintings Rarey did on noses of the squadron's planes. The journal entries are moving but brisk and give a very good idea of the conditions these men had to bear. The cartoons are great.

271. Enigma and the Code Breakers

http://www.iwm.org.uk/online/enigma/eni-intro.htm

Students who are interested in codes, ciphers, and ways of transmitting information during wartime will find much of interest here. Information on code breaking is presented interactively and the text is interspersed with photos, examples, sidebars, and other features to maintain interest.

272. Hiroshima: A Survivor's Story

http://teacher.scholastic.com/activities/wwii/hiroshima/index.htm

Eleven-year-old Mitsuo leaves his native Hawaii to live in Hiroshima, Japan, in March 1941. Readers follow his experiences in his new country up to and after the dropping of the atomic bomb. Each chapter is followed by links that allow readers to find out more about specific topics. A "Think About It" feature may be helpful for some readers. There is a transcript of a May 2000 student interview of the seventy-year-old Mitsuo at http://teacher.scholastic.com/activities/wwii/interview/trans.htm.

273. Immigration: Stories of Yesterday and Today

http://teacher.scholastic.com/immigrat/index.htm

Scholastic has compiled a rich resource in partnership with the Statue of Liberty-Ellis Island Foundation. Five young immigrants tell what it's like to arrive in the United States today, Seymour Rechtzeit describes his journey from Poland in 1920, and there's an interactive tour of Ellis Island. The charts and graphics are not attractively presented but the rest of the site is appealing.

274. In Search of Liberty Bell 7

http://www.discovery.com/exp/libertybell7/libertybell7.html

This excellent presentation of Gus Grissom's 1961 flight and the search for the capsule effectively uses the technique of rolling the mouse over graphics to reveal relevant text. The Latest on the Restoration is much more text-intensive, but students will enjoy Grissom's Story, which describes his three-word speech and how he nearly drowned as his capsule sank.

275. The Internet African American History Challenge

http://www.brightmoments.com/blackhistory/

Basic information is presented on twelve nineteenth-century African Americans, including Frederick Douglass, Harriet Tubman, Nat Turner, and Sojourner Truth. Students can test their knowledge and comprehension at three different levels. The reading level will challenge some students, but the presentation is enticing.

276. The Lower Eastside Tenement Museum: Virtual Tour

http://www.tenement.org/index_virtual.html

Explore 97 Orchard Street, a tenement building that housed many new migrants to New York City, and read the stories of the families who lived there. Nathalie Gumpertz must start a career in dressmaking when her husband disappears; Fannie Rogarshevsky struggles to make ends meet when her husband dies of tuberculosis. There are photographs of these and the other families residing in the building. The downstairs hallway is shown as a ruin, along with photos from the excavation of 97 Orchard Street; upper apartments are pictured as they would have looked in the late nineteenth and early twentieth centuries. You need QuickTime and RealPlayer to take advantage of this online exhibit.

277. Modern World History

http://www.bbc.co.uk//education/modern/

An excellent overview of world events from the end of World War I to the end of World War II, including the Russian Revolution, the Wall Street Crash, the Great Depression, and the rise of Nazism. The sections on the Crash and People at War will be of particular interest, the latter providing good descriptions of conditions in Britain during the Blitz. Students will meet certain unknown British terms, such as "hire purchase"—a form of installment purchase arrangement, but in general the information is clearly and concisely presented. Each section ends with a quiz. A timeline puts all the events into context.

278. Remember.org

http://www.remember.org/

Students interested in reading about the Holocaust will find a great deal of information here, from interactive maps of the camps to interviews with survivors, liberators, and rescuers. The Student Forum includes excerpts from books and submissions from classes. The Education section includes lesson plans and other teacher resources. The Museum of Tolerance has a page called Children of the Holocaust (http://www.wiesenthal.com/mot/children/list1.cfm) that tells the stories of many teenagers who were caught up in these horrors.

279. Solemates: The Century in Shoes

http://www.centuryinshoes.com/home.html

Shoes of the twentieth century are displayed by decade with accompanying historical notes on the fashions, social customs, and events of the times. There are also scenes from the decades and examples of shoe advertisements. Don't miss the Before This Century feature hidden down on the bottom of the screen.

280. Technology in 1900

http://www.pbs.org/wgbh/amex/kids/tech1900/

PBS presents three user-friendly features on the height of high-tech at the turn of the last century. "Built for Speed: Early Automobiles Hit the Road" explains the many pitfalls of motoring in its early days. "Music Video 1900 Style" is subtitled "The Marriage of Pop Music and Pictures." "Number Please!" tells how women replaced unruly teenage boys as the preferred operators of the new switchboards. This was not necessarily a triumph; the pay was low, discrimination high, and the rules numerous. Women who married were immediately dismissed, and operators in large cities had to request permission for bathroom visits. The Snapshot section lists predictions from 1900, such as "Automobiles will be cheaper than horses are today." Buzz allows users to conduct an amazingly realistic online interview.

281. Time 100: The Most Important People of the 20th Century

http://www.time.com/time/time100/

Meet the most fascinating people of the twentieth century: the leaders and revolutionaries, artists and entertainers, builders and titans, scientists and thinkers, and heroes and icons. Among other interesting features of this wide-ranging site are the Time Warp: 1900 vs. Now, which compares the status of items such as world population, unemployment, cars sold worldwide, and crude-oil production; the 100 Worst Ideas (including kudzu, aerosol cheese, and thong underwear for men); and the poll trying to establish the Event of the Century.

282. Two Legends of Aviation

http://www2.worldbook.com/students/feature_index.asp#space

Select Two Legends of Aviation from the menu of Aviation and Space Exploration topics to access this rich site on early aviation. For Charles Lindbergh you will find the World Book article on him as well as articles from 1927 and 1928 about his exploits. Similar information is provided on Amelia Earhart. The site is rounded out by the addition of a section on How Air Navigation

Has Changed, with a link to live transmissions of the Chicago Approach frequency, broadcasted from O'Hare.

283. The Underground Railroad

http://www.nationalgeographic.com/railroad/

The Underground Railroad comes to life online as you choose to make the dangerous journey to freedom. In addition to the journey itself (during which the reader has to make difficult choices), there is a timeline to give historical context and a map of the route. Faces of Freedom gives very brief biographies of characters including Lucretia Mott, Frederick Douglass, Allan Pinkerton, and Susan B. Anthony. A postcard allows you to email friends and let them know about the site.

284. USAF Museum History Gallery

http://www.wpafb.af.mil/museum/history/history.htm

A virtual gallery of planes—mainly military—from the earliest days of aviation to modern rockets. The length of the text descriptions of each aircraft varies considerably. Additional displays show weapons and engines.

285. Women Airforce Service Pilots (WASP) WWII: Posters

http://www.wasp-wwii.org/wasp/signs.htm

A collection of posters that illustrate the various demands the United States made on its citizens—both men and women—during World War II. There is very little text, but the attractiveness of the posters themselves may serve to introduce the topic and spur readers toward related books and more detailed Web sites. Click on Scrapbook to read the exciting story of one woman pilot's training flight and to see images and descriptions of life as a WASP.

Inspirational

BOOKS

286. Espeland, Pamela. *Succeed Every Day*. Free Spirit Publishing, 2001. 387pp. Paper $10.95 (1-57542-083-X). Nonfiction.

READING LEVEL: 5–6   INTEREST LEVEL: 14–18

Quotations by notables who may be familiar to today's teens—Colin Powell, Paul Simon, Rodney Dangerfield, Denzel Washington, John F. Kennedy ("Ask not what your country can do for you. Ask what you can do for your country")—introduce each item in this collection of readings. In each case, the message that follows is designed to promote a new perspective on an issue or to stimulate action to try something new. Following the mini-essay is an affirmation, "Today I'll . . . ," suggesting something teens might do, consider, reflect upon, or plan as they go about their day. The affirmations are short and meaningful and their brevity makes them manageable for teens reading below grade level.

287. Espeland, Pamela, and Elizabeth Verdick. *Making Every Day Count: Daily Goals for Young People on Solving Problems, Setting Goals, & Feeling Good About Yourself.* **Free Spirit Publishing, 1998. 383pp. Paper $9.95 (1-57542-047-3). Nonfiction.**

READING LEVEL: 4–6 INTEREST LEVEL: 12–18

Presents 366 quotations, advice, and affirmations to help readers face challenges, plan for the future, and appreciate their unique qualities. Each day begins with a reassuring quote. On January 1, Danny Kaye begins with "Life is a big canvas. Throw all the paint on it you can." The quotes and the brief essays that follow the quotes can be used as a springboard to positive thinking or can be a stimulus for journal writing. The shortness of the daily affirmations, the brief essays that follow, and the goals (the goal for January 1 is "Today, I'll list my goals for a year") will be manageable reading for reluctant and below-grade readers and will assist in setting goals for school work as well as personal growth.

288. Espeland, Pamela, and Rosemary Wallner. *Making the Most of Today: Daily Readings for Young People on Self-Awareness, Creativity & Self Esteem.* **Free Spirit Publishing, 1998. 381pp. Paper $9.95 (0-915793-33-4). Nonfiction.**

READING LEVEL: 4–6 INTEREST LEVEL: 12–18

A daily book of readings for all young people who want to be more self-aware, be more creative, and feel better about themselves. Each day of the year starts with an inspirational quote from people from all walks of life, to spur positive thought and action in a quest for self-growth. For May 31, Edgar Degas says "Painting is easy when you don't know how, but difficult when you do." A short statement follows about the difference between childhood creativity, which is spontaneous, and creativity after childhood, which forces us to follow rules. There are also springboard quotes from people who teens may recognize: Ntozake Shange, Eleanor Roosevelt, Paul McCartney, Alice

Walker, and so forth. Dipping into these short pieces will be very manageable for reluctant readers and will give teens a feeling of satisfaction in reading as the days go by.

289. Gaines, M. C., and Don Cameron, illus. *Picture Stories from the Bible: The Old Testament in Full-Color Comic-Strip Form.* **Bloch Publishing, 1980. 143pp. Hardcover $14.95 (0-934386-01-3). Nonfiction.**

READING LEVEL: 4   INTEREST LEVEL: 7–12

Although the vocabulary used in the balloons that accompany the very attractive, brightly colored, comic-style drawings in both this book and *Picture Stories from the Bible: The New Testament . . .* (1980) is not always as simple as one would like, these two titles cover the major stories of both the Old and New Testaments and present them in a clear and readable format. These two abridged versions of Bible stories were originally published in 1943. Young people constantly request Bible stories. This set is very popular with teenagers and adults who have a reading disability and cannot tackle a full-text version of the stories.

290. Gootman, Marilyn E. *When a Friend Dies: A Book for Teens About Grieving and Healing.* **Free Spirit Publishing, 1994. 102pp. Paper $9.95 (0-915793-66-0). Nonfiction.**

READING LEVEL: 4–5   INTEREST LEVEL: 12–18

Many teens experience the loss of a friend. This is an extraordinary book that will help teens through the grieving process and assist them in the belief that they will grow from this tragedy and can find meaning from the experience. There are quotes from teens who are struggling with grief over a friend's suicide, car crash, or murder and tips on how to handle grief and to channel anger and loss constructively by supporting associations that encourage the wearing of seat belts and other safety measures. The author issues heartfelt assurances that you won't be in a constant state of grief and that there is a natural healing process that we all must go through. Quotes at the end inspire thought and healing, for example: "We are healed of suffering only by experiencing it to the full" (Marcel Proust) and "No willpower could prevent someone's dying" (Annie Dillard).

291. Wilber, Jessica. *Totally Private & Personal: Journaling Ideas for Girls and Young Women.* **Free Spirit Publishing, 1996. 157pp. Paper $8.95 (1-57542-005-8). Nonfiction.**

READING LEVEL: 5–6   INTEREST LEVEL: 12–18

A collection of journaling ideas, writing tips, and self-help information from fourteen-year-old teen author Jessica. Teens will be inspired to begin to keep a journal by following Jessica's tips, which guide teens in an uncomplicated way through the writing process. Teens are encouraged to record their thoughts and feelings without regard to spelling or grammar, to decorate the page of their journals with drawings and collages, and to write daily. Different approaches to journal keeping are discussed: art journal, computer journal, friendship journal, scrapbook journal, and family journal, for example. Writing will lead to reading and teens who are reluctant readers can get a good start here, recording the daily events in their lives and reading about how other teens keep a daily journal.

Love, Sex, and Relationships

BOOKS

292. Ayer, Eleanor. *It's Okay to Say No: Choosing Sexual Abstinence.* **Rosen Publishing, 2000. 62pp. LB $17.95 (0-8239-3239-7). Nonfiction.**

READING LEVEL: 5–6 INTEREST LEVEL: 12–18
ACCELERATED READER: YES

Teens leaning toward abstinence may feel that it is an unpopular topic among their peers. This book will help them to stand up for their own beliefs by stressing the positive values of virginity, among them the freedom from unwanted pregnancies and sexually transmitted diseases. Testimonials from teens who are refraining from premarital sex and who are joining nationwide programs, such as True Love Waits, that stress relationship-building will reinforce and strengthen the resolve to wait until marriage. Tackling a tough topic for teens to understand, this book offers solid information on the benefits of abstinence. Glossary of terms.

293. Brooks, Sheldon. *Everything You Need to Know About Romance and the Internet: How to Stay Safe.* **Rosen Publishing, 2001. 64pp. LB $17.95 (0-8239-3399-7). Nonfiction.**

READING LEVEL: 4–6 INTEREST LEVEL: 12–18
ACCELERATED READER: YES

Meeting potential friends online has both positive and negative aspects. Teens who meet on the Internet may feel connected and attracted and this can easily lead to a cyber-romance. This book clearly outlines the safeguards that teens should take before attempting a face-to-face meeting with a cyber-friend. In addition, there is solid information about discussion groups, chat rooms, email, and online dating services. Teens are warned to beware of stalkers and other types of extreme behavior that can be encountered online. Teens will get a crash course in dating safety precautions, such as taking someone along when first meeting an online friend, meeting in a public place, keeping parents posted on where you are meeting, and establishing the time of your return. Includes list of emoticons, online shorthand, and good and poor netiquette. Color photos, glossary.

294. Frisch, Carlienne A. *Money Matters: A Teen Guide to the Economics of Divorce*. Rosen Publishing, 2000. 64pp. LB $19.95 (0-8239-3151-X). Nonfiction.

READING LEVEL: 4–6 INTEREST LEVEL: 12–18
ACCELERATED READER: YES

Teens whose parents are divorcing will frequently find their lifestyles alter as a result of a change in family income. From getting a part-time job or helping with younger siblings to accepting a move into smaller, cheaper quarters, the author guides teens on what to expect as they become members of single-parent households. Extended families, foster care, and the emancipated minor status are all introduced as challenges that teens may face as a result of parental divorce. Photos.

295. Isler, Claudia. *Caught in the Middle: A Teen Guide to Custody*. Rosen Publishing, 2000. 64 pp. LB $19.95 (0-8239-3109-9). Nonfiction.

READING LEVEL: 4–6 INTEREST LEVEL: 12–18
ACCELERATED READER: YES

For many teens, custody decisions are the most painful aspect of divorce. This book prepares teens for the instability that may occur in their lives as issues of joint custody, sole custody, foster care, and blended families are discussed by their separating parents. Teens are reassured that psychological, medical, and legal resources are available if they become depressed or confused by the changes in their lifestyles. A glossary appends the text, defining terms and phrases used in divorce proceedings.

296. Kuehn, Eileen. *Loss: Understanding the Emptiness*. Capstone Press, 2001. 64pp. LB $17.95 (0-7368-0746-2). Nonfiction.

READING LEVEL: 4–6 INTEREST LEVEL: 14–18
ACCELERATED READER: YES

The author defines loss and the many ways in which it affects teens and provides ideas on how to deal with loss in a positive way. There are tips on moving beyond the sometimes overwhelming feelings of emptiness and sound advice on how to get on with life. The real value of this title is that teens are reassured that loss of friendship, a job, a move from a familiar neighborhood, or the death of a family member, friend, or pet are naturally occurring losses in life that will heal if teens allow themselves the time for grieving. We all heal from loss at a different pace. A support group or counselor can make us feel that we are not alone in our feelings and can guide us toward change and a new life. Glossary and useful addresses for sources of counseling services.

297. Marecek, Mary. *Breaking Free from Partner Abuse: Voices of Battered Women Caught in the Cycle of Domestic Violence.* **Morning Glory Press, 1999. 94pp. Paper $8.95 (1-885356-53-6). Nonfiction.**

READING LEVEL: 4–5   INTEREST LEVEL: 15–18

Using poetry by abused women and case studies that illustrate how difficult it is for women of all ages to break the pattern of abuse in intimate relationships, the author tries to show the 28 million abused women in the United States that there can be a life free of emotional and physical battering. Many teenagers are caught in a familial cycle of abuse and often find their way into a relationship that continues this pattern. The haunting black-and-white illustrations can be a springboard for discussion of this very serious problem. The sad statistic that every twenty-eight seconds a woman is beaten in the United States introduces the reader to an issue that needs attention in the teen years.

298. Peacock, Judith. *Abstinence: Postponing Sexual Involvement.* **Capstone Press, 2001. 64pp. LB $17.95 (0-7368-0713-6). Nonfiction.**

READING LEVEL: 4–6   INTEREST LEVEL: 12–18
ACCELERATED READER: YES

Both straight and gay teens struggle with the decision to engage in sexual intercourse. Peer pressure, media influence, and drugs and alcohol force many teens into a sexual experience for which they are unprepared. This book features testimonials by teens who regret their early sexual experiences as well as statements by teens who have resolved to postpone any sexual activity that may lead to intercourse. It also includes tips on how to design your own personal abstinence program: wear a promise ring as a reminder to abstain from sex, be upfront with those you date, avoid risky situations and activities, stay in a group that supports abstinence; and advice for teens to build on their self-confidence so that they can remain firm in their resolve to abstain. Glossary. List of organizations that encourage teens to abstain from sex.

299. Peacock, Judith. *Dating and Sex: Defining and Setting Boundaries.* **Capstone Press, 2001. 64pp. LB $17.95 (0-7368-0716-0). Nonfiction.**

READING LEVEL: 5–6   INTEREST LEVEL: 12–18
ACCELERATED READER: YES

Both straight and gay teens love to dream about dating. This book helps teens learn about dating relationships, including discussion of healthy relationships, challenges that couples face, making a decision about sex, and handling breakups. Teens in relationships must learn how to communicate, cope with jealousy, and give their partner space. There is a chapter on birth control and on abstinence. As most teen relationships do not end in marriage, the chapter on recovery from a breakup is especially helpful for teens coping with loss. Glossary.

300. Sommers, Annie Leah, and Michael A. Sommers. *Everything You Need to Know About Virginity.* **Rosen Publishing, 2000. 64pp. LB $17.95 (0-8239-3115-3). Nonfiction.**

READING LEVEL: 4–6   INTEREST LEVEL: 13-18
ACCELERATED READER: YES

The authors focus on the concept of virginity in literature, in society, and within one's own personal value system. Teens have an opportunity to read about their peers' decisions to engage in sex or to practice abstinence. The message is clear—once virginity is lost it is gone forever—and the text supports teens who choose to postpone sex until marriage. Interviews feature both teens who regret having had sex on a whim and teens who say their decision to engage in sexual intimacy was correct because theirs is a meaningful, long-term, caring relationship not only based on sex. Color photos and diagrams of male and female sex organs complement the text.

301. Spencer, Lauren. *Everything You Need to Know About Falling in Love.* **Rosen Publishing, 2001. 54pp. LB $17.95 (0-8239-3395-4). Nonfiction.**

READING LEVEL: 4–6   INTEREST LEVEL: 12–18
ACCELERATED READER: YES

Falling in love, staying in love, taking love to the next stage, breaking up, same sex love, and eternal love are all issues of interest to teens. Managing teen love is tricky, and teens may find useful tips here as they leap into the vast cauldron of one of life's most complex emotions. Teens express themselves in frank sincere vignettes that demonstrate the complexities and beauty of teen love.

WEB SITES

302. Adoption

http://www.kidshealth.org/teen/your_mind /families/adoption.html

Colleen feels she is quite comfortable with the fact that she is adopted until the day her teacher announces a new class project: tracing family histories. With the usual skill of KidsHealth, the story addresses many of the issues that adoptive children struggle with. Also of interest will be the list of Well-Known Adopted Persons, Birth Parents, and Adoptive Parents at the National Adoption Information Clearinghouse (http://www.calib.com/naic/pubs/r_famous. htm), a site that gives information on state regulations on adoption and tracing birth parents and birth records.

303. American Love Stories

http://www.pbs.org/weblab/lovestories/stories/

PBS has collected stories under a number of topical headings, such as Communication, Extended Family, Greater Horizons, Love and Death, and Role Breaking. Many are in the first person; most are fairly brief, sometimes emotional and sometimes funny. Readers can browse through the titles and brief summaries of each account, using the handy pull-down menu. Try "Net Love" (under Love and Death) for a start, a plucky tale of Internet love for a disabled young man. Or (under Greater Horizons) "Mouse and Me," the tale of a long and strong nontraditional relationship that began in high school. There is an emphasis throughout the site on intimate relationships that cross "not just racial differences, but religious, ethnic, geographical, age and other boundaries as well."

304. Dealing with Divorce

http://www.kidshealth.org/teen/your_mind /families/divorce.html

Children of divorcing parents often blame themselves for the breakup, or feel they could have prevented it in some way. TeensHealth looks at a couple of important questions—How will this change my life? and Are my feelings normal?—and then gives a few practical tips on dealing with the situation.

305. It's Great to Wait: Sexual Abstinence Until Marriage

http://www.greattowait.com/

The Florida Department of Health runs this attractive site, which aims to reduce teen sexual activity, pregnancy, and sexually transmitted diseases. Topics discussed include peer pressure, self-esteem, difficulties in communicating with friends and parents, and AIDS. Real-life stories and testimonials illustrate how teens agonize over these issues and share some of their good and bad decisions. The section "How Should I Wait?" gives examples of effective communication under pressure. You need Shockwave 8.0 to take the quiz.

306. It's Not Your Fault

http://www.itsnotyourfault.org/

A British children's charity created this attractive site that offers information for children, teens, and parents involved in divorce. The section for teens examines the various emotions young people feel when faced with divorce and offers advice on coping with parents who are behaving oddly, on knowing when to seek help, on dealing with anger and confusion, and on the importance of communicating your needs. The site makes good use of graphics and includes personal stories from teens. A glossary is called Difficult Words Explained, and there is an online template for a Diary.

307. It's Your (Sex) Life: Your Guide to Safe and Responsible Sex

http://www.itsyoursexlife.com/

The Kaiser Family Foundation presents practical information on pregnancy and contraception, birth control options (complete with "groovy parts" and "drag factors"), sexually transmitted diseases, and how to talk about sex and negotiate with partners. The reading level varies from page to page, but the attractive presentation will entice teens to explore the site.

308. Iwannaknow

http://www.iwannaknow.org/

From the American Social Health Association, a teen-friendly, matter-of-fact sex education site. It not only discusses puberty, STDs, abstinence, protection, and the usual topics, but also—in a section called Sex on the Brain—tackles the difference between sex and love, the special pressures on gay teens, and ways to deal with peer pressure. There are lists of items to consider when deciding whether or not to indulge in sexual activities. Well written and clearly presented, with a frank and useful glossary.

309. Relationships

http://www.talkcity.com/theinsite/relationships/relationships.html

This site offers tips on how to deal with parents, siblings, friends, boyfriends/ girlfriends, and authority figures. You will find much of the standard advice here, but it's presented in an attractive way and accompanied by real-life stories.

310. Sex Etc.: A Website by Teens for Teens

http://www.sxetc.org/

Developed by the Network for Family Life Education at Rutgers University, this is a cool site with feature stories, "news" headlines, chat sessions, Ask-the-Expert, polls, and a message board. There's frank discussion of topics including relationships, sexually transmitted diseases, contraception, pregnancy, gay and lesbian teens, alcohol and drug abuse, health and happiness, and violence and abuse. Teens will find the Frequently Asked Questions (in the Ask the Experts section) particularly useful. Attractive, friendly, and informative.

311. Sex Has Consequences: Facts and Figures

http://www.teenpregnancy.org/teen/facts/factfig.html

How many teen girls in the United States get pregnant each year? You can't get pregnant the first time, right? What happens to the children of teen moms? These are just three of the questions answered at this site created by the National Campaign to Prevent Teen Pregnancy. The Teens Tell All section will be a popular resource, with quotes on topics including what it's like to be a teen parent, abstaining from sex, and dealing with parents.

312. Sexual Issues

http://www.smith.edu/ourhealthourfutures/sexualissues.html

Knowing Your Body, Are You Ready for Sex? Contraception, Teen Pregnancy, Sexually Transmitted Diseases, and "The Ideal Girl": Teen Lesbians and Bisexuals. These are the headings on this site created by teen girls as part of a program at Smith College. It provides a nice blend of practical information, comments and quotes from teens, statistics, and quizzes, all presented by the girls themselves. Some areas have a higher reading level than others. Note: Watch for Next signs indicating that there is more on a following page.

Nature and the Environment

BOOKS

313. Cohen, Daniel. *Tyrannosaurus Rex and Other Cretaceous Meat-eaters.* **Capstone Press, 1996. 48pp. LB $ 15.95 (1-56065-288-8). Nonfiction.**

READING LEVEL: 4–5 INTEREST LEVEL: 12–15
ACCELERATED READER: YES

The dinosaurs Tyrannosaurus rex, Stenonychosaurus, and Deinonychus lived from 140 million to 65 million years ago. These are tough words for teens with reading deficiencies to grasp but with illustrations, charts, photos of pale-ontologists at work, and the scientific words spelled out in parentheses, a fascinating age is brought to life. Daniel Cohen, a seminal author in the high/low field of writing, gives teens a full record of the size, setting, living conditions, and evolution of the time when dinosaurs roamed the earth. An exceptionally well-written book that will appeal to all teens.

314. Duden, Janice. *Helping Paws: Service Dogs.* **Perfection Learning, 1998. 56pp. Paper $8.95 (0-7891-2147-6). Nonfiction.**

READING LEVEL: 4 INTEREST LEVEL: 12–18
ACCELERATED READER: YES

Any teen who loves animals will enjoy this book about dogs that assist disabled people with many everyday chores, enabling them to lead happy and independent lives. It is difficult to imagine how limiting life can be if you are unable to do simple tasks such as opening doors or picking up things you dropped. A trained helping dog can perform these functions and at the same time provide companionship that makes life more meaningful. A mini course on training helping dogs gives the reader an insider look at how verbal commands enable the dog to respond immediately to its handler or partner. Color photos of disabled people with their helping dogs accompany dog job descriptions.

315. George, Charles, and Linda George. *Police Dogs.* **Capstone Press, 1998. 48pp. LB $15.95 (1-56065-752-9). Nonfiction.**

READING LEVEL: 3–4 INTEREST LEVEL: 12–18
ACCELERATED READER: YES

An inside look at the life of a working dog. Teens who love animals may want to consider becoming a trainer or police officer whose duties include using dogs to detect, restrain, and retrieve suspects. All aspects of the rigorous train-ing—obedience, scent, obstacle course, aggression—are described and high-lighted with color photos of dogs in action against crime. Case histories of dogs who solved crimes, such as the bloodhound who tracked down James Earl Ray (Martin Luther King's killer) after he escaped from prison, make this an exciting and inspiring career for teens to consider. Glossary.

316. Welsbacher, Anne. *Anacondas*. **Capstone Press, 2001. 32pp. LB $15.95 (0-7368-0785-3). Nonfiction.**

READING LEVEL: 2–3   INTEREST LEVEL: 12–14
ACCELERATED READER: YES

For those who love Discovery Channel documentaries on wild animals, this book brings to life all the excitement that the television screen delivers. It is a fact-filled, compact volume full of photos of the huge anacondas, showing their hunting techniques, their unique curved teeth, and their ability to suffo-cate their prey and to swallow it whole. A fascinating South American reptile. Color photos, glossary.

317. Wilcox, Charlotte. *The Greyhound*. **Capstone Press, 2001. 48pp. LB $15.95 (0-7368-0764-0). Nonfiction.**

READING LEVEL: 3–4   INTEREST LEVEL: 12–18
ACCELERATED READER: YES

This is one of a series of twenty-four books about learning about how to select, train, and care for a dog. Each book highlights the physical characteris-tics, personality, history, and special features of a popular breed. Beautiful full-color photos show the elegance of the greyhound, highlighting the aero-dynamic shape that reduces wind resistance and enables the dog to run at great speed. The reader follows the greyhound to the track (25 million people annually watch greyhounds race at fifty-five tracks around the United States). There's lots of food for thought here for teens who are craving dog owner-ship. In addition to facts about the dogs, the authors convey the tremendous sense of companionship and solace that dogs can provide their owners. Glos-sary and chart of Quick Facts About Dogs.

WEB SITES

318. Amazon Interactive

http://www.eduweb.com/amazon.html

An interactive exploration of the history, geography, environment, animals, and people of the Amazon. Does ecotourism benefit or harm the ecology and people of this region? Try your hand at taking over an ecotourism project.

319. Anaconda

http://www.nashvillezoo.org/anaconda.htm

Nashville Zoo presents information on the anaconda, which can reach an impressive 29 feet in length and can weigh more than 550 pounds. For a more exciting presentation, visit the highly interactive King Cobra site (http://www.nationalgeographic.com/features/97/kingcobra/index-n.html) and learn about these magnificent snakes that have inspired many myths and legends. This site will fascinate both young and old, and the sophisticated and bored.

320. Butterflies 2000: On the Wings of Freedom

http://library.thinkquest.org/C002251/index2.shtml

Two sections of this site have particular merit for this age group: The Astounding World of Butterflies and Butterflies and Humans. The former lists amazing facts—about giant and dwarf butterflies, about butterflies that fly 500 miles without a break, and about butterflies that get drunk on rotten fruit. Among topics covered in the latter are the butterfly's influence on the arts, its frequent use as a symbol in advertising and a motif in jewelry, and the significance of its name in many languages. Other areas of the site are more appropriate to younger students, but provide good, basic information, answering such questions as "where do butterflies sleep?" and detailing the "workaday" world of the butterfly.

321. Cats! Wild to Mild

http://www.lam.mus.ca.us/cats/

There's something for all cat lovers at this site from the Natural History Museum of Los Angeles County: cat facts, biology, behavior, history, conservation, cultural attitudes, etc. The presentation is excellent, with text interspersed with images, Shockwave and other features, and quizzes. You can either follow the guided tour through the site or select individual topics from the menu. The Working With Cats section consists of fascinating interviews with people who work in quite different cat-related fields. Another site that will be of interest is Extraordinary Cats (http://www.pbs.org/wnet/nature/excats/), which tells stories of heroic felines and gives some insight into the activities of cat breeders. This site is much more text-heavy than Cats! Wild to Mild.

322. Climate Kaleidoscope

http://climate.nms.ac.uk/

How do rain forests affect our climate? This is probably the best site on the subject of global warming, with clear, lucid descriptions of scientific facts and concepts. An excellent example of how to present information without talking down to students, and how to use a mix of graphics and photos judiciously. The Journey section relates the preparations for an expedition into the Brazilian rain forest and tells what expedition members eat and drink and which language they choose to speak.

323. Congo Gorilla Forest

http://www.congogorillaforest.com/

Take a virtual tour of the Bronx Zoo's gorilla rain forest and meet its residents. You will also learn about rain forests, which animals live there, and why they are threatened. The Congo Game will probably not be of interest to this age group. The conservation information is slightly marred by flashing requests to donate funds.

324. FBI Working Dogs

http://www.fbi.gov/kids/dogs/doghome.htm

FBI working dogs perform a variety of tasks: helping to find bombs, drugs, money, and people and to carry things, pick up items off the floor, and open doors. Readers are introduced to a number of dogs, who tell their own stories. Each dog's individual story is accompanied by a number of photos. The signposts on the right lead to more information on the FBI, divided by grade level.

325. Gators

http://www.roadsideamerica.com/set/ANIMgator.html

Roadside America calls itself "Your Online Guide to Offbeat Attractions." Anyone who reads *Odd Jobs* (entry no. 177) and is attracted to a life as an alligator wrestler will find food for thought here, and at the Nova site on a similar beast, Crocodiles! (http://www.pbs.org/wgbh/nova/crocs/), which offers lots of information, an interview with a crocodile expert, and a clickable crocodile. Here you'll find details of exactly how a croc uses those big teeth.

326. Global Warming: Focus on the Future

http://globalwarming.enviroweb.org/index.html

A well-constructed, well-illustrated overview of the status of global warming, the resultant rising waters (threatening parts of the world from Bangladesh and the Maldives to Washington, D.C.) and health problems, and what individuals can do to reduce the threat. The "games" are more educational than entertaining.

327. Life of Birds

http://www.pbs.org/lifeofbirds/

A companion to David Attenborough's TV program, this is a beautiful production in itself, with riveting explanations of how some of the film shots were accomplished. From the story of intelligent Japanese crows that exploit both cars and traffic lights to descriptions of the fastest, strongest, highest-flying . . . this offers something for everyone. Evolution and parenthood—even how birds breathe while singing—are discussed in clear terms. Students who want to know more about bird migration should look at Audubon's page called Bird Migration Facts (http://north.audubon.org/facts.html), part of the organization's site on snow geese.

328. My First Garden: Gardening FUNdamentals

http://www.urbanext.uiuc.edu/firstgarden/fundamentals/index.html

The University of Illinois Extension gives advice for youngsters with an interest in gardening. Clear, easy-to-understand sections cover Tools of the Trade, Garden Measuring, and When to Start Planting. There is also a printable Garden Planning List and instructions on how to read a seed package. Young gardeners are urged to keep a daily journal, recording their successes and failures, the varieties used, and the weather.

329. Nature: Extraordinary Dogs

http://www.pbs.org/wnet/nature/dogs/

Meet some wonderful dogs: dogs that herd sheep, predict epileptic seizures, rescue people from avalanches, and offer therapy to the bed-ridden. The Owning a Dog section helps readers understand the responsibilities involved in keeping a pet.

330. The Raptor Center at Auburn University

http://www.vetmed.auburn.edu/raptor/

Auburn College's eagle Tiger soared over the opening of the Winter Olympics in Salt Lake City. Students interested in Tiger and other birds of prey can see information both at the Auburn College Web site (http://

www.auburn.edu/) and at the college's Raptor Center, which gives basic information on eagles, falcons, hawks, kites, ospreys, and owls. There are also details on what to do if you find an injured bird, and a special page on Tiger, who was twenty-three years old when she flew at the Games. Eagle Symbolism introduces beliefs from around the world, from Wales to Ancient Sumeria. Falcons have reappeared around the United States in recent years, and have in many cases adopted city skyscrapers as a new habitat. There are several live falcon cams that are fun to watch in the spring as the young hatch and are fed by their parents, including Peregrine Watch, from Cleveland, Ohio (http://www.dnr.state.oh.us/wildlife/resources/falcon/columbus/falcons.html). The highlights from the year before are available for viewing year-round.

331. Vampire Bats

http://www.nationalgeographic.com/fieldtales/bats/

The crew filming *Vampire Bats* for a National Geographic Explorer episode tell their online audience about their adventures in bat-filled caves in Nicaragua. Wonderfully presented with photos and film clips. The Off Camera section tells the story of a young girl who died from a bat bite. Excellent bat information is also available at The Wild Ones: Bats (http://www.thewildones.org/Animals/bat.html) and for a more frivolous approach to learning, try the park ranger's interview with a friendly vampire bat at http://www.nps.gov/bibe/batintvw.htm.

332. Virtual Shark Buffet: Feed Your Need

http://www.discovery.com/stories/nature/sharkweek/sharkweek.html

Sharks are much maligned, according to most experts, but our fascination with them—and fear of them—continues unabated. This site offers something for everyone, from basic information on various kinds of shark in the Shark Tank to a more challenging account of shark encounters in Shark Reality. There is an Interview with a Shark for those who like their information in light doses and a Shark Cam trained on an aquarium tank. (To be thoroughly disabused of any false notions you have about sharks, visit Shark Myths at http://www.marinelab.sarasota.fl.us/~rhueter/sharks/myths.phtml.)

333. The Year of the Ocean

http://www.enn.com/yoto/index.asp

In honor of the Year of the Ocean (1998), the Environmental News Network created a fascinating site that covers oceans from all perspectives: science, technology, fisheries, conservation, commerce, arts and entertainment, recreation, and coastal living. Every possible aspect is included and the multimedia offerings are many and varied. The news items have not been updated since mid-2000, but those remain interesting.

Reference

BOOKS

334. Parnwell, E. C. *The New Oxford Picture Dictionary.* **Oxford University Press, 1989. 140pp. Paper $10.95 (0-19-434355-3). Nonfiction.**

READING LEVEL: DICTIONARY FORMAT   INTEREST LEVEL: 7–12

The New Oxford Picture Dictionary presents more than 2,400 words clearly depicted in full-color contextualized illustrations. Vocabulary is introduced within eighty-two topics such as the space program, occupations, and sports. An index includes all vocabulary words with a clear, easy-to-follow pronunciation guide. The dictionary is useful both in reading programs and in work with non-English-speaking students.

WEB SITES

335. American Sign Language and Interpreting

http://www.nad.org/infocenter/infotogo/asl/index.html

The National Association of the Deaf provides a fact sheet about American Sign Language and discusses how long it takes to learn it. For an online dictionary of ASL signs, with video illustrations, turn to American Sign Language Browser (http://commtechlab.msu.edu/sites/aslweb/). This requires the Quicktime plug-in.

Science, Technology, Space Exploration

WEB SITES

336. Amusement Park Physics: Roller Coaster

http://www.learner.org/exhibits/parkphysics/coaster.html

Learn about the history and design of roller coasters, with a little physics and discussion of safety measures thrown in. Carousels, bumper cars, and free fall rides are also covered. There are links to other sites of interest and a glossary.

337. ArtEdventures: Color Theory vs. Dr. Gray and His Dechromatizer

http://www.sanford-artedventures.com/play/color2/a1.html

On an ordinary day at the Museum of World Art . . . an evildoer steals the colors from the famous paintings. Readers learn about primary, secondary, and tertiary/intermediary colors and can test their skill in combining colors. Key words are linked to a glossary. Students who click on Study Art at the bottom of the page will find easy-to-read information on the following topics: Elements and Principles of Art, Art Concepts, Media, Styles, and Artists. Many of these reinforce understanding with interactive and printable activities (creating tints and shades, looking at proportion, making 3-D shapes, and so forth).

338. Astronomy Picture of the Day

http://antwrp.gsfc.nasa.gov/apod/astropix.html

Every day NASA presents a new image or photo that is always worth seeing. The accompanying information is written by a professional astronomer but is clear and comprehensible. You can browse through the archives searching for specific heavenly bodies. Some of the most interesting are of auroras, meteors, and of our planet, particularly those showing Earth at night and the distribution of lights (http://antwrp.gsfc.nasa.gov/apod/ap001127.html, http://antwrp.gsfc.nasa.gov/apod/ap000708.html, and http://antwrp.gsfc.nasa.gov/apod/ap990728.html), respectively the whole world, the United States, and Asia.

339. Building Big

http://www.pbs.org/wgbh/buildingbig/

Explore the structural concepts underlying bridges, domes, skyscrapers, dams, and tunnels, and meet the engineers who design them. Not only do you get the facts about famous examples of each kind of structure, but you get to work with different forces, materials, loads, and shapes in the interactive labs. For example, experiment with adding load to a bridge until it collapses; then work on strengthening the structure to avert future problems. The skyscraper section will be of particular interest; it includes information on the World Trade Center, updated to reflect the towers' collapse.

340. Comets

http://whyfiles.org/011comets/

In typically accessible language, the Why Files presents a lively account on comets and their origins. This was created when Hale-Bopp was approaching Earth, but the facts remain relevant. You can move from one document to the next using the numbers across the bottom of the page.

341. Gene Stories: Who Am I?

http://www.bbc.co.uk/science/genes/who_am_i/

Why am I like my parents? Why am I the shape I am? Students will find much of interest in this BBC site. They may need help with some of the scientific vocabulary, but many sections will pose less challenge: the discussions of identical twins and of body shape under Nature/Nurture and of thrill-seekers and of owls versus larks under Behavior, for example. Quizzes, graphics, and photos add to the interest.

342. Glacier

http://www.glacier.rice.edu/

What is it like to live and work in Antarctica? How do you get there? What do you wear? Full of maps, photographs, facts, anecdotes, and graphics, this site tells what it's like to go on an Antarctic expedition. You'll read about the initial preparations, the journey south, and the conditions at base and remote camps. Additional sections explain about climate and weather studies in Antarctica, glacier formation and movement, and the oceans of the world. There is coverage of the responsibilities of the scientists. Students will need help with some of the more technical information, but should be able to handle the accounts of the expedition more easily. Even if they skip some sections, they will find much of interest here. Glossaries are provided throughout.

343. Greatest Engineering Achievements of the 20th Century

http://www.greatachievements.org/greatachievements/index.html

The National Academy of Engineering has selected twenty achievements of the last century for inclusion here, ranging from the automobile and airplane to electrification, health technologies, and the Internet. A brief summary of each achievement is accompanied by a useful timeline. Histories of each achievement are more difficult depending on the nature of the product, and students may need help with these.

344. How Things Fly

http://www.nasm.si.edu/galleries/gal109/

What makes an airplane fly? How does a spacecraft stay in orbit? Why does a balloon float in the air? To get the answers to these and many other questions, click on the Floor Plan of this National Air and Space Museum exhibit or access the information through the How Do Things Fly? graphic. Principles such as drag, thrust, and lift are clearly explained. Readers should be encouraged to click on the Did You Know?, In the Museum, and Try This Yourself links at the bottom of many pages. The Resource Center includes several activities and links to other related Web sites.

345. Liftoff to Space Exploration

http://liftoff.msfc.nasa.gov/

Students with an interest in space exploration should bookmark this site and visit it frequently. NASA created it specifically for teens age 13 and over. The site keeps you up-to-date on developments throughout NASA and has special sections on Spacecraft, Human Journey, The Universe, Fundamentals (tools of science and engineering), and Tracking. Students may need help with the scientific vocabulary.

346. Living in Space

http://www.spaceflight.nasa.gov/living/index.html

What do astronauts eat? What do they wear? How do they shower and use the toilet in space? Don't they get bored? These and many other important questions are answered here, with videos of astronauts dancing, running, and playing ball. There's also information on work schedules and sleep allotments. Links at the top of the page take you to additional details on the space program's history, with a gallery of images.

347. Space-Age Living: Building the International Space Station

http://school.discovery.com/schooladventures/spacestation/

When completed in 2006, the International Space Station will be a little "city in space." It's being constructed in space, with sixteen countries collaborating on the complex project. Here you'll find the mission "basics," meet some of the people involved, and learn about the technological challenges. The site also answers important questions such as What will the astronauts do for fun? The reading level varies by sections of the site. Everyone will enjoy Putting It Together, an interactive demo of the station's construction.

Sports and Recreation

BOOKS

348. Atwood, Jane. *Capoeira: A Martial Art and a Cultural Tradition*. Rosen Publishing, 1998. 64pp. LB $19.95 (0-8239-1859-9). Nonfiction.
READING LEVEL: 5–6 INTEREST LEVEL: 12–18
ACCELERATED READER: YES

Capoeira is a beautiful and unique form of martial art, originating in Brazil, performed by African slaves hundreds of years ago. It combines combat, play, dance, music, theater, ritual, and self-defense. It is a complex sport that requires skill, agility, and concentration. Capoeira will be an Olympic sport in 2004. Includes background information on the founders of the art, glossary, photos of basic movements, and list of schools where capoeira is taught.

349. Brooke, Michael. *The Concrete Wave: The History of Skateboarding*. Warwick Publishing, 1999. 196pp. Paper $19.95 (1-894020-54-5). Nonfiction.
READING LEVEL: 6 AND UP INTEREST LEVEL: 12–18

This book, the first published to document the history of one of the world's most cutting-edge sports—skateboarding—will serve as more of a browsing book for teenagers interested in the sport's most perilous feats and dreaming of accomplishing these extreme moves for fun and competition. The book features hundreds of photos of skaters and memorabilia and includes interviews with Tony Alva and Tony Hawk. Many passages are written at a higher reading level than grade six, but teens will be attracted by the spectacular nature of the photos and the general information on the sport, which includes a list of skating pros over the last forty years, short bios of legends, skateboard films, skateboarding parks, and even a section on *Thrasher* (the skateboarding magazine—always stolen from libraries). Beautifully painted and designed skateboards and their owners pictured throughout. Color photos.

350. Cebulash, Mel. *Bases Loaded: Great Baseball of the 20th Century.* **New Readers Press, 1993. 64pp. Paper $5.00 (0-88336-742-4). Nonfiction.**

READING LEVEL: 4   INTEREST LEVEL: 12 AND UP

One of a series of books that detail notable sporting events, this title presents seven memorable moments in baseball, focusing on the player. Babe Ruth's called shot, Willie Mays' famous catch, Reggie Jackson's four consecutive World Series homers—these are all baseball legends that may not be familiar to today's young people. The stories are seven to nine pages long. Great descriptive passages will draw boys in and will appeal especially to those who do not have the reading skills to tackle a novel.

351. Cebulash, Mel. *Fast Break: Great Basketball of the 20th Century.* **New Readers Press, 1993. 64pp. Paper $5.00 (0-88336-744-0). Nonfiction.**

READING LEVEL: 4   INTEREST LEVEL: 12 AND UP

This title details eight memorable moments in basketball, focusing on great players at their best: Wilt's 100-point game and Magic leading the Lakers to overcome a seven-point lead in the last two minutes of the NBA finals against the Celtics, to name just two. The stories are seven to eight pages long.

352. Cebulash, Mel. *Lights Out: Great Fights of the 20th Century.* **New Readers Press, 1993. 63pp. Paper $4.75 (0-88336-741-6). Nonfiction.**

READING LEVEL: 4   INTEREST LEVEL: 12 AND UP

This title presents seven great boxing matches, featuring athletes including Ali, Louis, and Hearns. The stories are eight to nine pages long and include great descriptive passages that should appeal to boys, especially those who do not have the reading skills to get through a novel. The clear focus on the fights makes these stories particularly easy to follow and a good choice for stoking an interest in reading about sports.

353. Cebulash, Mel. *Third and Goal: Great Football of the 20th Century.* **New Readers Press, 1993. 63pp. Paper (0-88336-743-2). Nonfiction.**

READING LEVEL: 4   INTEREST LEVEL: 12 AND UP

This title details eight memorable moments in football, focusing mainly on the player at the center of the action, with comments on the contributions of the rest of the team and reminders that football is indeed a team game. The moments portrayed are not all well known. The story of disabled kicker Tom Dempsey's longest field goal in NFL history is particularly well done. The accounts are each six to eight pages in length. Great descriptive passages should draw boys into this one, especially those who do not have the reading skills to get through a sports biography.

354. Devine, Monica. *The Iditarod: The Greatest Winner Ever*. Perfection Learning, 1977. 55pp. Paper $8.95 (0-7891-1955-2). Nonfiction.

READING LEVEL: 3   INTEREST LEVEL: 12–15
ACCELERATED READER: YES

Kara wanted more than anything to win the Iditarod. Her dogs were well trained and her stock of provisions seemed to provide for almost every possible type of disaster. The race went well until a moose attacked and killed her lead dog. Overcoming this setback, she struggled onward, making her way toward the finish in spite of a blizzard that howled through the night . . . But as she and her dogs were racing across an ice pack, she saw fellow racer Alex walking in circles, clearly disoriented. As much as Kara wanted to win, her job now was to save Alex before hypothermia set in. Stripping him of his wet clothes, she wrapped him in sleeping bags and she and her dogs warmed his body until his color and consciousness returned. Saving a life turns out to be the greatest win of all for Kara, and there's always next year's Iditarod to look forward to. Nonfiction, reads like fiction. Beautiful color photos and drawings. Glossary.

355. George, Charles, and Linda George. *Ice Climbing*. Capstone Press, 1999. 48pp. LB $15.95 (0-7368-0052-2). Nonfiction.

READING LEVEL: 3–4   INTEREST LEVEL: 14–18
ACCELERATED READER: YES

Words such as *couloir, crampon, crevasse, alpenstock*, and *rappel* are not usually found in high-interest, low-reading-level books. But teens with an interest in the extreme sport of ice climbing will soon be speaking and reading about these terms as they learn about the tools and equipment needed to survive as an ice climber. Ice climbing can take place on a vertical slope (like a frozen waterfall), in a crevasse, or on alpine ice in mountainous areas. Very special training and team cooperation are essential for survival in a sport that is fast gaining in popularity. Glossary of terms and beautiful color photos accompany the text.

356. Glaser, Jason. *Bungee Jumping*. Capstone Press, 1999. 48pp. LB $15.95 (0-7368-0168-5). Nonfiction.

READING LEVEL: 3–4   INTEREST LEVEL: 15–18
ACCELERATED READER: YES

Bungee jumping, even under the best conditions, is an extreme sport with great risk for potential injury. It involves using safety gear to attach bungee cords to the feet or to a harness on the body. The cords stretch as the individual falls from a plane, hot air balloon, or other high place, and allow one to fall great distances without hitting the ground. Children under the age of 18 cannot bungee-jump without their parents' permission. An entertaining read about an exciting sport that explores the history, stunts, competitions, and safety measures needed to tackle a jump. Color photos, glossary.

357. Hayhurst, Chris. *Mountain Biking! Get on the Trail*. Rosen Publishing, 2000. 64pp. LB $19.95 (0-8239-3013-0). Nonfiction.

READING LEVEL: 5–6   INTEREST LEVEL: 12–18
ACCELERATED READER: YES

The style of this book resembles a colorful magazine piece on the extreme sport of mountain biking. Action shots of biking up, down, and across terrain that requires skill, daring speed, and stamina make the reader want to drop everything and grab a specially designed bike, a helmet, and other accoutrements detailed in this fast-paced book. Mountain bikes, originally designed in Marin County, California, in the 1970s, and called Clunkers, now come in hundreds of styles, and are manufactured all over the United States. Various competitive events are defined, replete with photos of bikers traveling 70 mph, and sidebars enhance our appreciation for this growing sport that has enormous appeal to teenagers. A glossary of terms appends the text.

358. Hopkins, Ellen. *Fly Fishing*. Capstone Press, 2002. 48 pp. LB $14.95 (0-7368-0914-7). Nonfiction.

READING LEVEL: 4–5   INTEREST LEVEL: 12–18
ACCELERATED READER: YES

Describes the equipment, skills, conservation issues, and safety concerns of fly fishing. Very clear instructions give step-by-step guidance on how to use flies (lures to attract fish) with beautiful color photos of young people casting and fishing in streams and lakes. Charts on fly styles and a color section on typical North American fish species. Glossary.

359. Keller, Kristin Thoennes. *Hiking*. Capstone Press, 2002. 48pp. LB $14.95 (0-7368-0916-3). Nonfiction.

READING LEVEL: 4–5   INTEREST LEVEL: 12–18
ACCELERATED READER: YES

The woods offer a chance to clear the cobwebs from the brain and find natural beauty. All teens with an interest in the outdoors will appreciate the advice on selecting the proper equipment, learning safety skills in the woods, and learning how to read a topographical map. Color photos, glossary of hiking terms.

360. Labanowich, Stan. *Wheelchair Basketball.* **Capstone Press, 1998. 46pp. LB $15.95 (1-56065-614-X). Nonfiction.**
READING LEVEL: 3–4   INTEREST LEVEL: 12–18
ACCELERATED READER: YES

An inspiring book that introduces the history of wheelchair basketball and its rules, equipment, and training. The game of basketball was begun in 1891 by D. James Naismith. The first players threw a soccer ball into peach baskets. Wheelchair basketball was invented during World War II to give thousands of wounded and amputee soldiers an opportunity to play sports in a competitive environment. Color photos show players using a variety of throws and techniques in specially designed wheelchairs costing $2,000. Glossary of basketball terms and useful addresses of wheelchair basketball associations appended.

361. Mattern, Joanne, and James Mattern. *TeamWork: Working Together to Win.* **Perfection Learning, 2002. 59pp. Paper $8.95 (0-7891-5514-1). Nonfiction.**
READING LEVEL: 5–6   INTEREST LEVEL: 12–18
ACCELERATED READER: YES

The authors show how successful teams work together and blend their strengths and weaknesses into a winning combination. From sports history, we read how quarterback Joe Namath put the New York Jets on the map by leading them to victory in Superbowl III and how in 1980 the U.S. Olympic Hockey Team, although regarded as the underdog, beat Russia and then Finland to secure the gold medal. There are also championship stories about the Chicago Bulls, the 1999 New York Yankees World Series, women's basketball, the U.S. World Cup Soccer Team, and other great examples of sports teamwork. Glossary and photos.

362. Parr, Danny. *Extreme Bicycle Stunt Riding Moves.* **Capstone Press, 2001. 32pp. LB $15.95 (0-7368-0781-0). Nonfiction.**
READING LEVEL: 3–4   INTEREST LEVEL: 12–18
ACCELERATED READER: YES

Discusses with great enthusiasm the sport of extreme bicycle stunt riding, including the moves involved in the sport and the rules and equipment for safe riding. Since 1995, when ESPN TV network started an extreme sports competition called the X Games, this sport has been increasing in popularity. This competition includes the four styles of freestyle bicycle stunt riding: dirt, flatland, street, and vert riding. Includes stunt riding slang (for example, a "brain bucket" is a bike helmet), a list of bicycling associations, and a glossary.

363. Roberts, Jeremy. *Rock and Ice Climbing! Top the Tower*. Rosen Publishing, 2000. 63pp. LB $19.95 (0-8239-3009-2). Nonfiction.
READING LEVEL: 5–6 INTEREST LEVEL: 12–18
ACCELERATED READER: YES

Young people who are strong of body and mind may want to try one of sport's most extreme, grueling, and dangerous arenas—rock and ice climbing. Special equipment, a trainer, and faith in one's climbing team are essential for anyone contemplating life on the edge of cliffs that meet the body at 180 degrees and offer views 5,000 feet down. Beautiful photos of young people rock- and ice-climbing illustrate a book that will inspire even the most reluctant reader to turn page after page, seeking the secret to success on a rope! Glossary of terms under the heading "X-Planations" enhances an exciting reading experience.

364. Ryan, Pat. *Street Luge Racing*. Capstone Press, 1998. 48pp. LB $15.95 (1-56065-538-0). Nonfiction.
READING LEVEL: 3–4 INTEREST LEVEL: 12–18
ACCELERATED READER: YES

Introduces the history of the sport, native to California, that combines skateboarding and ice luging. A street luge is a wooden or metal sled with skateboard wheels, about 8 feet long and capable of reaching speeds of 60 to 70 miles per hour. The record speed for a street luge racer is 78 mph. Street luge racing is considered a professional sport. Because of the high speed of the luge and possibility of serious injury, racers formed the Road Racers Association in 1990 to make the sport much safer. There are now many clubs and associations for those interested in this extreme, and exciting, activity. Hair-raising color photos of racers competing in full protective gear give the reader an impression of continuous challenge in a growing sport. Glossary of sporting terms.

365. Sullivan, George. *Burnin' Rubber: Behind the Scenes in Stock Car Racing*. Millbrook Press, 1998. 48pp. LB (0-7613-1256-0). Nonfiction.
READING LEVEL: 4–5 INTEREST LEVEL: 12–18

Cars traveling at an average speed of 212.8 miles an hour on the nation's premier tracks are captured in beautiful color action shots that complement an easy-to read text. All the big names—Jeff Gordon, Dale Earnhardt, Ernie Ivan,

Bill Elliot, Rusty Wallace—are pictured here with their classic cars. This is a big-money sport, as the author explains, and it has to be. "The typical Winston Cup car chews up 360 sets—a total of 1,440 tires—each racing season. At $300 apiece, that's $432,000 for tires." There is also detailed information on behind-the-scenes automotive and engine design and a description of the teamwork needed to make race day a winning event.

366. Sullivan, George, and Anne Canevari Green, illus. *Don't Step on the Foul Line: Sports Superstitions.* **Millbrook Press, 2000. 61pp. LB $14.95 (0-7613-1558-6). Nonfiction.**

READING LEVEL: 5–6   INTEREST LEVEL: 12–18

What makes a baseball star sit in a stadium office during a game? Or put on his socks in exactly the same order before each game? Or carry a Teddy Bear with him? What would make grown men wear their hats inside out? Winning, of course, and these are but a few of the superstitions that many players indulge. Line drawings complement the text.

WEB SITES

367. Ancient Greece: The Olympics

http://www.bbc.co.uk/schools/landmarks/ancientgreece/classics/olympics/intro.shtml

Thespis and Melinna are your Greek guides to the Games in this animated BBC Online Cartoon Classic. Roll your mouse over the illustrations to read various comments and descriptions of the activities. This is also how you navigate through the site. You must click on the correct part of the picture to move to the next page. However, the clues make this quite easy and the correct selection is outlined in yellow

368. Baseball's 25 Greatest Moments

http://www.sportingnews.com/baseball/25moments/

Historic moments in baseball are recounted, complete with details of date, location, and players, and followed by quotes by people who were there. The aftermath of each event is also given, in a kind of "where are they now?" treatment. Links take you to Moments That Changed the Game, Unusual and Unforgettable Moments, and Individual Feats. A good site for those who enjoy dates, details, and statistics. A similar site is Olympic Hockey: 25 Greatest Moments (http://tsn.sportingnews.com/olympics/25greatest/1.html).

369. Fly Fishing

http://www.orvis.com/

Select Fly Fishing from the main menu of the Orvis site to access a wide range of resources for novice and expert devotees of this sport. Beginners will particularly welcome the glossary, frequently asked questions, and casting and fishing tips. This is a commercial site but it succeeds in providing useful, practical information to its customers.

370. Iditarod.com

http://www.iditarod.com/index.shtml

Click on General Information to read about the history of this race in "The 1925 Serum Run to Nome," background material on Alaska, and a portrait of a musher, which discusses the training and preparation necessary for participating in this grueling race. A rich site, with lots to offer including maps of the trail and a Veterinary Corner that discusses the dogs and their health and welfare.

371. Learn2 Behave When Lost in the Woods

http://www.learn2.com/04/0434/0434.asp

The no-nonsense Learn2 approach offers enough graphics and bullets to make almost any subject accessible to reluctant readers even when the vocabulary is at a high level. This is a useful site for anyone setting off on a trip in the backwoods. Related tutorials are linked from the first page: Build a Campfire; Improvise a Compass; Choose the Right Tent; and Shop for Hiking Boots.

372. National Baseball Hall of Fame

http://www.baseballhalloffame.org/index.htm

Packed with information for fans and report writers, this site lacks glitz. There are brief biographies of the inductees and names can be accessed by alphabetical order, date of induction, birthplace, voting percentage, defensive position, and so forth. Perhaps the most interesting part of the site is the online exhibits, which include The 3,000-Hit Club and From Rookies to Legends, telling the stories of Lou Gehrig and Cal Ripken, Jr., and of Tony Gwynn and Stan Musial. For those who need more visual stimulation, much of the same information can be found in the History section of MLB.com (http://www.mlb.com/NASApp/mlb/mlb/history/mlb_history_timeline.jsp). Here you will find more detail about recent baseball events and a sketchier approach to the past.

373. Negro Baseball Leagues

http://www.blackbaseball.com/

For most of the first half of the twentieth century, black Americans could not play major league baseball. This site is dedicated "to the generation of ballplayers who were denied the opportunity to play in the major leagues because of factors other than their ability to play the game of baseball." Some of the history and other descriptions are at a high reading level, but the biographical information on players including Satchel Paige, Josh Gibson, and Ray Dandridge will be of interest to fans.

374. Pro Football Hall of Fame

http://www.profootballhof.com

Read a decade-by-decade history of pro football, the stories of how the teams' names were selected, and brief biographical details on Hall of Fame inductees. There are links to all the teams and features that change on a regular basis.

375. Science of Cycling

http://www.exploratorium.edu/cycling/index.html

Cycling is a very efficient form of transportation but is used mainly for recreation in the United States. This site explores the human energy that drives bicycles and also looks at the mechanical components of bicycles and the aerodynamic properties of today's efficient designs. Avid cyclists will enjoy the site, although some sections will be challenging. The timeline and section on human power are probably the best places to start. The latter includes several features (on a band called Bicycle, on two race champions, and two audio/video interviews) as well as information on diet and how muscles work. Students may need help with the sections on the equipment and aerodynamics. The Exploratorium also offers similar sites on hockey (http://www.exploratorium.edu/hockey/index.html) and skateboarding (http://www.exploratorium.edu/skateboarding/index.html).

376. The Sport of Life and Death: The Mesoamerican Ballgame

http://www.ballgame.org/main.asp?section=2

Explore the first team sport in history, looking at the composition of the ball, the clothes the contestants wore, their mascots, the court, and the rules of the game—including sacrificing losing players. Readers will—with no effort—absorb a lot of knowledge about the cultures of the Aztecs, Mayans, and other residents of Mesoamerica. Playing the game involves answering questions based on information given in the rest of the site. This site, created by the

National Endowment for the Humanities and the Mint Museum of Art, requires a recent version of your Web browser and Flash plug-in.

377. Sumo

http://wpni01.auroraquanta.com/pv/sumo

The Washington Post presents a photoessay on the ancient sport of sumo wrestling. You can click through the photos in order or select particular topics such as Behind the Scenes, Tradition, and The Fans. Each photo has an informative caption.

378. What to Bring on a Hike

http://www.cmc.org/cmc/hike_eqp.html

The Colorado Mountain Club lists the essentials of hiking: ten essentials, adequate outdoor clothing, proper equipment, and a first aid kit. Click at the bottom of the page to move to the accompanying information on Backcountry Safety and Survival. REI (http://www.rei.com/), the well-known source for outdoor gear of all kinds, also has a wealth of useful information on its Web site. Unfortunately, some of this is at a high reading level. Select Camp/Hike and then Health/Safety to access advice on planning and equipping yourself for hiking or camping.

Teen Culture and Issues

BOOKS

379. Acker, Kerry. *The Goth Scene*. Rosen Publishing, 2000. 64pp. LB $17.95 (0-8239-3223-0). Nonfiction.

READING LEVEL: 4–6   INTEREST LEVEL: 12–18
ACCELERATED READER: YES

An extremely thorough and readable survey of the contemporary Goth scene. Goth culture traces its origins back to the late 200s and early 300s, when invading Goths pillaged and looted the Roman Empire and acquired the reputation of being barbaric. In the Middle Ages, Gothic art and architecture incorporated stone gargoyles with grotesque features, and in the eighteenth and nineteenth century Gothic novels celebrated the supernatural and delighted in creating an overall atmosphere of gloom. Today's teens' interest in Goth subculture stems from the British punk rock music of the 1970s, when bands such as Bauhaus and Siouxsie and the Banshees performed music that expressed dark emotions, dressed primarily in black, and applied ghoulish white makeup. Drawing on the 1999 Columbine tragedy, the author presents an excellent portrait of this contemporary cult that can serve as resource material for a term paper topic for older teens reading below grade level. Photos and glossary.

380. Cruz, Barbara C. *School Dress Codes: A Pro/Con Issue.* **Enslow Publishers, 2001. 64pp. LB $17.95 (0-7660-1465-7). Nonfiction.**

READING LEVEL: 5–6 INTEREST LEVEL: 12–18
ACCELERATED READER: YES SCHOLASTIC COUNTS: YES

Dress codes are a great topic for a school debate and the information presented here is accessible to all students, especially those who read below grade level. Other items that denote status in teen culture such as cell phones, beepers, tattoos and body piercings, and extreme make-up are also reviewed, considering their acceptability in a school setting. The author cites instances of violence in schools that have been attributed to dress: the six-year-old who was killed for wearing a red sweater because it implied she was connected to a local gang and teens who have been attacked for wearing Starter jackets (professional sport team jackets) or leather bomber jackets. The issue of proper attire for school is bound to get teens thinking, talking, and reading! Color photos, glossary.

381. Morgenstern, Mindy. *The Real Rules for Girls.* **Girl Press, 1999. 111pp. Paper $15.95 (0-9659754-5-2). Nonfiction.**

READING LEVEL: 5–6 INTEREST LEVEL: 14–18

Girls will push themselves beyond their reading level in this original and hip book packed with the kind of helpful hints a girl can use to navigate and succeed in life: Guys really *do* like girls who talk about themselves, ignore your mother's advice not to call a boy first and do it, and so forth. The book is divided into sections on romance, work, social life, family, and money, and punctuated with sidebars, photos, and quotes by prominent women—for example, "If high heels were so wonderful, men would be wearing them" (Sue Grafton) and "If you obey all the rules, you will miss all the fun" (Katharine Hepburn). Lots for musing and discussion.

382. Pollack, Sudie, M.A. *Will the Dollars Stretch? Teen Parents Living on Their Own: Virtual Reality Through Stories & Check-Writing Practice.* **Morning Glory Press, 2001. 108pp. Paper $8.95 (1-885356-78-1). Nonfiction.**

READING LEVEL: 5–6   INTEREST LEVEL: 12–18

This book is a must for any teen contemplating parenthood without a good source of income, child care, caring partner, or a guarantee of paid education. And diapers??? All the details of daily life must be carefully budgeted when wages are minimum and health care is hit-or-miss. The personal expenses of moms, dads, and baby (as well as car insurance and maintenance) are additional burdens that can push teen parents quickly into debt. Budgeting charts can get teens into the habit of recording expenses, balancing checkbooks, watching for sales, and trying to live within their means. Designed for a high school home economics course, this nuts-and-bolts, real-life look at money and the services needed to support a child is a survival guide that any teen should peruse before taking that big step toward parenthood. Black-and-white photos and charts.

WEB SITES

383. Brainevent.com

http://www.brainevent.com/

Teens with an interest in world events and the environment will like this user-friendly site, which calls itself "a place where kids can come together to find out about the world, flex their mental muscles, share their opinions, give voice to their musings, and be inspired to social action." Several of the features are written by teens. There is information on culture, on sports around the world, and on environmental issues. Teens can seek emotional and medical advice and can participate in many polls, quizzes, and debates. Quizzes that would be good starting places include Name That Decade, How Superstitious Are You? Are You a Marketing Target? and Bad Fads.

384. Consumer Education for Teens

http://www.wa.gov/ago/youth/

Developed for teens by teens in Washington state, this site offers general tips on saving and looking after your money, followed by sections on specific items of interest to teens—joining music clubs, selecting a tattoo artist, buying a car, credit cards, return policies, health clubs, and so forth.

385. Consumer Jungle

http://www.consumerjungle.org/s_default.htm

The Credit Cave, Car-fari, and Jingle in the Jungle (dealing with cell and other phones) are just three of the sections of this site that may be a tad too cute for totally cool teens. However, it's an ambitious effort to make learning consumer sense easy for young adults, and it's worth guiding students toward it.

386. A Guide to the Business of Babysitting

http://www.urbanext.uiuc.edu/babysitting/

What should a babysitter do when the parents who are supposed to drive her home have clearly been drinking? How do you discipline somebody else's child? The answers to these and many other practical questions are here. From defining what makes a good babysitter to advice on financial arrangements to planning play activities, this is a wonderful, well-planned site. Sample conversations show how to tackle difficult topics; there's even a flyer to personalize and distribute to potential customers.

387. The Human Face

http://www.bbc.co.uk/science/humanbody/humanface/index.shtml

Can you tell if a smile is genuine? What does your face reveal about you? Looks are a major preoccupation for teens, who will enjoy this fascinating collection of information on the human face and how we use it. Major parts of the site are Face to Face, which deals with expressions; Identity, which discusses recognition and various ways we try to fit in and includes a moving story about a woman with a rare and deforming genetic disorder; and Beauty. The reading level of the Expert Articles is considerably higher than the rest of the site.

388. Me, Myself, and I

http://www.talkcity.com/theinsite/me/me_myself_and_I.html

Practical and straightforward talk on topics of interest to teens: drugs, sex, health, self-image, anger, depression, jealousy, love, and loneliness, to name just a few. But this site also tackles issues of spirituality and inner strength and offers two questionnaires on values. Interviews and anecdotes accompany each section of the site.

389. SmartGirl

http://www.smartgirl.org/

SmartGirl is by and for teen girls. The site consists mainly of reviews of movies, music, books, magazines, Web sites, computer games, TV products, and beauty products—all written by visitors to the site. The Learning, Life and Love section allows girls to anonymously post love letters and poetry; Issues and Information is full of links to other sites of interest; Speak Out includes current and archived surveys. This site won't attract teens who need glitz and animation but takes a more gentle approach that will appeal to shyer teens.

390. Teen Advice Online

http://www.teenadviceonline.org/

Dating, loneliness, depression, school—all these are part of this international site that combines articles by teenaged counselors with anonymous (and signed) real stories, personal thoughts, and poetry by other teens. Counselors, who are between the ages of 13 and 23, are required to be "responsible, mature, and motivated to help" and must agree to answer a certain number of questions a week. The grammar and vocabulary run the gamut from the very poor to the more sophisticated. But the subject matter is compelling, and, even if they are exposed to errors, the teens will at least be reading and will keep on doing so.

391. Teens Helping Teens

http://www.ldteens.org/

Dyslexic teens have banded together to create a site that displays their own art and writing and offers advice and support to other learning-disabled students. There's a listing of famous people who are/were learning disabled, a compilation of study tips, and a passage from Nelson Rockefeller, also dyslexic, urging students to persevere in the face of tough problems. He lists accomplishments that he's achieved despite this disability, such as being able to conduct press conferences in three languages. This is not a pretty site, but young people with real reading problems may find it helpful.

392. Teenwire

http://www.teenwire.com/index.asp

The Planned Parenthood Federation of America has adopted the successful style of online magazines for this site for teenagers. Teens will feel comfortable with this attractive, lively presentation. The feature articles may change from time to time, but the basics remain: information and advice on all matters related to relationships, sexually transmitted diseases, birth control, and abortion. Particularly interesting areas of the site are World Views, which talks about teen life and issues in other countries; Taking Action, which tackles all kinds of social issues; In Focus, which looks in depth at a single issue; and Hothouse, a teen 'zine. One neat feature is the "quick definition" (key a word into the field shared with the search function, click on "quick definition," and the information you're seeking will appear in a pop-up). The reading level is uneven, but the format is sure to generate strong interest. Many parts of the site are available in Spanish.

393. Virtual Homelessness

http://www.centrepoint.org.uk/start.asp

British teens threatened with homelessness have slightly different options from American teens, but the underlying choices remain the same: whether to stay in a bad home situation or leave and try to cope on their own. This site allows you to select from a number of alternatives for three different teens. Each choice spawns a new set of circumstances and challenges to overcome. It's interesting to go back and make new choices and see how the outcomes differ. Centrepoint is an organization specializing in housing young people at risk in some of the major cities of England.

Transportation

BOOKS

394. Abramovitz, Melissa. *Mine Hunting Ships*. Capstone Press, 2001. 48pp. LB $15.95 (0-7368-0758-6). Nonfiction.

READING LEVEL: 3–4 INTEREST LEVEL: 12–18
ACCELERATED READER: YES

Mine hunting ships save lives. The Navy's fleet of these ships uses sonar to detect underwater mines. Then specially designed equipment called sweeps neutralize mines in a large area. The sweeps cut the cables of moored mines, the mines float to the surface, and divers explode them. This is one book in a series that explores military vehicles (titles include *PT Boats, Submarines, Nuclear Submarines,* and *Supercarriers*), demonstrating the important functions of these vehicles in and out of battle. Glossary, color photos.

395. Burgan, Michael. *The World's Fastest Military Airplanes.* **Capstone Press, 2001. 47pp. LB $15.95 (0-7368-0568-0). Nonfiction.**

READING LEVEL: 3–4   INTEREST LEVEL: 12–18
ACCELERATED READER: YES

This volume explains how jet planes operate and their use in the military. Planes featured include the F-15 Eagle, the SR-71A Blackbird, the AV-8B Harrier, and the F-22 Raptor. These planes fly faster than the speed of sound, and their speed is measured with a mach number. An experimental X-15 reached a mach level of 6.7! Sometimes you can hear these planes flying overhead—their signature sound is a sonic boom. Charts, graphs, and photos of planes in flight will introduce reluctant readers to terms used in physics and technology. Glossary.

396. Hopkins, Ellen. *Air Devils: Sky Racers, Sky Divers, and Stunt Pilots.* **Perfection Learning, 2000. 64pp. Paper $8.95 (0-7891-5146-4). Nonfiction.**

READING LEVEL: 4   INTEREST LEVEL: 12–18
ACCELERATED READER: YES

A history of aircraft from the times when cavemen covered themselves with feathers hoping to emulate birds in flight to racers who cruise the skies at record speeds of 529 miles per hour. Includes biographical information on historical figures in flight: Lindbergh, Amelia Earhart, and the women pilots, the WASPs who ferried the fighter planes of World War II. Glossary and photos. Words in bold are listed in the glossary.

397. Lally, Linda Jean. *The Volkswagen Beetle.* **Capstone Press, 1999. 48pp. LB $15.95 (0-7368-0185-5). Nonfiction.**

READING LEVEL: 3–4   INTEREST LEVEL: 12–18

A beloved car has made a comeback. This book traces the history of the popular bug-shaped car, from its origins in Nazi Germany to its appeal among college students in the 1960s to the nostalgic version introduced in 1998. A very informative section on the changes in the car's engine design punctuated by clear diagrams will motivate any teenage boy. Includes a glossary of automotive terms.

398. Sweetman, Bill. *Stealth Bombers: The B-2 Spirits.* **Capstone Press, 2001. 32pp. LB $15.95 (0-7368-0791-8). Nonfiction.**

READING LEVEL: 3–4   INTEREST LEVEL: 12–18
ACCELERATED READER: YES

An exceptionally well-written title on the B-2 Spirit, its uses, engines, weapons, and future in the U.S. Air Force. One of the most advanced aircraft ever built, the B-2 made its first test flight in 1989. For eleven weeks in 1999, B-2 pilots bombed Serbian airbases, bridges, railroads, and power plants in an effort to convince the Serbian government to pull its soldiers out of Kosovo. Flying distances of 6,000 miles, the B-2 can refuel from a tanker aircraft. Pilots fly without radios, which makes their location undetectable. The Air Force plans to use the B-2 until 2020. In the meantime, the current B-2 will undergo computer updates and plans are in process to equip the B-2 with a satellite radio link. Other titles in the series—*Attack Helicopters, High Altitude Spy Planes*, and *Supersonic Fighters*—will also engage the most reluctant of readers. Color photos and glossary of aircraft and flight terms.

WEB SITES

399. Concorde: Facts and Figures

http://www.britishairways.com/concorde/docs/facts/index.html

A look at Concorde's design and achievements. The history stops before the Paris crash, but if you click on Concorde Enhancements at the top of the page, you'll get all the changes that have been made to the plane since the accident (these include both safety measures that allowed it to return to service and new, even more luxurious interiors). Click Next at the bottom of each page to progress through the site. The Concorde Experience is an interesting look at the flight from the passenger's point of view. A very glitzy Flash presentation that focuses on the luxury aspect of travel by Concorde—from the fine wines and liqueurs to the sculpted seats and fine linen towels in the bathrooms—can be seen at http://www.british-airways.com/regional/usa/experience/intro.html.

400. Model T Road Trip

http://www.hfmgv.org/education/smartfun/welcome.html

The automobile was still beyond the means of many American families at the end of World War I. Here you can follow a fictional family's excitement in the summer of 1919 as they choose and purchase a car, and then set off on a trip. The story is told through the journal of the daughter. This is an extensive site and students will want to tackle it in stages. Links throughout the diary take you to information about life at that time. You will find car ads, quotes from neighbors, descriptions of road conditions and "autocamping," and details of how to change a Model T's tire. . . . All this is interspersed with photos and some video clips. A very rich site created by the Henry Ford Museum and Greenfield Village. Students who enjoy this may also want to try

Road Trip! (http://www.pbs.org/wgbh/amex/kids/summer/trip.html), a virtual tour of some of America's favorite vacation spots.

401. The New Beetle

http://www.vw.com/newbeetle/

VW invites visitors to the site to "Get info. Look at pretty pictures. Or just wander aimlessly." A pull-down menu helps focus your wanderings around this really cool site. Round for a Reason is the section that describes safety features in the new Beetle's design. The explanation—under the heading Thinking Round—of the new Beetle's round shape and the history of the strength of arches (going back to their Etruscan origins) is fascinating. The special effects are exciting enough to keep the attention even of readers who are uninterested in technical specifications. Navigation can be subtle; watch for small boxes that you can select and use your mouse to find rollovers that display different photos. Students interested in Lindbergh will find his personal 1959 VW, restored and exhibited with related objects (Lindbergh's maps, flashlights, tools, cans of food, etc.) at http://www.mnhs.org/events/artifacts/VW.html. The text offers many things to many people; some students will be interested in the personal side of Lindbergh's choice of a Beetle (a small car for a tall, wealthy man), others in the technical side of restoring such a car. They may struggle with the vocabulary in areas not of interest.

402. Outback Travelling

http://www.rfds.org.au/obtravel-info.htm

"Please drive carefully, we don't want to fly you home!" is the message from Australia's Royal Flying Doctor Service at the top of this page on surviving travel in the Outback. Preparations may include carrying as much as 10 liters of water per person per day, learning to identify as many as twenty-one poisonous kinds of snake, and knowing how to negotiate around the "road trains" that travel across Australia's interior. Carrying a radio and the contact frequencies for the flying doctors is highly advisable. This site also includes fascinating, illustrated, real-life stories of rescues (http://www.rfds.org.au/real-life.htm) and a more challenging history of the flying doctor service (http://www.rfds.org.au/history.htm) that features a Where Does It Hurt? chart that doctors use to make long-distance diagnoses.

403. Smart

http://www.thesmart.co.uk/

Most American teens will be struck dumb by the size of Europe's tiniest new "micro" car: the Smart. DaimlerChrysler's answer to crowded city streets is a

3-cylinder, 8.2-foot-long two-seater with a six-speed manual gearbox, a top speed of 84 mph, and ultra-low fuel consumption. Two of these cars can park in a normal parking space. You can build your own virtual Smart car here (the price is in pounds sterling, which should keep this in the fantasy realm), choosing the color, interior, and various options and accessories. You can even buy Smartware fashion at the site and download Smart screensavers to enliven your PC. There are plenty of specifications (guide students to an online calculator to convert from metric to U.S. measurements; a useful one can be found at http://www.mikesart.net/giantglossarycom/Converters_and_Calculators/all_in_one/), and the News area tells Smart's story.

404. Virgin Atlantic: Fantastic Story

http://www.virgin-atlantic.com/main.asp?page=1.3

A timeline outlines the successful rise of Richard Branson's empire and introduces some Virgin Atlantic innovations, including in-flight beauty treatments, individual video screens, defibrillators, and delivery to the plane on "limo bikes." Some world events are included to give context. Let the timeline run at its own pace. The History section of this site gives some basic information on Branson and his early fame as creator of Virgin Records. The Advertising section allows you to download some of the airline's best-known creative efforts. There's also a photo library in the Press Office.

The World Around Us

BOOKS

405. Jordan, Shirley. *From Smoke Signals to Email.* Perfection Learning, 2000. 64pp. Paper $8.95 (0-7891-5144-8). Nonfiction.

READING LEVEL: 5   INTEREST LEVEL: 12–18
ACCELERATED READER: YES

From earliest times, man has devised ways to communicate over distances. This book gives an overview of the many methods of communication developed, from the use of runners, sign language, newspapers, the telegraph, Pony Express, radio, typewriter, telephone, airmail, and television, culminating in the first email message sent in 1972. Teens will be fascinated by the roles that each new invention played in advancing the role of communications. Includes brief biographical sketches of key inventors in the communications field such as Marconi and Bell. Black-and-white illustrations and photos, glossary, index.

406. Margolis, Jeff. *Everything You Wanted to Know About Teens Who Kill.* Rosen Publishing, 2000. 62pp. LB $17.95 (0-8239-2883-7). Nonfiction.

READING LEVEL: 4–6   INTEREST LEVEL: 12–18
ACCELERATED READER: YES

In the 1990s America was witness to an unusually high number of episodes of teen violence. This book explores how and why teens have been killing each other and adults, and provides advice and suggestions about how to be safe in the neighborhood and at school. From Kipland Kinkle to Columbine, this book provides an overview of the motives and tragic consequences of teen violence. Photos, glossary.

407. Sullivan, George. *100 Years in Photographs.* Scholastic, 1999. 96pp. Paper $8.99 (0-590-22858-7). Nonfiction.

READING LEVEL: 5–6   INTEREST LEVEL: 12–18

Black-and-white photographs highlighting the major events of the 20th century are featured in a style reminiscent of a scrapbook and organized decade by decade. All the photos, many of them classic, are accompanied by an explanation of their significance. Among the images are Babe Ruth batting in 1927, a four-year-old Shirley Temple breaking into film, the Beatles' first New York appearance in 1964, the 1967 Kent State massacre, and the 1995 Murrah Building bombing. More than 200 dramatic photographs will give teens instant snapshots of the important historical events of the past hundred years.

WEB SITES

408. Bad Fads Museum

http://www.badfads.com/home.html

Remember when we used to iron our hair/throw boomerangs/build fallout shelters/wear mood rings/stuff ourselves into phone booths? The Bad Fads featured here may include some of your fondest memories, but for today's teens they reveal fascinating examples of early weirdness. The descriptions are short enough to maintain interest.

409. BrainPop

http://www.brainpop.com/

BrainPop is just plain irresistible. The *Chicago Tribune* has called it "brain candy for kids." It combines cartoons, movies, information, and fun in one entertaining bundle that teaches about health, science, and technology. Movies on hot issues are linked with entertaining quizzes that will feed an urge for knowledge. You can move around the site for free, but if you register you can gain points for everything you do, making you eligible for various prizes.

410. Geographia

http://www.geographia.com/

Whether you want to visit modern downtown Moscow, ancient sites in Malaysia, tropical islands, or frozen arctic wastes, you're sure to find something of interest here. Contents change regularly, and many of the links are to sites that are not related to Geographia. The reading level varies according to subject matter.

411. Gestures Around the World

http://www.webofculture.com/worldsmart/gestures.asp

In Greece, you slightly nod your head upward or lift your eyebrows upward to signal "no." To wish someone good luck in Austria, you should make two fists and imitate pounding on the table. These and many other nuggets of international etiquette are combined with advice that seems to be mere common sense (don't chew gum; don't talk loudly; and so forth). You have to register to access this site, but it's an easy process, and there is no charge. A related part of this site deals with Colors (http://www.webofculture.com/worldsmart/design_colors.asp), telling what various colors signify in different countries. For example, white is the color of death and mourning in China and Taiwan, but is seen as "clean, pure, antiseptic, elegant" in the United States.

412. Greatest Places Online

http://www.greatestplaces.org/book_pages/top.html

An unusually beautiful site, created by the Science Museum of Minnesota, this introduces seven geographically diverse locations: the Amazon, Greenland, the Iguazu Falls of South America, Madagascar, the Namib Desert, the Okavango Delta in Botswana, and Tibet. In addition to well-balanced text, there are maps where they're needed, video as appropriate, animal sounds, a game or two, questions and answers—in short, ideal use of all the media that appeal. You can even use it to send e-cards to keypals.

413. Hold Onto Your Hats!

http://www.civilization.ca/hist/hats/hat00eng.html

This Canadian Museum of Civilization exhibition looks at the role hats play in society, and what each hat says about its wearer. Among the topics examined are Protection and Practicality, Religion and Ritual, Authority and Status, Identity and Belonging, Fashion and Image, Hat Lore, and Game.

414. Life in Korea: Cultural Spotlight

http://www.lifeinkorea.com/Culture/spotlight.cfm

Life in Korea takes an in-depth look at various interesting aspects of the country's culture, including oriental astrology, tae kwon do, Korean food, the celebration of a child's first birthday, and traditional clothing. Links at the top of the page will take you to Scenes of Korea and a section on Ceremonies and Festivals.

415. Lonely Planet

http://www.lonelyplanet.com/

Lonely Planet makes online travel fun. Read up on individual destinations, on travel by theme (beaches, deserts, food, and so forth), on travel news (in The Scoop), and on measures you can take before you leave to stay healthy on the road. On The Road presents tall tales and yarns, and visitors can relate their own stories at several locations on the site.

416. Looking @ Earth

http://www.nasm.si.edu/galleries/lae/css_gal110.htm

The National Air and Space Museum presents a fascinating account of the ways man has looked at the Earth from on high and how information gained from this exploration has led to the ability to predict weather, forecast wildfire and volcanic activity, and monitor human activities. Start the tour in the Windows on the World gallery with its vistas of our world from ever-increasing distances. In all cases, the accompanying text is easy to find and follow; the navigation at the bottom of each page takes you to the next. First Looks shows how early aerial exploration and photography developed, using kites, camera-carrying rockets, balloons, even pigeons. Applications of aerial photography in the areas of geology, archaeology, disaster assessment, and the environment are explored in Onwards and Upwards, while the Sky Spies—perhaps the section with the highest interest level—discusses military intelligence and the bravery and skill of the pilots who fly reconnaissance aircraft.

417. My World

http://pbskids.org/africa/myworld/index.html

Although this PBS site may at first be dismissed as one intended for younger children, it introduces high school students in Africa, who relate the events of their daily lives. Visitors to the site can also play a virtual thumb piano and help the hero of a Swahili folktale succeed in his quest.

418. National Library of Jamaica

http://www.nlj.org.jm/

The Historical Titbits section is rewarding; click on Jamaica for an overview of the island nation. There's a page of recommended Web sites, with the criteria for selection clearly selected. As always, the CIA World Factbook is a good source for general information. The URL for the CIA article on Jamaica is http://www.cia.gov/cia/publications/factbook/geos/jm.html.

419. The New Americans: Perceptions and Misconceptions

http://www.pbs.org/kcet/newamericans/4.0/4.0perception.html

Part of a larger site, this interesting section looks at Americans' attitudes toward immigrants. Which films have influenced the way you think about newcomers? Look at some misconceptions about immigrants' contributions to (or demands from) society. Read a list of notable immigrants. And finally, a link to the Immigration and Naturalization Service's Naturalization Self Test. Test your own ability to answer questions posed by INS officers. The site states that citizenship applicants will be "evaluated on . . . ability to speak, read, write, and understand English" at their interview.

420. On the Line: Virtual Journey of Ghana

http://www.ontheline.org.uk/explore/journey/ghana/ghandex.htm

Take a virtual trip to Ghana and learn about daily life in the African nation by following a young girl through her routine activities. Other sections show the country's sports, arts and crafts, music and dance, and food. Click on Guide Book to find more in-depth (and more challenging) material on the country's history, geography, environment, society, and education system. On the Line, creators of this site, also provides similar, equally fascinating sites on Togo, Burkina Faso, Mali, Algeria, Spain, France, and the United Kingdom. (These countries are all situated on the zero meridian.) Click on Home to find this menu.

421. Oxfam

http://www.oxfam.org.uk/

Visit Oxfam's site in times of crisis—and peace—to explore what the charitable organization is achieving around the world. In mid-2002, there was an excellent piece in the Cool Planet section (http://www.oxfam.org.uk/coolplanet/index.html) on banana farming and trade. In Amazing World (http://www.oxfam.org.uk/coolplanet/kidsweb/amazing.htm), information could be found on countries including Afghanistan, Bangladesh, Bolivia, Bosnia, Brazil, Ethiopia, Ghana, India, Kenya, Mozambique, Pakistan, Sudan, and Vietnam. A special section is devoted to the life of refugees in Afghanistan, showing conditions in the camps and the daily struggle to find adequate food, fuel, and water. The Development section (http://www.oxfam.org.uk/development.htm) includes case studies (including, in mid-2002, an interesting article on the important role animals play in the lives of poor communities), a glossary of development terms, and an overview of how the agency works.

422. Standing Tall

http://www.popsci.com/popsci/science/article/0,12543,187978-1,00.html

A fascinating article at *Popular Science*'s Web site looking at new concerns about safety in skyscrapers following September 11, 2001. This is a lengthy and detailed essay, but the subject matter is compelling, and, although the text is long and dense, it is clearly written. Of particular interest would be page 2, "Skyscraper Self-Defense"; page 3, "The Right Stuff," which points out that the World Trade Center towers did a good job of withstanding the impact of the planes; and page 4, "Getting People Out." Page 9 shows images, many of them views taken by robots in the rubble of the WTC.

423. Tornado Project Online

http://www.tornadoproject.com/

Which state gets the most tornadoes? Where's the safest place to be in a tornado? Amazing stories of debris found miles from the site of a tornado . . . All this plus facts, photos, FAQs, informative trivia (in the Storm Cellar), real-life tornado stories, and Other Neat Stuff make this a really interesting site.

424. Urban Legends Reference Pages

http://www.snopes2.com/

Heard the one about the man who's been waiting for a flight at Charles de Gaulle airport for more than ten years? Or the nude passenger left on the roadside by an unknowing driver? These two stories are apparently true. Many others are pure fabrication. Very few are edifying, but they're interesting enough to keep you reading!

425. Volcano World

http://volcano.und.nodak.edu/

Explore the world's volcanoes; investigate current eruptions; view St. Helens before, during, and after; and read interviews with volcanologists in which they discuss what they like about their profession and how they deal with the constant dangers involved. The Kids' section also contains items of interest and is not confined to material for younger children.

426. The World Today

http://www.popexpo.net/eMain.html

The world's population reached 6 billion on October 12, 1999. Will it stabilize before it reaches unmanageable proportions? Everyone should read this interactive discussion of all the issues, laid out amazingly clearly by the Musée de l'Homme in Paris. A thought-provoking site that effectively combines simplicity and interactivity.

Part II

◆

Young Adult Materials for the Reluctant Reader

Young Adult Materials

Deanna McDaniel

TEENS ARE INTERESTED in a wide range of subjects. All you have to do is convince them that the book or magazine you are showing them is a good one. The following lists highlight titles that are perennial favorites.

Books

The books recommended here are not specifically targeted at the reluctant reader but that have sufficient appeal to entice a poor reader. Both good and bad readers of all ages will tackle harder books if they are really interested in them. Reluctant readers will be attracted to books that are about an especially interesting subject or that have been booktalked in an especially appealing way. Booktalks are particularly effective when they concern books with plots that leave your audience hanging.

This is an age group that really enjoys fantasy and science fiction. Once they find a good series, they like to read all of them, so have as many on hand as possible! Teens also like horror and life-and-death stories. They are interested in issues of all kinds as they are at a stage in their lives when they are forming opinions on many topics.

The following is a listing of fiction and nonfiction titles that will entertain and inform your readers, all published since 1990. Unlike the books recommended in the Core Collection—which are organized by subject—these are simply listed alphabetically by author. The authors of these books tend to be better known than authors of high-low books, and the authors themselves may be a source of appeal for teens. Let your readers take their pick—you may be surprised by what they choose!

427. Abelove, Joan. *Go and Come Back: A Novel.* DK Ink, 1998. 192pp. Hardcover $16.95 (0-7894-2476-2). Fiction.

A young tribeswoman living in a Peruvian jungle village in the Andes tells about two anthropologists who have come to observe them. A fascinating glimpse at a very different culture, along with a wry look at what is considered "different."

428. Almond, David. *Kit's Wilderness.* Delacorte Press, 2000. 240pp. Hardcover $15.95 (0-385-32665-3). Fiction.

Thirteen-year-old Kit goes to live with his grandfather in an old coal-mining town in England and finds the town haunted by ghosts.

429. Anderson, Laurie Halse. *Fever, 1793.* Simon & Schuster, 2000. 256pp. LB $16.00 (0-689-83858-1); paper $5.99 (0-689-84891-9). Fiction.

Sixteen-year-old Matilda is separated from her sick mother and forced to deal with the horrors of a yellow fever epidemic.

430. Anderson, Laurie Halse. *Speak.* Farrar, Straus & Giroux, 1999. 208pp. Hardcover $16 (0-374-37152-0); paper $7.99 (0-141-31088-X). Fiction.

Melinda attends a senior party right before the beginning of her freshman year, with disastrous results.

431. Armstrong, Jennifer, and Todd Brewster. *The Century for Young People.* Random House, 1999. 256pp. Hardcover $29.95 (0-385-32708-0). Nonfiction.

Full of pictures and entertaining facts, this book is fun to browse through and useful for reports. Covers 1900 to 2000.

432. Ash, Russell. *Incredible Comparisons.* DK, 1996. 64pp. Hardcover $19.95 (0-7894-1009-5). Nonfiction.

Teachers will like to use this book. Students will have fun with it. A large visual guide that compares sizes, heights, weights, and numbers in capacity, population, growth, weather, disasters, speed, and more.

433. Avi. *Midnight Magic.* Scholastic, 1999. 256pp. Hardcover $15.95 (0-590-36035-3); paper $4.99 (0-439-24219-3). Fiction.

The year is 1491. Mangus the magician and his apprentice are summoned to the castle to see if the duke's daughter is indeed being haunted by a ghost.

434. Bachrach, Susan D. *Tell Them We Remember: The Story of the Holocaust with Images from the United States Holocaust Memorial Museum.* Little, Brown, 1994. 109pp. Paper $14.95 (0-316-07484-5). Fiction.

While a sobering account, this is a meaningful compilation that students will spend time with.

435. Banyai, Istvan. *Re-zoom.* Viking, 1995. 64pp. LB $15.99 (0-670-86392-0); paper $6.99 (0-140-55694-X). Fiction.

A wordless picture book that is nothing but fun! Art teachers will want to use it when they are teaching perspective, but teenagers will just enjoy it on their own terms.

436. Biesty, Stephen, and Richard Platt. *Man-of-War.* Dorling Kindersley, 1993. 32pp. Hardcover $16.95 (1-56458-321-X). Nonfiction.

Biesty is known for his detailed cutaway illustrations. This title shows life aboard a British warship of the Napoleonic era.

437. Biesty, Stephen, and Richard Platt. *Stephen Biesty's Incredible Explosions.* DK Publishing, 1996. 32pp. Hardcover $19.95 (0-789-41024-9). Nonfiction.

Cutaway illustrations of various items including a space station, airport, and windmill.

438. Bloor, Edward. *Tangerine.* Harcourt Brace, 1997. 304pp. Hardcover $17.00 (0-15-201246-X); paper $4.99 (0-439-28603-4). Fiction.

Paul fights for the right to play soccer, while slowly beginning to remember how his eyesight became damaged.

439. Brewster, Hugh. *Anastasia's Album.* Hyperion, 1996. 64pp. Hardcover $17.95 (0-7868-0292-8). Nonfiction.

Another of those books that is simply fun to browse through. Large-spread pictures of Anastasia's life, along with information about the mystery surrounding her disappearance.

440. Bridges, Ruby, and Margo Lundell. *Through My Eyes.* Scholastic, 1999. 63pp. Hardcover $16.95 (0-590-18923-9). Nonfiction.

Another large-format book full of wonderful photographs. Ruby Bridges tells what it was like to be at a New Orleans school going through the process of integration. A touching story from the eyes of a six-year-old.

441. Bunting, Eve. *Blackwater*. HarperTrophy, 2000. 146pp. Paper $4.95 (0-06-440890-6). Fiction.

Two teens have drowned, and Brodie must decide whether to confess that he caused the accident.

442. Busenberg, Bonnie. *Vanilla, Chocolate & Strawberry: The Story of Your Favorite Flavors*. Lerner Publications, 1994. 112pp. Hardcover $23.95 (0-8225-1573-3). Nonfiction.

Describes how these came to be popular flavors, details the history of their use, and includes some entertaining recipes.

443. Cabot, Meg. *The Princess Diaries, Volume I: A Novel*. HarperCollins, 2000. 304pp. Paper $5.95 (0-380-81402-1). Fiction.

Mia, a backward New York City teenager, is shocked to learn that her father is the Prince of Genovia, and she is a princess and heir to the throne.

444. Cabot, Meg. *The Princess Diaries, Volume II: Princess in the Spotlight*. HarperCollins, 2001. 240pp. LB $15.89 (0-06-029466-3). Fiction.

Mia continues to cope with being a princess and a typical New York teenager.

445. Cabot, Meg. *The Princess Diaries, Volume III: Princess in Love*. HarperCollins, 2002. 240pp. Hardcover $15.99 (0-06-029467-1). Fiction.

More of Mia's adventures.

446. Cadnum, Michael. *Zero at the Bone*. Viking, 1996. o.p. Fiction.

When Anita fails to return home from work, her family tries to cope with her disappearance.

447. Carlson, Lori M. *Cool Salsa: Bilingual Poems on Growing Up Latino in the United States*. Henry Holt, 1994. 136pp. Paper $5.50 (0-449-70436-X). Nonfiction.

This wonderful collection of poems will be read even if you do not have a large Latino population.

448. Carter, David A., and James Diaz. *The Elements of Pop-Up: A Pop-Up Book for Aspiring Paper Engineers*. Little Simon, 1999. Pop-up $35.00 (0-689-82224-3). Nonfiction.

Nothing but fun! Lots of great ideas for creating pop-ups with easy-to-follow directions.

449. Cochran, Thomas. *Roughnecks.* Harcourt Brace, 1997. 256pp. Paper $6.00 (0-15-202200-7). Fiction.

Travis prepares for the final game of his high school football career. Good for sports fans, especially those who love football.

450. Cole, Brock. *The Facts Speak for Themselves.* Front Street, 1997. 192pp. Paper $16.95 (1-886910-14-6). Fiction.

Thirteen-year-old Linda gradually reveals how her life with her mother led to her rape and the murder she witnessed.

451. Coman, Carolyn. *What Jamie Saw.* Front Street, 1995. 127pp. Paper $4.99 (0-140-38335-2). Fiction.

Nine-year-old Jamie finds himself in a frightening position after he sees his mother's boyfriend try to throw his baby sister against a wall.

452. Conford, Ellen. *Crush: Stories.* HarperCollins, 1998. 138pp. Paper $4.95 (0-06-440778-0). Fiction.

Nine episodes in the school life of students at Cutter's Forge High.

453. Cooney, Caroline B. *Burning Up: A Novel.* Dell/Laurel-Leaf, 2001, 1999. 240pp. Paper $5.50 (0-440-22687-2). Fiction.

When a friend is murdered, Macey uncovers prejudice she had not imagined in her community.

454. Cooney, Caroline B. *Driver's Ed.* Delacorte, 1994. 199pp. Paper $5.50 (0-440-21981-7). Fiction.

Three teenagers' lives are changed when they steal a stop sign from an intersection.

455. Cooney, Caroline B. *The Face on the Milk Carton.* Delacorte, 1996, 1990. 184pp. Paper $5.99 (0-440-22065-3). Fiction.

A photograph on a milk carton leads Janie on a search for her real identity.

456. Cooney, Caroline B. *The Terrorist.* Scholastic, 1997. 198pp. Paper $4.50 (0-590-22854-4). Fiction.

Laura tries to find the person responsible for the death of her brother, who was killed by a terrorist bomb.

457. Cooney, Caroline B. *The Voice on the Radio.* Delacorte, 1996. 224pp. Paper $5.50 (0-440-21977-9). Fiction.

In this sequel to *The Face on the Milk Carton* and *Whatever Happened to Janie?*, Janie discovers that her boyfriend has betrayed her and her family on his college radio program.

458. Cooney, Caroline B. *Whatever Happened to Janie?* Delacorte, 1993. 217pp. Paper $5.50 (0-440-21924-8). Fiction.

Sequel to *The Face on the Milk Carton.* Two families' lives are upset when Janie discovers that the people who raised her are not her real parents.

459. Coville, Bruce, and Michael Hussar. *Oddly Enough: Stories by Bruce Coville.* Harcourt Brace, 1994. 163pp. Paper $3.99 (0-671-51693-0). Fiction.

A collection of nine short stories featuring angels, unicorns, vampires, werewolves, and other strange creatures.

460. Creech, Sharon. *Love That Dog: A Novel.* HarperCollins, 2001. 112pp. LB $14.89 (0-06-029289-X). Fiction.

A cleverly written story about a student who learns to love poetry. This book is an English teacher's dream; students will enjoy the humor and the great ending.

461. Creech, Sharon. *Walk Two Moons.* HarperCollins, 1994. 280pp. Paper $5.95 (0-06-440517-6). Fiction.

Thirteen-year-old Sal and her grandparents retrace her mother's journey after she leaves suddenly. A moving story for readers of any age who have lost someone they love.

462. Crutcher, Chris. *Athletic Shorts: Six Short Stories.* Dell/Laurel-Leaf, 1991. 160pp. Hardcover $16.95 (0-688-10816-4). Fiction.

Chris Crutcher is a favorite of teens. This is a collection of stories about characters in other Crutcher titles. Fans will enjoy reading more about characters they already know.

463. Crutcher, Chris. *Ironman: A Novel.* Greenwillow Books, 1995. 228pp. Paper $4.99 (0-440-21971-X). Fiction.

While training for a triathlon, a seventeen-year-old learns about anger management and his relationship with his father.

464. **Daldry, Jeremy.** *The Teenage Guy's Survival Guide.* Little, Brown, 1999. 176pp. Paper $8.95 (0-316-17824-1). Nonfiction.

Kids will enjoy the humor in this informational guide for teenage boys that covers dating, sex, body changes, and social life.

465. **Danziger, Paula, and Ann M. Martin.** *P.S. Longer Letter Later.* Scholastic, 1998. 234pp. Paper $4.99 (0-590-21311-3). Fiction.

Two friends continue their friendship via mail when they move to different states.

466. **Deem, James M.** *Bodies from the Bog.* Houghton Mifflin, 1998. 42p. Hardcover $16.00 (0-395-85784-8). Nonfiction.

Information about the remains of prehistoric bog bodies and what they reveal about their civilization. Gruesome and interesting photographs will grab readers' attention.

467. **Dowell, Frances O'Roark.** *Dovey Coe.* Atheneum, 2000. 192pp. Paper $4.99 (0-689-84667-3). Fiction.

Twelve-year-old Dovey Coe is accused of murder in 1928 North Carolina.

468. **Draper, Sharon M.** *Forged by Fire.* Atheneum, 1997. 176pp. Paper $4.99 (0-689-81851-3). Fiction.

A teenager has spent years protecting his fragile sister from their abusive father.

469. **Draper, Sharon M.** *Tears of a Tiger.* Atheneum, 1994. 180pp. Paper $4.99 (0-689-80698-1). Fiction.

The death of a high school basketball star affects his friend, who was driving the car, and their schoolmates.

470. **Fine, Anne.** *Flour Babies.* Little, Brown, 1994. 178pp. Paper $4.50 (0-440-21941-8). Fiction.

Simon discovers many things about himself when he is forced to take care of a "flour" baby for three tortuous weeks.

471. **Fletcher, Ralph J., and Joe Baker.** *I Am Wings: Poems About Love.* Atheneum, 1994. 48pp. Hardcover $14.00 (0-02-735395-8). Nonfiction.

This collection of poems covers the relationship of two teens, from first glance to goodbye.

472. Freymann, Saxton, and Joost Elffers. *How Are You Peeling? Foods with Moods.* A. Levine, 1999. 48pp. Hardcover $15.95 (0-439-10431-9). Nonfiction.

Once again, this is a book for both teachers and students. Carvings of vegetables illustrate emotions. Fun!

473. Giberga, Jane Sughrue. *Friends to Die For.* Dial Books, 1997. 231pp. Paper $4.99 (0-140-38599-1). Fiction.

Christina reevaluates her life when a friend is murdered after a party they both attended.

474. Glenn, Mel. *The Taking of Room 114: A Hostage Drama in Poems.* Lodestar Books, 1997. 182pp. Hardcover $16.99 (0-525-67548-5). Nonfiction.

Written before Columbine, this set of poems reflects the thoughts of different people affected when a history teacher takes his class hostage.

475. Greenberg, Jan, and Sandra Jordan. *Chuck Close, Up Close.* DK Ink, 1998. 48pp. Paper $10.95 (0-7894-2658-7). Nonfiction.

The artists in your population will enjoy this book about the artist and his works, which are amazingly photographic.

476. *Guinness World Records 2002.* Guinness World Records Ltd., 2002. 288pp. Hardcover $27.95 (1-892051-06-0). Nonfiction.

A yearly compilation of statistics, pictures, and pop figures. Teenagers will spend hours browsing through this edgy book.

477. Haddix, Margaret Peterson. *Among the Betrayed.* Simon & Schuster, 2002. 160pp. Hardcover $15.95 (0-689-83905-7). Fiction.

Continues the story in *Among the Hidden* and *Among the Impostors.*

478. Haddix, Margaret Peterson. *Among the Hidden.* Simon & Schuster, 1998. 160pp. Paper $4.99 (0-689-82475-0). Fiction.

Lucas is the third child in a society where families are only allowed to have two children. Amazingly, he meets another "third" child.

479. Haddix, Margaret Peterson. *Among the Impostors.* Simon & Schuster, 2001. 176pp. Hardcover $16.00 (0-689-83904-9). Fiction.

Sequel to *Among the Hidden.* Lucas enters a boarding school under an assumed name.

480. Haddix, Margaret Peterson. *Don't You Dare Read This, Mrs. Dunphrey.* Aladdin, 1997. 125pp. Paper $4.99 (0-689-81543-3). Fiction.

In her journal for English class, Trish writes about her life in which her abusive father leaves, and her mother and brother follow him.

481. Haddix, Margaret Peterson. *Just Ella.* Simon & Schuster, 1999. 240pp. Paper $4.99 (0-689-83128-5). Fiction.

Ella finds that life at the castle is not what she expected when she marries Prince Charming.

482. Haddix, Margaret Peterson. *Running Out of Time.* Simon & Schuster, 1995. 240pp. Paper $4.99 (0-689-83128-5). Fiction.

A teenager discovers that the 1840s village in which she lives is actually a twentieth-century tourist site. It is up to her to stop the diphtheria epidemic that has taken hold of it.

483. Haddix, Margaret Peterson. *Takeoffs and Landings.* Simon & Schuster, 2001. 208pp. Hardcover $16.00 (0-689-83299-0). Fiction.

An overweight boy and his popular sister seem to switch places when they go on a speaking engagement with their mother.

484. Hesse, Karen. *Out of the Dust.* Scholastic, 1997. 227pp. Paper $4.99 (0-590-37125-8). Fiction.

A beautiful set of poems by Karen Hesse, in which Billie Jo relates the hardships of growing up in the Dust Bowl during the Depression.

485. Hesse, Karen. *Witness: A Novel.* Scholastic, 2001. 176pp. Hardcover $16.95 (0-439-27199-1). Fiction.

Another set of beautiful poems that illustrate what happens in a small Vermont town in the 1920s when the Ku Klux Klan tries to infiltrate.

486. Hesse, Karen, and Robert Andrew Parker. *Stowaway.* M. K. McElderry Books, 2000. 328pp. Hardcover $17.95 (0-689-83987-1). Fiction.

The fictionalized journal of a young stowaway aboard Captain Cook's *Endeavor.*

487. Hesser, Terry Spencer. *Kissing Doorknobs.* Delacorte, 1998. 149pp. Paper $5.50 (0-440-41314-1). Fiction.

A fourteen-year-old describes how her obsessive-compulsive behavior affects her family and friends.

488. Hobbs, Will. *Beardance.* Atheneum, 1993. 197pp. Paper $4.95 (0-380-72317-4). Fiction.

Cloyd, a Ute Indian, tries to help two grizzly cubs and complete his spirit mission. Sequel to *Bearstone.*

489. Holtwijk, Ineke, and Wanda Boeke. *Asphalt Angels.* Front Street/Lemniscaat, 1999. 184pp. Hardcover o.p. Fiction.

Based on real street kids in Rio de Janeiro, this volume follows the life of a young boy and how he adapts to homelessness.

490. Jackson, Donna, and Charlie Fellenbaum. *The Bone Detectives: How Forensic Anthropologists Solve Crimes and Uncover Mysteries of the Dead.* Little, Brown, 1996. 48pp. Paper $6.95 (0-316-82961-7). Nonfiction.

Fascinating reading. Explores the world of forensic anthropology.

491. Janulewicz, Mike. *Yikes! Your Body, Up Close!* Simon & Schuster, 1997. 32pp. LB $15.00 (0-689-81520-4). Nonfiction.

Visual magnification of different parts of the body. Stunning photographs.

492. Johnson, Angela. *Toning the Sweep.* Scholastic, 1994. 103pp. Paper $4.99 (0-590-48142-8). Fiction.

While visiting her grandmother, a young teen hears stories that help her understand her family better.

493. Kehret, Peg. *Small Steps: The Year I Got Polio.* Albert Whitman, 1996. 184pp. Paper $5.95 (0-807-57458-9). Nonfiction.

This children's author describes having polio as a teenager and its lasting effects. Teens who don't know about this disease or the vaccinations programs will find this documentary fascinating, especially as it is told from a teenager's point of view.

494. Kindl, Patrice. *Owl in Love.* Houghton Mifflin, 1993. 204pp. Paper $5.99 (0-140-37129-X). Fiction.

A fourteen-year-old girl who can transform herself into an owl develops a crush on her science teacher. A great blend of fantasy and teenage angst.

495. King, Martin Luther, Jr. *I Have a Dream.* Scholastic, 1997. 40pp. Hardcover $16.95 (0-590-20516-1). Nonfiction.

Martin Luther King's famous speech, with pictures from well-known children's illustrators.

496. Kirberger, Kimberly. *Chicken Soup for the Teenage Soul: 101 Stories of Life, Love, and Learning.* Health Communications, 1997. 352pp. Paper $12.95 (1-55874-463-0). Nonfiction.

Heartwarming stories, poems, and cartoons for teenagers.

497. Klass, David. *You Don't Know Me.* Farrar, Straus & Giroux, 2001. 262pp. Hardcover $17.00 (0-374-38706-0). Fiction.

John creates alternative realities in his mind as he tries to cope with his mother's abusive boyfriend and problems at school.

498. Konigsburg, E. L. *Silent to the Bone.* Atheneum, 2000. 261pp. Hardcover $16.00 (0-689-83601-5). Fiction.

Branwell loses his power of speech when he is wrongly accused of seriously injuring his baby sister. Only his friend can work out what really happened.

499. Koss, Amy Goldman. *The Girls.* Dial Books for Young Readers, 2000. 128pp. Paper $4.99 (0-142-30033-0). Fiction.

One member of a girls' clique has a strong hold on the others.

500. Krull, Kathleen, and Kathryn Hewitt. *Lives of the Athletes: Thrills, Spills (And What the Neighbors Thought).* Harcourt Brace, 1997. 96pp. Hardcover $20.00 (0-15-200806-3). Nonfiction.

Part of a series that covers all kinds of people. Offers little-known facts about well-known people in an often humorous way.

501. Krull, Kathleen, and Kyrsten Brooker. *They Saw the Future: Oracles, Psychics, Scientists, Great Thinkers, and Pretty Good Guessers.* Atheneum, 1999. 108pp. Hardcover $19.99 (0-689-81295-7). Nonfiction.

More trivia about well-known people.

502. Lavender, David Sievert. *Snowbound: The Tragic Story of the Donner Party.* Holiday House, 1996. 96pp. Hardcover $16.95 (0-8234-1231-8). Nonfiction.

A very readable account of this horrifying story of starvation and possible cannibalism.

503. Lawrence, Iain. *The Smugglers.* Dell, 2000, 1999. 208pp. Paper $4.99 (0-440-41596-9). Fiction.

In eighteenth-century England, a young boy becomes involved in a dangerous smuggling scheme involving his father's schooner.

504. Lawrence, Iain. *The Wreckers.* Delacorte, 1998. 224pp. Paper $4.99 (0-440-41545-4). Fiction.

In this sequel to *The Smugglers*, John is shipwrecked.

505. Levine, Gail Carson. *Ella Enchanted.* HarperCollins, 1997. 232pp. Paper $5.95 (0-06-440705-5). Fiction.

Another version of the Cinderella story, in which we learn that Cinderella was born with a curse and must obey all orders.

506. Litvin, Jay, and Lee Salk. *How to Be a Super Sitter.* VGM Career Horizons, 1991. 118pp. Paper $12.95 (0-8442-2481-2). Nonfiction.

Advice to young sitters. Full of good ideas.

507. Matas, Carol. *After the War.* Simon & Schuster, 1996. 144pp. Paper $4.99 (0-689-80722-8). Fiction.

After her release from the Buchenwald prison camp, a young girl leads children to Palestine.

508. Mazer, Harry. *Twelve Shots: Outstanding Short Stories About Guns.* Bantam Doubleday Dell, 1997. 229pp. Paper $5.50 (0-440-22002-5). Fiction.

Twelve short stories illustrate how guns can change lives.

509. Miklowitz, Gloria D. *Past Forgiving.* Simon & Schuster, 1995. 153pp. Paper $16.00 (0-671-88442-5). Fiction.

A young girl eventually comes to terms with an abusive boyfriend.

510. Murphy, Jim. *Blizzard.* Scholastic, 2000. 135pp. Hardcover $18.95 (0-590-67309-2). Nonfiction.

Murphy is well known for his fascinating historical documentation. This title covers the massive snowstorm that hit the Northeast, particularly New York City, in 1888. Absorbing reading.

511. Murphy, Jim. *The Great Fire.* Scholastic, 1995. 144pp. Hardcover $17.95 (0-590-47267-4). Nonfiction.

This one will also fascinate readers. It separates fact from fiction concerning the great Chicago fire of 1871.

512. Myers, Walter Dean. *The Greatest: Muhammed Ali.* Scholastic, 2001. 172pp. Hardcover $16.95 (0-590-54342-3). Nonfiction.

An affectionate yet candid biography of the well-known fighter by a well-known author.

513. Myers, Walter Dean. *Slam!* Scholastic, 1996. 266pp. Paper $4.99 (0-590-48668-3). Fiction.

A young teenager is counting on his basketball talents to get out of the inner city, but his coach turns out to be an obstacle.

514. Myers, Walter Dean, and Christopher Myers, illus. *Monster.* HarperCollins, 1999. 288pp. Hardcover $15.95 (0-06-028077-8); paper $6.95 (0-06-440731-4). Fiction.

A compelling book that will be widely read. Written as a film script, it portrays a young teenager on trial as an accomplice to murder.

515. Naylor, Phyllis Reynolds. *Jade Green: A Ghost Story.* Atheneum, 1999. 176pp. Paper $4.99 (0-689-82002-X). Fiction.

Judith wonders if she is causing the mysterious events in her uncle's haunted house.

516. Ousseimi, Maria. *Caught in the Crossfire: Growing Up in a War Zone.* Walker and Co., 1995. 120pp. Hardcover $20.85 (0-802-78364-3). Nonfiction.

The author documents children growing up during conflicts around the world. Washington, D.C., is classed as a war zone, based on interviews with children there.

517. Paulsen, Gary. *Brian's Return.* Delacorte, 1999. 128pp. Paper $5.50 (0-440-41379-6). Fiction.

A sequel to the well-known *Hatchet.* Brian finds he is no longer able to live in the city after surviving in the wilderness.

518. Paulsen, Gary. *Brian's Winter.* Delacorte, 1996. 144pp. Paper $5.50 (0-440-22719-4). Fiction.

An alternate sequel to *Hatchet,* in which Brian is not rescued but is forced to survive the winter in the wilderness.

519. Paulsen, Gary. *Guts: The True Stories Behind Hatchet and the Brian Books*. Delacorte, 2001. 144pp. Hardcover $16.95 (0-385-32650-5). Nonfiction.

A good read for Paulsen fans. The author describes his life and how it inspired the character of Brian Robeson, one of his favorite subjects.

520. Paulsen, Gary. *Soldier's Heart: A Novel of the Civil War*. Delacorte, 1998. 128pp. Paper $5.50 (0-440-22838-7). Fiction.

Based on a real person, this documents the life of a fifteen-year-old who enlists to fight in the Civil War.

521. Pellowski, Michael, and Howard Bender. *The Art of Making Comic Books*. Lerner, 1995. 78pp. Paper $8.95 (0-8225-9672-5). Nonfiction.

Fun for all, especially young artists.

522. Philbrick, W. R. *Freak the Mighty*. Blue Sky Press, 1993. 176pp. Paper $4.99 (0-439-28606-9). Fiction.

A learning-disabled teen befriends a handicapped teen. The two make a positive team.

523. Philbrick, W. R. *Max the Mighty*. Blue Sky Press, 1998. 166pp. Paper $4.99 (0-590-57964-9). Fiction.

A companion book to *Freak the Mighty*. Max befriends a young girl trying to escape her abusive stepfather.

524. Pierce, Tamora. *Alanna: The First Adventure*. Random House, 1987, 1983. 240pp. Paper $5.50 (0-679-80114-6). Fiction.

A good fantasy and adventure story. Alanna aspires to be a knight even though she is a girl. The first in a series.

525. Pierce, Tamora. *Tris's Book*. Scholastic, 1998. 256pp. Paper $4.99 (0-590-55409-3). Fiction.

Tris and her fellow mages-in-training join their magical forces.

526. Pullman, Philip, and Leonid Gore. *Clockwork, Or, All Wound Up*. Scholastic/Arthur Levine Books, 1998. 112pp. Paper $4.99 (0-590-12998-8). Fiction.

Entertaining fantasy. A story and a nightmare meet, with interesting consequences.

527. Rees, Celia. *Witch Child*. Candlewick Press, 2000. 272pp. Hardcover $15.99 (0-7636-1421-1). Fiction.

Based on a true story. Mary Newbury tells the story of her journey from England to America and her experience living as a witch near Puritans.

528. Reinhard, Johan. *Discovering the Inca Ice Maiden: My Adventures on Ampato*. National Geographic Society, 1998. 48pp. Hardcover $17.95 (0-792-27142-4). Nonfiction.

An account of the discovery of a 500-year-old Peruvian ice mummy.

529. Reiss, Kathryn. *Dreadful Sorry*. Harcourt Brace Jovanovich, 1993. Paper $4.99 (0-590-48406-0). Fiction.

Molly has nightmares about a girl who died more than eighty years ago.

530. Rennison, Louise. *Angus, Thongs and Full-Frontal Snogging: Confessions of Georgia Nicolson*. HarperCollins, 1999. 272pp. Paper $6.95 (0-06-447227-2). Fiction.

This is a title that will get passed around! The fictional diary of a fourteen-year-old British girl. Full of humor, this book also introduces readers to English culture and slang. There is a dictionary at the back.

531. Roehm, Michelle, and Jerry McCann. *Girls Who Rocked the World 2: Heroines From Harriet Tubman to Mia Hamm*. Gareth Stevens, 2000. 160pp. Paper $8.95 (1-58270-025-7). Nonfiction.

Portrays women from all walks of life: scientists, authors, performers, and politicians.

532. Sachar, Louis. *Holes*. Farrar, Straus & Giroux/Frances Foster Books, 1998. 240p. $6.50 (0-440-41480-6). Fiction.

An adventure story and a mystery, this highly entertaining novel will keep readers guessing. Stanley Yelnats is sent to a correctional camp in the Texas desert where he discovers a centuries-old secret about his family.

533. Sheldon, Dyan. *Confessions of a Teenage Drama Queen*. Candlewick Press, 1999. 272pp. Hardcover $16.99 (0-7636-0822-X). Fiction.

Mary Elizabeth, in a brand-new school, finds herself competing with the most popular girl for the lead in the school play.

534. Silverstein, Shel. *Falling Up: Poems and Drawings.* HarperCollins, 1996. 184pp. Hardcover $17.95 (0-06-024802-5). Nonfiction.

Another great collection of poems from the author of *Where the Sidewalk Ends.*

535. Sleator, William. *The Beasties.* Dutton Children's Books, 1997. 198pp. Paper $5.99 (0-141-30639-4). Fiction.

Doug and his sister move to a wilderness area where they encounter strange creatures whose lives are endangered.

536. Snedden, Robert. *Yuck! A Big Book of Little Horrors.* Simon & Schuster, 1996. o.p. Nonfiction.

Amazing microscope photographs illustrate the bugs and germs in our houses.

537. Spinelli, Jerry. *Wringer.* HarperCollins, 1997. 228pp. Paper $5.95 (0-06-440578-8). Fiction.

In the spirit of *The Chocolate War*, a young boy must decide if he has the courage not to participate as a wringer in the annual pigeon shoot.

538. Springer, Nancy. *Toughing It.* Harcourt Brace, 1994. 144pp. Paper $4.95 (0-15-200011-9). Fiction.

A teenager comes to terms with his anger over his brother's death in a motorcycle accident.

539. Stoker, Bram, and Tudor Humphries. *Dracula.* DK, 1997. 64pp. Hardcover $14.95 (0-7894-1489-9). Fiction.

One of a series of illustrated classics. Sidebars offer fascinating facts about the story and the author.

540. Sykes, Shelley. *For Mike.* Delacorte, 1998. 197pp. Paper $4.99 (0-440-22693-7). Fiction.

Jeff's best friend disappears, and gradually the secret surrounding his disappearance begins to unfold.

541. *Taste Berries for Teens: Inspirational Short Stories and Encouragement on Life, Love, Friendship, and Tough Issues.* Bettie B. Young, ed. Health Communications, 1999. 344pp. Paper $12.95 (1-55874-669-2). Nonfiction.

In the *Chicken Soup for the Soul* tradition, a collection of inspirational stories for teens.

542. Thomas, Peggy. *Talking Bones: The Science of Forensic Anthropology*. Facts on File, 1995. 136pp. Hardcover $25.00 (0-8160-3114-2). Nonfiction.

Includes actual cases in which forensics was used successfully to solve crimes.

543. Trueman, Terry. *Stuck in Neutral*. HarperCollins, 2000. 128pp. Paper $6.95 (0-064-47213-2). Fiction.

Fourteen-year-old Shawn, crippled by cerebral palsy, thinks his father may be planning to kill him.

544. Welden, Amelie, and Jerry McCann. *Girls Who Rocked the World: Heroines From Sacagawea to Sheryl Swoopes*. Gareth Stevens, 1999. 117pp. Hardcover $22.60 (0-8368-2454-7). Nonfiction.

Women of achievement from all walks of life.

545. Werlin, Nancy. *The Killer's Cousin*. Dell, 1998. 240pp. Paper $4.99 (0-440-22751-8). Fiction.

This would be an entertaining title to booktalk. After being acquitted of murder, David begins to discover who really did it.

546. Wick, Walter. *Walter Wick's Optical Tricks*. Scholastic, 1998. 48pp. Hardcover $13.95 (0-590-22227-9). Nonfiction.

Fun! A series of optical tricks, with explanations.

547. Williams, Carol Lynch. *The True Colors of Caitlynne Jackson*. Delacorte, 1997. 176pp. Paper $4.50 (0-440-41235-8). Fiction.

Caily and her younger sister learn to fend for themselves after their mother leaves.

548. Williams-Garcia, Rita. *Like Sisters on the Homefront*. Lodestar Books, 1995. 176pp. Paper $5.99 (0-140-38561-4). Fiction.

This is a strong African American title. When it is discovered that she is pregnant, Gayle is sent to Georgia where she experiences the warmth of family.

549. Windsor, Patricia. *The Blooding*. Scholastic, 1996. 288pp. Paper $4.50 (0-590-43308-3). Fiction.

Good horror fiction for teens. A young girl discovers that the father of the children she is taking care of is a werewolf.

550. Wolf, Bernard. *HIV Positive.* Dutton Children's Books, 1997. o.p. Nonfiction.

Shows the effects of AIDS by illustrating the life of a 29-year-old mother who has the disease.

551. Wulffson, Don L. *The Kid Who Invented the Popsicle: And Other Surprising Stories About Inventions.* Cobblehill/Dutton, 1997. 114pp. Paper $4.99 (0-141-30204-6). Nonfiction.

Documents inventions, often accidental, of everyday objects from animal crackers to zippers.

552. Zindel, Paul. *The Doom Stone.* HarperCollins, 1995. 192pp. Paper $4.95 (0-7868-1157-9). Fiction.

A creature is stalking and killing people in the area surrounding Stonehenge.

553. Zindel, Paul. *Loch: A Novel.* HarperCollins, 1994. 224pp. Paper $4.95 (0-7868-1099-8). Fiction.

Two teens searching for living prehistoric creatures discover that the purpose of the expedition is not what it seems.

554. Zindel, Paul. *Reef of Death.* HarperCollins, 1998. 177pp. Paper $5.99 (0-7868-1309-1). Fiction.

A young teen fights an evil scientist and a deadly underwater sea creature.

Magazines

A typical class of eighth graders walks into the media center. The teacher gives them one set of instructions: "You have thirty minutes to spend *reading.*" Some sit down in front of computers to do research or browse the permissible Web sites, some stroll over toward the fiction, some toward the nonfiction, and the rest walk over and look for a magazine to grab. Which are the disabled or reluctant readers? They could be any of these students, but nine times out of ten the disabled or reluctant readers will be by the magazines. Why? Because they don't usually have to worry about the reading level. If they can't read the words, the ads and glitzy pictures will still provide entertainment. They don't have to follow hard-to-read instructions on a computer screen, and they can enjoy the same magazines as their fellow students who are far better readers. They don't have to go through the agony of searching for a book they can *read* (never mind enjoy) while their peers are right beside them.

Today's teenagers are avid consumers of books and magazines. They want fashion, music, sports, news, and celebrity spotlights. They are sexually and politically aware. These teens need current and accurate information that reflects their lifestyle, whatever it may be. They will let you know what they like and dislike—all you have to do is ask!

Don't forget the broad range of maturity that exists among teens. Some are ready for more sophisticated stuff; others are happy being younger for a while. There are many good periodicals out there for teen readers; the trick is being aware of content and knowing the topics that interest them.

Many teens enjoy online "zines." We have not included them in this listing for two reasons: Zines tend to come and go, enjoying brief periods of popularity before fading away; and zine sites may have unmoderated message boards or chat rooms with inappropriate language for this age group. Many of the periodicals below do have Web sites at which teens can read selected articles from current and archived issues.

555. *Beckett Baseball Card Monthly.* Statabase Inc., 15850 Dallas Parkway, Dallas, TX 75248. 1–800–840–3137. http://www.beckett.com. Monthly. News and notes from the world of baseball card collecting.

556. *Beckett Basketball Card Monthly.* Statabase Inc., 15850 Dallas Parkway, Dallas, TX 75248. 1–800–840–3137. http://www.beckett.com. Monthly. News and notes from the world of basketball card collecting.

557. *Beckett Football Card Monthly.* Statabase Inc., 15850 Dallas Parkway, Dallas, TX 75248. 1–800–840–3137. http://www.beckett.com. Monthly. News and notes from the world of football card collecting.

558. *BMX Plus.* Daisy/Hi-Torque Publishing Co., 25233 Anza Drive, Valencia, CA 91355. 1–800–767–0345. http://www.bmxmag.com. Monthly. Products and tips on riding and maintaining your bike.

559. *Boys' Life.* Boy Scouts of America, 1325 W. Walnut Hill Lane, P.O. Box 157209, Irving, TX 75015-2079. 1–972–580–2088. http://www.boyslife.org. Monthly. Keep in mind that this is an official publication of the Boy Scouts of America; it will appeal to younger teen boys and has lots of good articles covering all kinds of subjects.

560. *Career World: Your Guide to Career Paths.* Weekly Reader Corp., 3001 Cindel Drive, Delran, NJ 08075. 1–800–446–3355. Published six times during the school year from September to May. Not just a publication for college-bound students, this also covers a wide array of career possibilities, along with advice on how to survive in the real world.

561. *Cat Fancy.* Fancy Publications Inc., 3 Burroughs, Irvine, CA 92618. 1–800–365–4421. http://www.catfancy.com. Monthly. Information and tips for cat owners.

562. *Cicada.* Carus Publishing Co., Cricket Magazine Group, 315 Fifth St., Peru, IL 61354. 1–800–827–0227. http://www.cicadamag.com. Bimonthly. Comics, art work, poetry, and book reviews by teen readers.

563. ***Circus: America's Rock Magazine.*** 6 West 18th St., New York, NY 10011. 1-212-242-4902. http://www.circusmagazine.com. Monthly. More than twenty years in print, this rock'n'roll monthly remains ever-popular and much requested.

564. ***Cosmo Girl.*** Hearst Communications Inc., 224 West 57th St., New York, NY 10019. 1-800-827-3221. http://cosmogirl.com. Monthly except June and December. Advertised as "A cool new magazine for teens," this is a teen version of *Cosmopolitan*, with an emphasis on fashion.

565. ***Current Events.*** Weekly Reader Corp., 200 First Stamford Place, P.O. Box 120023, Stamford, CT 06912-0023. 1-800-446-3355. http://www.weekly reader.com. Weekly. Comes with a teacher's edition. Up-to-date news written for students.

566. ***Current Health.*** Weekly Reader Corp., 3001 Cindel Drive, Delran, NJ 08075. 1-800-446-3355. Published eight times during the school year, September through May. Covers all sorts of health issues for teens, including drugs, personal health, nutrition, and fitness and exercise.

567. ***Current Science.*** Weekly Reader Corp., 200 First Stamford Place, P.O. Box 120023, Stamford, CT 06912-0023. 1-800-446-3355. http://www.weekly reader.com/cs. Published eight times during the school year, September through May. Covers all sorts of current science issues for teens.

568. ***Dirt Bike.*** Daisy/Hi-Torque Publishing Co., 25233 Anza Drive, Valencia, CA 91355. 1-800-767-0345. http://www.dirtbikemagazine.com. Monthly. Devoted to all facets of dirt bike racing: bikes, new products, evaluations.

569. ***Dog Fancy.*** Fancy Publications Inc., 3 Burroughs, Irvine, CA 92618. 1-800-365-4421. http://www.dogfancy.com. Monthly. Information and tips for dog owners.

570. ***Electronic Gaming Monthly.*** Ziff Davis Media, Inc., 28 East 28th St., New York, NY 10016. 1-800-779-1174. http://www.egmmag.com. Monthly. For the video game aficionado. Full of advertisements, gaming tips, and new product information.

571. ***Faces.*** Cobblestone Publishing Co., 30 Grove St., Suite C, Peterborough, NH 03458. 1-603-924-7209. http://www.cobblestonepub.com. Monthly except June, July, and August. Our schools and communities are ethnically diverse today. This publication explores a different country and culture each month. Besides being a wonderful research tool, this is a great publication to promote better understanding among different kinds of peoples.

572. ***Fantasy & Science Fiction.*** Mercury Press Inc., 143 Cream Hill Rd., West Cornwall, CT 06796. No phone number available. http://www.fsfmag.com. Monthly except for a combined October/November issue. In its fifty-second year of publication. Teens are often science fiction and fantasy fans. Includes novelets, short stories, poems, and book reviews.

573. Fine Scale Modeler. Kalmbach Publishing Co., 21027 Crossroads Circle, P.O. Box 1612, Waukesha, WI 53187. 1-800-446-5489. http://www.finescale.com. Monthly except for June and August. News, products, and how-to articles.

574. Football Digest. Century Publishing Co., 990 Grove St., Evanston, IL 60201-4370. 1-847-491-6440. http://www.centurysports.net. Published ten times a year, monthly September through April, and bimonthly June and August. News for football fans.

575. Gamepro. P.O Box 37579, Boone, IA 50037-0579. 1-415-974-7447. http://www.gamepro.com. Monthly. Bills itself as "the world's largest multiplatform gaming magazine." Has a section for each game platform with reviews of several different games.

576. Girls' Life Magazine. Monarch Services, Inc., 4517 Harford Rd., Baltimore, MD 21214. 1-888-999-3222. http://www.girlslife.com. Bimonthly. Unlike *Boys' Life*, this is not published by a scouting organization. With a completely new look, this magazine covers fashion, beauty, and advice, while keeping to the younger end of the teen years. Parents not ready for *Cosmogirl* and *YM* will like this one.

577. Hit Parader. Hit Parader Publications Inc., 40 Violet Ave., Poughkeepsie, NY 12601. 1-914-454-7420. http://www.hitparader.com. Monthly. For heavy metal fans.

578. Horse & Rider. Horse & Rider Inc., Primedia Enthusiast Publications, 656 Quince Orchard Rd., Suite 600, Gaithersburg, MD 20878. 1-800-829-3340. http://www.HorseandRider.com. Monthly. Competition and horse care for Western riding.

579. Horse Illustrated. Fancy Publications Inc., 3 Burroughs, Irvine, CA 92618. 1-800-365-4421. http://www.horseillustratedmagazine.com. Monthly. Training and riding tips, and all kinds of features covering many different kinds of horses.

580. Hot Rod Magazine. Petersen Publishing Co., P.O. Box 56249, Boulder, CO 80322-6249. 1-800-800-4681. http://hotrod.com. Monthly. Information and entertainment for hot rodders.

581. J-14: Just for Teens. Bauer Publishing Co., 270 Sylvan Ave., Englewood Cliffs, NJ 07632. 1-800-215-7275. http://www.j14.com. Monthly. More celebrity news: music, horoscope, TV, quizzes, and more.

582. Junior Scholastic. Scholastic, Inc., 2931 McCarty St., P.O. Box 3710, Jefferson City, MO 65102-3710. 1-800-Scholastic. http://www.juniorscholastic.com. Biweekly during the school year, eighteen issues. Along with teacher's guide (and corresponding state standards), covers current events around the world.

583. *Mad*. E.C. Publications, 1700 Broadway, New York, NY 10019. No phone number available. http://www.madmag.com. Monthly. *Mad*'s unique brand of humor and satire remains a perennial favorite.

584. *Merlyn's Pen: Fiction, Essays, and Poems by America's Teens*. Merlyn's Pen Inc., P.O. Box 910, Greenwich, RI 02818. 1-800-247-2027. http://www.merlyns pen.com. Published annually in November. Features the work of students from all over the country. Aspiring writers will want to know about this publication and how to contribute and/or enter contests.

585. *MH-18: Fitness/Sports/Girls/Life*. Rodale Inc., 33 E. Minor St., Emmaus, PA 18098. 1-800-666-2106. http://www.MH-18.com. Quarterly. Much like *Seventeen, YM*, and the like, only for boys, featuring advice, fashion, sports, and fitness.

586. *Model Airplane News*. Air Age Inc., 100 East Ridge, Ridgefield, CT 06877-4606. 1-800-827-0323. http://www.modelairplanenews.com. Monthly. Tips and tricks, all kinds of model information, product reviews, and how-tos.

587. *Model Aviation*. The Academy of Model Aeronautics Inc., 5161 East Memorial Drive, Muncie, IN 47302. 1-765-287-1256. http://www.modelaircraft.org. Monthly. The official publication of the Academy of Model Aeronautics. Includes tips and announcements from the academy.

588. *Muse*. Carus Publishing Co., 315 Fifth St., Peru, IL 61354. 1-800-827-0227. http://www.musemag.com. Monthly except for combined May/June and July/August issues. A science and discovery magazine.

589. *National Geographic World*. National Geographic Society, 1145 17th St., N.W., Washington, DC 20036-4688. 1-800-647-5463. http://www.national geographic.com/world. Monthly. All kinds of science information: special effects from movies, animals, sports, and more. Geared to the younger teen.

590. *New Moon*. New Moon Publishing, 2127 Columbus Ave., P.O. Box 3620, Duluth, MN 55803-3620. 1-800-381-4743. http://www.newmoon.org. Bimonthly. Positive articles and role models, featuring girls around the world.

591. *The New York Times Upfront: The News Magazine for Teens*. Scholastic Inc., 2931 East McCarty St., P.O. Box 3710, Jefferson City, MO 65102-3710. 1-800-724-652-7842 (1-800-Scholastic). http://www.upfrontmagazine.com. Weekly. Published jointly by the *New York Times* and Scholastic, this is the weekly news, geared to student level.

592. *News for You*. New Readers Press, 1320 Jamesville Ave., Syracuse, NY 13210. 1-800-448-8878. http://www.news-for-you.com. Weekly. Presents the news stories of the week, rewritten to make them more accessible to students reading below grade level. Also people in the news, a look at work, sports, crossword, and cartoon.

593. *Nintendo Power.* Nintendo of America Inc., 4820 150th Ave. N.E., Redmond, WA 98502. 1-800-255-3700. http://www.nintendo.com. Monthly. Lots of advertisements for Nintendo's products, but Nintendo video gamers will want this magazine.

594. *Odyssey.* Cobblestone Publishing Co., 30 Grove St., Suite C, Peterborough, NH 03458. 1-800-821-0115. http://www.odysseymagazine.com. Published nine times a year (monthly, September through May). Science trivia, feature articles, and activities.

595. *Plays: The Drama Magazine for Young People.* Kalmbach Publishing Co., 21027 Crossroads Circle, P.O. Box 1612, Waukesha, WI 53187. 1-800-446-5489. http://www.playsmag.com. Monthly from October through May (except for one issue for January–February). Monthly plays for kids to have fun with, from middle and lower grades to junior and senior high and classic readings.

596. *Science World.* Scholastic Inc., 2931 East McCarty Street, P.O. Box 3710, Jefferson City, MO 65102-3710. 1-800-Scholastic. http://www.scholastic.com. Biweekly during the school year, fourteen issues. Current science news, along with worksheets for the teacher to use.

597. *Seventeen.* P.O. Box 55192, Boulder, CO 80321-5192. 1-800-388-1749. http://www.seventeen.com. Monthly. With an emphasis on fashion and beauty, there is also advice and info on celebrities.

598. *Slap Skateboard Magazine.* High Speed Productions Inc., 1303 Underwood Ave., San Francisco, CA 94124. 1-415-822-3083. http://www.slapmagazine.com. Monthly. With more and more cities building recreation areas for skateboarders, this magazine will continue to grow in popularity. Devoted to techniques, products, and contests, with lots of visuals.

599. *Soccer America.* Soccer America, 1235 10th St., Berkeley, CA 94710. 1-510-528-5000. http://socceramerica.com. Biweekly except at year's end. This magazine has a nice international flavor. Follows U.S. and international soccer at both the college and professional level, along with playing tips.

600. *Sports Illustrated for Kids.* Time Inc., Time & Life Building, Rockefeller Center, New York, NY 10020-1393. 1-800-992-0196. http://www.sikids.com. Monthly. For those not comfortable with *Sports Illustrated* and its swimsuit edition, this publication is aimed at the younger end of the teen spectrum.

601. *Teen Beat.* Primedia Magazine Inc., 470 Park Ave. S., 8th floor, New York, NY 10016. 1-904-447-2465. Monthly. Teen celebrities, fashion, and beauty, with lots of posters, surveys, and contests.

602. *Teen Magazine.* Primedia Specialty Group Inc., 6420 Wilshire Blvd., Los Angeles, CA 90048-5515. 1-800-800-8336. http://www.teenmag.com. Monthly. Fashion and celebrities.

603. *Teen Newsweek*. Weekly Reader Corp., 200 First Stamford Place, P.O. Box 120023, Stamford, CT 06912-0023. 1-800-446-3355. http://www.weekly reader.com/teennewsweek/index.html. Weekly. Current news written for teens.

604. *Teen People*. Teen People, P.O. Box 61690, Tampa, FL 33661-1690. 1-800-284-0200. http://www.teenpeople.com. Published ten times a year. Teen celebrities, fashion, and beauty.

605. *Teen Voices Magazine*. Women Express Inc., Teen Voices, 515 Washington St., 6th floor, Boston, MA 02111. 1-888-882-TEEN. http://www.teenvoices.com. Quarterly. An "interactive, educational forum that challenges media images of women," this magazine has something for everyone.

606. *Time for Kids*. Time, Inc., Time & Life Building, 1271 Ave. of the Americas, New York, NY 10020-1393. 1-800-777-8600. http://www.timeforkids.com. Weekly during the school year. Much like *Sports Illustrated for Kids*, this is geared toward the younger end of the teen spectrum. It will prove invaluable for those needing a quick current events article or just a quick read about the news.

607. *World Wrestling Federation Magazine*. World Wrestling Federation Entertainment Inc., 1241 East Main St., Stamford, CT 06902. 1-815-734-1204. http://www.wwf.com. Monthly. News for WWF fans.

608. *YM*. 15 East 26th St., 4th floor, New York, NY 10010. No phone number available. http://www.ym.com. Monthly. Formerly *Young Miss*. More fashion, beauty, celebrities, and advice.

609. *Young Money*. Young Money, P.O. Box 637, Loveland, OH 45140. 1-800-214-8090. http://www.youngmoney.com. Monthly. Great information about money, written for teens: careers, colleges, entrepreneurship, money matters.

The following is a selected list of periodicals published for the adult market, but finding some appeal among teenagers.

Baseball Digest	*Guitar Player*
Basketball Digest	*Motorcyclist*
Football Digest	*People*
Car and Driver	*Popular Science*
Car Craft	*Popular Mechanics*
Chess Life	*Rolling Stone*
Consumer Reports	*Skiing*
Cycle World	*Sports Illustrated*
Ebony	*Sporting News*

Appendices

Appendix I:
Resources on the Web

General Library Sites and Web Indexes

Blue Web'n

http://www.kn.pacbell.com/wired/bluewebn

"A library of Blue Ribbon learning sites," all well chosen and organized by subject and grade level.

Digital Librarian: A Librarian's Choice of the Best of the Web

http://www.digital-librarian.com

An excellent resource organized by subject area. Sadly, teens is not one of them. Nonetheless, a good place to start.

Kathy Schrock's Guide for Educators

http://school.discovery.com/schrockguide

If you are not familiar with the World Wide Web and its potential use in education and literacy, bookmark this site. It gives you subject access not only to Web sites, but also to slide shows, critical evaluation tools, and information on WebQuests and TeacherQuests. An invaluable resource.

Librarians' Index to the Internet

http://lii.org

Rather than searching randomly on Google, browse through the offerings indexed on this excellent site maintained by librarians. A Kids and Teens area includes thoughtful annotations.

Children's/YA Sites

Children's Literature Web Guide
http://www.ucalgary.ca/~dkbrown

A great compilation of resources and links including best book lists and author Web sites.

Cool Sites for Kids
http://www.ala.org/alsc/children_links.html

Just what the name says.

Great Sites!
http://www.ala.org/parentspage/greatsites

More than 700 "amazing, spectacular, mysterious, wonderful web sites for kids and the adults who care about them," from the American Library Association.

Internet Public Library
http://www.ipl.org

The Internet Public Library features a special collection for teens that includes information compiled by staff of the library and a more general listing of recommended sites under headings including Money Matters, Dating and Stuff, Health, Issues and Conflicts, Sports, and Style.

Teen Hoopla: An Internet Guide for Teens
http://www.ala.org/teenhoopla

The American Library Association's page for teens.

Vandergrift's Young Adult Literature Page
http://scils.rutgers.edu/%7Ekvander/YoungAdult/index.html

Extensive information on YA literature.

Literacy/ESL Materials

Learning Resources
http://literacynet.org/cnnsf

CNN San Francisco presents abridged news stories with interactive glossaries and other activities. Intended for adults, but good for teens too.

Learning English
http://www.bbc.co.uk/worldservice/learningenglish/index.shtml

Hone your knowledge and reading skills at the same time. An attractive site that makes excellent use of the Web's interactivity.

The Literacy Volunteer Connection
http://literacyvolunteer.homestead.com/index.html

"Information and inspiration for literacy volunteers."

Teen Reading
http://www.ala.org/teenread/

Links to surveys, resources, teen reading lists, tips to encourage reading.

Web English Teacher
http://www.webenglishteacher.com

Links to ESL resources, professional resources, YA fiction sites, and so forth.

Web Quests

Web quests allow students to learn by visiting Web sites. The quests may involve some Web surfing, but should be based on pre-evaluated assigned sites, in combination with print resources.

The WebQuest Page
http://webquest.sdsu.edu/webquest.html

This site is an excellent introduction to the genre, with information on creating quests and a database of quests that are available on the Web, organized by subject and intended audience.

Keypals

The electronic equivalent of penpals, keypal networks are popular and useful in encouraging young people to communicate with others around the world.

E-Mail Keypals for Language Fluency
http://www.kyoto-su.ac.jp/~trobb/keypals.html

An article that originally appeared in *Foreign Language Notes* (Foreign Language Educators of New Jersey), Vol. 38, No. 3, pp. 8-10, Fall 1996.

EPals.com
http://www.epals.com/

Intercultural E-Mail Classroom Connections
http://www.iecc.org
Helps teachers form overseas partnerships.

Hoax Sites

Hoax—or spoof—sites can be entertaining and can be used effectively to teach students how to evaluate sites' content.

Some of our favorites are:

Congress Passes Americans With No Abilities Act
http://www.theonion.com/onion3324/noabilities.html

Mankato, Minnesota
http://lme.mnsu.edu/mankato/mankato.html

Star Wars
http://www.geocities.com/SunsetStrip/Alley/7028/swosg.htm

Appendix II:
High/Low Publishers List

THIS LIST PROVIDES contact information for publishers of books listed in Part I of *High/Low Handbook*.

American Guidance Service
4201 Woodland Road
Circle Pines, MN 55014-1796
800-328-2560; fax 800-471-8457
http://www.agsnet.com/

Atheneum Books for Young Readers
Simon & Schuster
1230 Avenue of the Americas
New York, NY 10020
800-223-2336; fax 800-943-9831
http://www.simonsays.com/

Bloch Publishing Inc.
118 East 28th Street
Suite 501-503
New York, NY 10016-8413
212-532-3977; fax 212-779-9169
http://blochpub.com/

BUSTA Books
A division of Amber Books
1334 East Chandler Boulevard, Suite
  5-D67
Phoenix, AZ 85048
480-460-1660
http://www.amberbooks.com

Capstone Press
151 Good Counsel Drive
PO Box 669
Mankato, MN 56002
800-747-4992; fax 888-262-0705
http://www.capstonepress.com/

Clarion Books
A division of Houghton Mifflin
222 Berkeley Street
Boston, MA 02116-3764
1-800-225-3362
http://www.houghtonmifflinbooks.com/
  clarion/

Dark Horse
http://www.darkhorse.com/
Distributed by LPC
22 Broad St.
Milford, CT 06460
203-874-2308
http://www.lpcgroup.com

ECW Press
2120 Queen Street East
Suite 200
Toronto, ON M4E 1E2
416-694-3348; fax 416-698-9906
http://www.ecwpress.com/

Enslow Publishers Inc.
PO Box 398
40 Industrial Road
Berkeley Heights, NJ 07922-0398
800-398-2504, 908-771-9400; fax 908-
  771-0925
http://www.enslow.com/

Free Spirit Publishing
217 Fifth Avenue North, Suite 200
Minneapolis, MN 55401-1299
800-735-7323; fax 612-337-5050
http://www.freespirit.com/

Girl Press
PO Box 480389
Los Angeles, CA 90048
http://www.girlpress.com

Globe Fearon
4350 Equity Drive
PO Box 2649
Columbus, OH 43216-2649
800-526-9907; fax 800-393-3156
http://www.globefearon.com

Image Comics
1071 North Batavia Street, Suite A
Orange, CA 92867
http://www.imagecomics.com/
Distributed by LPC
22 Broad Street, Suite 34
Milford, CT 06460
203-874-2308
http://www.lpcgroup.com

Institute for Healthcare Advancement
15111 East Whittier Boulevard, Suite 460
Whittier, CA 90603
800-434-4633; fax 562-907-1963
http://www.iha4health.org/

Millbrook Press
2 Old New Milford Road

Brookfield, CT 06804
800-462-4703; fax 203-740-2223
http://www.millbrookpress.com/

Mitchell Lane Publishers
34 Decidedly Lane
PO Box 619
Bear, DE 19701
302-834-9646
http://www.angelfire.com/biz/
  mitchelllane/index.html

Morning Glory Press
6595 San Haroldo Way
Buena Park, CA 90620-3748
888-612-8254; fax 888-327-4362
http://www.morningglorypress.com/

New Readers Press
A division of Laubach Literacy
  International
1320 Jamesville Avenue
Syracuse, NY 13210
800-448-8878; fax 315-422-5561
http://www.newreaderspress.com/

Newmarket Press
18 East 48th Street
New York, NY 10017
212-832-3575; fax 212-832-3629
http://www.newmarketpress.com/

Perfection Learning Corporation
1000 North Second Avenue
PO Box 500
Logan, IA 51546-0500
800-831-4190; fax 800-543-2745
http://www.perfectionlearning.com/

Rosen Publishing Group
29 East 21st Street
New York, NY 10010
800-237-9932; fax 888-436-4643
http://www.rosenpublishing.com/

Scholastic Inc.
557 Broadway
New York, NY 10012
1-800-Scholastic
http://www.scholastic.com/

TOKYOPOP
http://www.tokyopop.com/
Distributed by LPC
22 Broad Street
Milford, CT 06460
203-874-2308
http://www.lpcgroup.com

Townsend Press
1038 Industrial Drive
West Berlin, NJ 08091-9164
800-772-6410; fax 800-225-8894
http://www.townsendpress.com/

Warwick Publishing
161 Frederick Street
Toronto, ON M5A 4P3
416-596-1555
http://www.warwickgp.com/

Author Index

AUTHORS AND ILLUSTRATORS of books recommended in *High/Low Handbook* are arranged alphabetically by last name, followed by book titles, which are also arranged alphabetically. References are to main entry numbers, not page numbers. Authors of Web sites are not included.

Title Index

THIS INDEX CONTAINS both main entry titles and internal titles cited within the entries. References are to main entry numbers, not page numbers. Each entry is identified as a book, magazine, or Web site.

Subject Index

SUBJECTS ARE ARRANGED alphabetically and subject heads may be divided into nonfiction (e.g., African Americans) and fiction (e.g., African Americans — Fiction). Both main entry titles and internal titles cited within the entries are included. References are to main entry numbers, not page numbers. Each entry is identified as a book, magazine, or Web site.

The Darkest Secret: Passages (Book), 93

Destiny's Child: The Complete Story (Book), 127

Freedom Knows No Color: Passages to History (Book), 77

The Freedom Side (Book), 81

The Gun (Book), 18

Lost and Found (Book), 41

A Matter of Trust (Book), 41

Nobody Knows: Hopes and Dreams: The Africans (Book), 70

The Price of Friendship: Passages 2000 (Book), 40

Secrets in the Shadows (Book), 41

Selected from I Know Why the Caged Bird Sings and The Heart of a Woman (Book), 5

The Shadow Man: Passages (Book), 99

The Shining Mark: Passages (Book), 100

Someone to Love Me (Book), 41

Strawberry Autumn: Passages to History (Book), 80

To Be Somebody: Passages 2000 (Book), 44

The Underground Railroad (Book), 261

Until We Meet Again (Book), 41

When a Hero Dies: Passages (Book), 104

African Americans — History
See also Underground Railroad
The Internet African American History Challenge (Web site), 275
Negro Baseball Leagues (Web site), 373

African Americans — Poetry
I Wanna Be the Kinda Father My Mother Was (Book), 110

AIDS
The AIDS Handbook: Written for Middle School Kids, By Middle School Kids (Web site), 229
HIV Positive (Book), 550
whatudo.org: HIV/AIDS facts, opinion, and action (Web site), 255

Airlines
Virgin Atlantic: Fantastic Story (Web site), 404

Airplane pilots
Air Devils: Sky Racers, Sky Divers, and Stunt Pilots (Book), 396

Choosing a Career as a Pilot (Book), 193

Fighter Pilots: Life at Mach Speed (Book), 178

A Light in the Sky (Book), 59

Airplanes
See also Aeronautics; Airplanes — Military; Models and model making
Concorde: Facts and Figures (Web site), 399

Airplanes — Military
Attack Helicopters (Book), 398
Fighter Pilots: Life at Mach Speed (Book), 178
High Altitude Spy Planes (Book), 398
Stealth Bombers: The B-2 Spirits (Book), 398
Supersonic Fighters (Book), 398
The Thunderbirds: The U.S. Air Force Aerial Demonstration Squadron (Book), 184
USAF Museum History Gallery (Web site), 284
The World's Fastest Military Airplanes (Book), 395

Alcoholism
See also Children of alcoholics
Just One Night (Web site), 240
Kick the Habit: For a Healthier You (Web site), 241

Alcoholism — Fiction
Maitland's Kid: Passages (Book), 35

Ali, Muhammed
The Greatest: Muhammed Ali (Book), 512

Alligators
See Crocodiles and alligators

Amazon
Amazon Interactive (Web site), 318

Amazon — Fiction
Go and Come Back: A Novel (Book), 427

Andre the Giant
Andre the Giant (Book), 160

Angelou, Maya
Selected from I Know Why the Caged

B

Babyface, *aka* Kenny Edmonds
Babyface: In Love with Love (Book), 128

Babysitting
A Guide to the Business of Babysitting (Web site), 386
How to Be a Super Sitter (Book), 506

Baseball
Baseball's 25 Greatest Moments (Web site), 368
Bases Loaded: Great Baseball of the 20th Century (Book), 350
Beckett Baseball Card Monthly (Magazine), 555
Crossing the Color Barrier: Jackie Robinson and the Men Who Integrated Major League Baseball (Web site), 158
MLB.com (Web site), 372
National Baseball Hall of Fame (Web site), 372
Negro Baseball Leagues (Web site), 373

Baseball — Biography
BabeRuth.com: The Official Web Site of the Sultan of Swat (Web site), 170
Bases Loaded: Great Baseball of the 20th Century (Book), 350
Derek Jeter (Book), 168

Basketball
The Band (Book), 2
Beckett Basketball Card Monthly (Magazine), 556
Fast Break: Great Basketball of the 20th Century (Book), 351
Wheelchair Basketball (Book), 360

Basketball — Biography
Fast Break: Great Basketball of the 20th Century (Book), 351
Player File: 22 Sheryl Swoopes (Web site), 173
Sheryl Swoopes (Book), 172

Basketball — Fiction
Harlem Beat #1 (Book), 106
Slam! (Book), 513

Bats
Ranger Mary Kay Interviews a Non-Vampire Bat (Web site), 331
Vampire Bats (Web site), 331
The Wild Ones: Bats (Web site), 331

Beauty
Cosmo Girl (Magazine), 564
Girls' Life Magazine (Magazine), 576
The Human Face (Web site), 387
Seventeen (Magazine), 597
Teen Beat (Magazine), 601
YM (Magazine), 608

Behavior
See also Emotions
Gestures Around the World (Web site), 411
Teen Health Centre: Taming Your Temper (Web site), 250

Bible stories
Picture Stories from the Bible: The New Testament in Full-Color Comic-Strip Form (Book), 289
Picture Stories from the Bible: The Old Testament in Full-Color Comic-Strip Form (Book), 289

Bicycles and bicycling
BMX Plus (Magazine), 558
Dirt Bike (Magazine), 568
Extreme Bicycle Stunt Riding Moves (Book), 362
Lance Armstrong Foundation (Web site), 242
Mountain Biking! Get on the Trail (Book), 357
Science of Cycling (Web site), 375

Biography
See also specific occupations, e.g., Artists; specific sports, e.g. Baseball; and names of individuals, e.g., Selena
Academy of Achievement (Web site), 120
Girls Who Rocked the World: Heroines From Sacagawea to Sheryl Swoopes (Book), 544
Girls Who Rocked the World 2: Heroines From Harriet Tubman to Mia Hamm (Book), 531
The Kid Who Invented the Popsicle: And

Other Surprising Stories About Inventions (Book), 551

They Saw the Future: Oracles, Psychics, Scientists, Great Thinkers, and Pretty Good Guessers (Book), 501

Time 100: The Most Important People of the 20th Century (Web site), 281

Birds

Auburn College (Web site), 330

Bird Migration Facts (Web site), 327

Life of Birds (Web site), 327

Peregrine Watch (Web site), 330

The Raptor Center at Auburn University (Web site), 330

Blind

Tangerine (Book), 438

Blizzards

Blizzard (Book), 510

Lost in a Blizzard: The Towner Bus Tragedy (Book), 215

Body piercing

Bodies of Cultures: A World Tour of Body Modification (Web site), 267

The Dangers of Tattooing and Body Piercing (Book), 227

Bosnia and Herzegovina — History — Fiction

Gingerbread Heart: Passages 2000 (Book), 31

Boxing

Lights Out: Great Fights of the 20th Century (Book), 352

Boxing — Biography

The Greatest: Muhammed Ali (Book), 512

Lights Out: Great Fights of the 20th Century (Book), 352

Boys

Boys' Life (Magazine), 559

Boys — Societies and clubs — Fiction

Business as Usual: West 7th Street Series (Book), 12

The Gumma Wars: West 7th Street Series (Book), 13

Who's Responsible: West 7th Street Series (Book), 14

Branson, Richard

Virgin Atlantic: Fantastic Story (Web site), 404

Brazil

Climate Kaleidoscope (Web site), 322

Brazil, Bobo

Bobo Brazil (Book), 162

Bullies — Fiction

Chuck Farris and the Tower of Darkness (Book), 83

The Gotcha Plot (Book), 48

The Truth Test (Book), 24

Butterflies

Butterflies 2000: On the Wings of Freedom (Web site), 320

C

Calhoun, Haystacks

Haystacks Calhoun (Book), 163

Camps and camping — Fiction

The Monster in the Mountains: Passages to Suspense (Book), 98

Canada

Hold Onto Your Hats! (Web site), 413

Careers

See also Careers — Fiction; Careers — Military; Careers — Nontraditional; Careers without college

ADA.org: Teens (Web site), 228

America's Career InfoNet (Web site), 196

The Career Key (Web site), 197

Career World: Your Guide to Career Paths (Magazine), 560

CareerZone (Web site), 198

Cats! Wild to Mild (Web site), 321

Choosing a Career as a Firefighter (Book), 188

Bird Sings and The Heart of a Woman (Book), 5
Through My Eyes (Book), 440

Civil rights — Fiction
Nobody Knows: Hopes and Dreams: The Africans (Book), 70

Civil War (U.S.)
The Civil War: Moments in History (Book), 258

Civil War (U.S.) — Fiction
Soldier's Heart: A Novel of the Civil War (Book), 520

Clemente, Roberto
Roberto Clemente (Web site), 262

Cleopatra
Cleopatra of Egypt: From History to Myth (Web site), 269

Climbing
Ice Climbing (Book), 355
Rock and Ice Climbing! Top the Tower (Book), 363

Close, Chuck
Chuck Close, Up Close (Book), 475

Codes and ciphers
Enigma and the Code Breakers (Web site), 271

Colorado — Fiction
Riding High: Janet Dailey's Love Scenes (Book), 11

Colors
ArtEdventures: Color Theory vs. Dr. Gray and His Dechromatizer (Web site), 337

Comets
Comets (Web site), 340

Comics
The Art of Making Comic Books (Book), 521
The Art of The Matrix (Book), 206
Cicada (Magazine), 562
DC Comics (Web site), 109
Mad (Magazine), 583
Marvel.com (Web site), 109

Communications
From Smoke Signals to Email (Book), 405

Consumer education
Become a Spice Trader (Web site), 266
Consumer Education for Teens (Web site), 384
Consumer Jungle (Web site), 385
Vanilla, Chocolate & Strawberry: The Story of Your Favorite Flavors (Book), 442
Will the Dollars Stretch? Teen Parents Living on Their Own: Virtual Reality Through Stories & Check-Writing Practice (Book), 382
Young Money (Magazine), 609

Cooking
Vanilla, Chocolate & Strawberry: The Story of Your Favorite Flavors (Book), 442

Court cases
American Justice II: Six Trials That Captivated the Nation (Book), 260

Creative ability
Making the Most of Today: Daily Readings for Young People on Self-Awareness, Creativity & Self Esteem (Book), 288

Criminals and crime
The Bone Detectives: How Forensic Anthropologists Solve Crimes and Uncover Mysteries of the Dead (Book), 490
Talking Bones: The Science of Forensic Anthropology (Book), 542

Criminals and crime — Fiction
The Vandal: Passages (Book), 103

Crocodiles and alligators
Crocodiles! (Web site), 325
Gators (Web site), 325

Culture
Faces (Magazine), 571
On the Line: Virtual Journey of Ghana (Web site), 420

Current events
Brainevent.com (Web site), 383

Current Events (Magazine), 565
Junior Scholastic (Magazine), 582
The New York Times Upfront: The
News Magazine for Teens (Magazine),
591
News for You (Magazine), 592
Teen Newsweek (Magazine), 603
Time for Kids (Magazine), 606

Curtis, Christopher Paul
Christopher Paul Curtis (Web site), 126
Christopher Paul Curtis: A Real-Life
Reader Biography (Book), 125

D

Dating
Dating and Sex: Defining and Setting
Boundaries (Book), 299

Dating — Fiction
Crush: Stories (Book), 452
Past Forgiving (Book), 509

Death and dying
See also Grief

Death and dying — Fiction
Please Don't Ask Me to Love You: Pas-
sages (Book), 39
Tears of a Tiger (Book), 469
The Terrorist (Book), 456
Toughing It (Book), 538
Walk Two Moons (Book), 461

Dental care
ADA.org: Teens (Web site), 228

Dental students — Fiction
The Next Life: The Indians: Hopes and
Dreams 2 (Book), 69

Depression, Great — Fiction
Hear That Whistle Blow: Passages to History (Book), 79

Depression (mental state)
Bipolar Disorder: A Roller Coaster of
Emotions (Book), 226

Teen Health Centre: Mental Health: The
Road to Recovery (Web site), 250
TeensHealth: Depression (Web site), 251

Destiny's Child
Destiny's Child: The Complete Story
(Book), 127

Diaries
"Dad" Rarey's Sketchbook Journals of the
379th Fighter Squadron (Web site), 270
Totally Private & Personal: Journaling
Ideas for Girls and Young Women
(Book), 291

Diaries — Fiction
Angus, Thongs and Full-Frontal Snogging:
Confessions of Georgia Nicolson
(Book), 530
Donner Party: A Diary of a Survivor
(Book), 61

Dictionaries
The New Oxford Picture Dictionary
(Book), 334

Dieting
See also Eating disorders
How Dieting Works (Web site), 237

Dinosaurs
Tyrannosaurus Rex and Other Cretaceous
Meat-eaters (Book), 313

Disabilities
See also Learning disabilities
Courageous Comebacks: Athletes Who
Defied the Odds (Book), 154
Helping Paws: Service Dogs (Book), 314
Lance Armstrong Foundation (Web site),
242
Wheelchair Basketball (Book), 360

Disabilities — Fiction
Freak the Mighty (Book), 522
Stuck in Neutral (Book), 543
Summer Friends (Book), 22

Disasters
See also Donner Party; Shipwrecks
Blizzard (Book), 510
Escape! (Web site), 217
The Great Fire (Book), 511

E

F

G

H

I

Hit Parader (Magazine), 577
Selena: A Real-Life Reader Biography
(Book), 138

Mystery and detective stories
An Alien from Cyberspace: Passages to
Suspense (Book), 89
An Alien Spring: Passages (Book), 90
Burning Up: A Novel (Book), 453
The Chain: Passages to Suspense (Book),
91
The Darkest Secret: Passages (Book), 93
Dovey Coe (Book), 467
Dreadful Sorry (Book), 529
The Facts Speak for Themselves (Book),
450
For Mike (Book), 540
Friends to Die For (Book), 473
The Ghost of Mangrove Manor: Passages
to Suspense (Book), 96
Holes (Book), 532
Midnight Magic (Book), 433
Mission Sabotage (Book), 82
The Monster in the Mountains: Passages
to Suspense (Book), 98
The Shadow Man: Passages (Book), 99
The Shining Mark: Passages (Book), 100
Silent to the Bone (Book), 498
Summer of Shame: Passages (Book), 101
Tangerine (Book), 438
To Slay the Dragon: Passages (Book), 102
Tony Jefferson in Beyond a Doubt
(Book), 86
Tony Jefferson in Broken Trust (Book),
86
Tony Jefferson in Burning Question
(Book), 86
Tony Jefferson in Double Back (Book), 86
The Vandal: Passages (Book), 103
When a Hero Dies: Passages (Book), 104

Mythology
Adventures: Timeless Tales (Book), 116
Age of Bronze, Vol. 1: A Thousand Ships
(Book), 107
Folktales: Timeless Tales (Book), 113
Love Stories: Timeless Tales (Book), 114
Myths: Timeless Tales (Book), 117
Tales of Wonder: Timeless Tales (Book),
115
Urban Legends Reference Pages (Web
site), 424

N

New York City — Fiction
Action on the Cape (Book), 15
Broken Chains (Book), 15
Hitting the Ice (Book), 15
The Longest Night: Uptown, Downtown
(Book), 15
Looking for Trouble (Book), 15
Love on the Subway (Book), 15
Never So Good: The Jamaicans: Hopes
and Dreams 2 (Book), 68
The Road South (Book), 15
Selected from The Lost Angel (Book), 10
Wheels of Danger (Book), 15

**Newspapers and periodicals (student) —
Fiction**
Bridge to the Moon: Passages (Book), 30

O

Oceans
The Year of the Ocean (Web site), 333

Olympic Games
Ancient Greece: The Olympics (Web
site), 367
Baseball's 25 Greatest Moments (Web
site), 368
Olympic Hockey: 25 Greatest Moments
(Web site), 368

P

Parenthood
See also Teenage parents
Pat King's Family (Book), 21
What to Do When Your Child Gets Sick
(Book), 223

Paulsen, Gary
Gary Paulsen (Web site), 135

Gary Paulsen: A Real-Life Reader Biography (Book), 134

Peer pressure — Fiction
Confessions of a Teenage Drama Queen (Book), 533
The Girls (Book), 499
To Be Somebody: Passages 2000 (Book), 44
Wringer (Book), 537

Photoessay
100 Years in Photographs (Book), 407

Physics
Amusement Park Physics: Roller Coaster (Web site), 336

Poetry
Cicada (Magazine), 562
Cool Salsa: Bilingual Poems on Growing Up Latino in the United States (Book), 447
Falling Up: Poems and Drawings (Book), 534
I Am Wings: Poems About Love (Book), 471
I Wanna Be the Kinda Father My Mother Was (Book), 110
Love That Dog: A Novel (Book), 460
Merlyn's Pen: Fiction, Essays, and Poems by America's Teens (Magazine), 584
Out of the Dust (Book), 484
The Taking of Room 114: A Hostage Drama in Poems (Book), 474
Witness: A Novel (Book), 485

Police
Bicycle Patrol Officers (Book), 181
Choosing a Career in Law Enforcement (Book), 195
Police Dogs (Book), 315

Polish Americans — Fiction
Ties to the Past: The Poles: Hopes and Dreams 2 (Book), 72

Political activists — Fiction
The Petition: Passages 2000 (Book), 38

Post-traumatic stress disorder — Fiction
Gingerbread Heart: Passages (Book), 31

Memories Are Forever (Book), 36

Potter, Harry — Fictitious character
Harry Potter (Web site), 137
J. K. Rowling: A Real-Life Reader Biography (Book), 136

Pregnancy
First 9 Months (Web site), 234
Sex Has Consequences: Facts and Figures (Web site), 311
The Visible Embryo (Web site), 253

Princesses — Fiction
Ella Enchanted (Book), 505
Just Ella (Book), 481
The Princess Diaries, Volume I: A Novel (Book), 443
The Princess Diaries, Volume II: Princess in the Spotlight (Book), 444
The Princess Diaries, Volume III: Princess in Love (Book), 445

Private schools — Fiction
The Haunting of Hawthorne: Passages (Book), 97

Puberty
The "What's Happening to My Body?" Book for Boys: A Growing-Up Guide for Parents and Sons (Book), 221
The "What's Happening to My Body?" Book for Girls: A Growing-Up Guide for Parents and Daughters (Book), 222

Puerto Ricans — Biography
Jennifer Lopez: A Real-Life Reader Biography (Book), 132
Ricky Martin: A Real-Life Reader Biography (Book), 133

Puerto Ricans — Fiction
Here and There: The Puerto Ricans: Hopes and Dreams 2 (Book), 64

Q

Quests — Fiction
The Quest: American Expressions (Book), 50

Quotations
Making Every Day Count: Daily Goals for Young People on Solving Problems, Setting Goals, & Feeling Good About Yourself (Book), 287
Succeed Every Day (Book), 286

R

Racing
See Automobiles; Street luge racing

Rain forests
Amazon Interactive (Web site), 318
Climate Kaleidoscope (Web site), 322

Rape — Fiction
The Facts Speak for Themselves (Book), 450
Past Forgiving (Book), 509
Speak (Book), 430

Rationing
American Home Front (Web site), 263

Refugees
Diary of a War Child: The Memoir of Gertrud Schakat Tammen as Told to Diana Star Helmer (Book), 151
Once Upon a War: The Memoir of Gertrud Schakat Tammen as told to Diana Star Helmer (Book), 152

Refugees — Fiction
Who Is My Neighbor? The Salvadorans: Hopes and Dreams 2 (Book), 74

Relationships
Relationships (Web site), 309

Relief organizations
Oxfam (Web site), 421

Resumes
Writing a Resume (Book), 192

Robinson, Jackie
Crossing the Color Barrier: Jackie Robinson and the Men Who Integrated Major League Baseball (Web site), 158
The Sporting News: Jackie Robinson (Web site), 158

Roller coasters
Amusement Park Physics: Roller Coaster (Web site), 336

Rowling, J. K.
Harry Potter (Web site), 137
J. K. Rowling: A Real-Life Reader Biography (Book), 136

Runaways — Fiction
Don't Blame the Children: Passages (Book), 94
The Ghost Boy: Passages (Book), 95
Please Don't Ask Me to Love You: Passages (Book), 39
To Slay the Dragon: Passages (Book), 102

Ruth, Babe
BabeRuth.com: The Official Web Site of the Sultan of Swat (Web site), 170

S

Salvadoran Americans — Fiction
Who Is My Neighbor? The Salvadorans: Hopes and Dreams 2 (Book), 74

Sammartino, Bruno
Bruno Sammartino (Book), 171

School stories
Confessions of a Teenage Drama Queen (Book), 533
Crush: Stories (Book), 452
Flour Babies (Book), 470
The Girls (Book), 499
The Gotcha Plot (Book), 48

Structures
Building Big (Web site), 339

Struggles — Fiction
Struggles: American Expressions (Book), 9

Substance abuse
See Alcoholism; Drugs and drug abuse;
Solvent abuse

Sumo
Sumo (Web site), 377

Superstitions
Don't Step on the Foul Line: Sports
Superstitions (Book), 366

Superstitions — Fiction
The Chain: Passages to Suspense (Book),
91

Survival
See also Donner Party
Escape! (Web site), 217
The Iditarod: The Greatest Winner Ever
(Book), 354

Survival — Fiction
Brian's Return (Book), 517, 519
Brian's Winter (Book), 518, 519
Hatchet (Book), 517, 518, 519

Suspense
Driver's Ed (Book), 454
The Face on the Milk Carton (Book), 455
For Mike (Book), 540
The Killer's Cousin (Book), 545
The Smugglers (Book), 503
The Voice on the Radio (Book), 457
Whatever Happened to Janie? (Book), 458
The Wreckers (Book), 504

Swoopes, Sheryl
Player File: 22 Sheryl Swoopes (Web site),
173
Sheryl Swoopes (Book), 172

Syrian Americans — Fiction
Many Miles: The Arabs: Hopes and
Dreams 2 (Book), 67

T

Tae kwon do
Life in Korea: Cultural Spotlight (Web
site), 414

Tall tales
Folktales: Timeless Tales (Book), 113
Tall Tales: Timeless Tales (Book), 112

Tammen, Gertrud Schakat
Diary of a War Child: The Memoir of
Gertrud Schakat Tammen as Told to
Diana Star Helmer (Book), 151
Once Upon a War: The Memoir of
Gertrud Schakat Tammen as told to
Diana Star Helmer (Book), 152

Tattooing
Bodies of Cultures: A World Tour of
Body Modification (Web site), 267
The Dangers of Tattooing and Body
Piercing (Book), 227

Technology
BrainPop (Web site), 409
Building Big (Web site), 339
Greatest Engineering Achievements of the
20th Century (Web site), 343
Looking@ Earth (Web site), 416
Technology in 1900 (Web site), 280

Teen advice
See also main entries, e.g., Divorce; Peer
pressure; Puberty; Self-esteem; Sex edu-
cation
Girls' Life Magazine (Magazine), 576
MH-18: Fitness/Sports/Girls/Life (Maga-
zine), 585
Seventeen (Magazine), 597
Teen Advice Online (Web site), 390
Teen Health Centre: Mental Health: The
Road to Recovery (Web site), 250
Teen Voices Magazine (Magazine), 605
YM (Magazine), 608

Teenage parents
Nurturing Your Newborn (Book), 220
Will the Dollars Stretch? Teen Parents
Living on Their Own: Virtual Reality

Through Stories & Check-Writing
Practice (Book), 382

Teenage parents — Fiction
Pat King's Family (Book), 21

Tenement life
The Lower Eastside Tenement Museum:
Virtual Tour (Web site), 276

Tenement life — Fiction
Coming to America: The Story of Immigration (Book), 58
Little Italy: Hopes and Dreams: The Italians (Book), 65

Terrorism
The Taking of Room 114: A Hostage
Drama in Poems (Book), 474
The Terrorist (Book), 456
Terrorists, Spies, and Assassins (Web site),
123

***Titanic* (ship)**
Finding the Titanic (Book), 212
Posted Aboard R.M.S. Titanic (Web site),
218
The Titanic: Disaster at Sea (Book), 214
Tour Titanic (Web site), 218

Tornadoes
Tornado Project Online (Web site), 423

Travel
Geographia (Web site), 410
Lonely Planet (Web site), 415

Trust — Fiction
Gingerbread Heart: Passages 2000 (Book),
31

Tubman, Harriet
The Underground Railroad (Book), 261

20th century
100 Years in Photographs (Book), 407
Solemates: The Century in Shoes (Web
site), 279
Time 100: The Most Important People of
the 20th Century (Web site), 281
Women of the Century: One Hundred
Years of American Heroes (Web site),
124

U

Underground Railroad
The Underground Railroad (Book), 261
The Underground Railroad (Web site),
283

Underground Railroad — Fiction
Freedom Knows No Color: Passages to
History (Book), 77
Selected from A Different Kind of Christ-
mas (Book), 56

United States Air Force
The Air Force in Action (Book), 185
Fighter Pilots: Life at Mach Speed (Book),
178
The Thunderbirds: The U.S. Air Force
Aerial Demonstration Squadron (Book),
184
U.S. Air Force (Web site), 205
Women Airforce Service Pilots (WASP)
WWII: Posters (Web site), 285

United States Army
The Army in Action (Book), 190

United States Marine Corps
The Marine Corps in Action (Book), 174

United States Navy
U.S. Navy Special Forces: Seal Teams
(Book), 175

United States Postal Service
Air Mail Pioneers (Web site), 262
Tour *Titanic* (Web site), 218

Urban legends
Urban Legends Reference Pages (Web
site), 424

V

Vampires
Dracula and Other Vampire Stories
(Book), 88